FOOD AND NUTRITION

The Prevention Total Health System™

FOOD AND NUTRITION

by Nancy Nugent and
the Editors of **Prevention**® Magazine

 Rodale Press, Emmaus, Pennsylvania

Printed in the United States of America on recycled paper containing a high percentage of de-inked fiber.

Library of Congress Cataloging in Publication Data

Nugent, Nancy.
  Food and nutrition.

  (The Prevention total health system)
  Includes index.
  1. Food. 2. Nutrition. I. Prevention (Emmaus, Pa.) II. Title. III. Series.
TX353.N83   1983   641.3   83-10963
ISBN 0-87857-464-6 hardcover

  4 6 8 10 9 7 5 3   hardcover

The Prevention Total Health System™
Series Editors: William Gottlieb, Mark Bricklin
Food and Nutrition Editors: William Gottlieb, Jim Nechas
Writers: Mark Bricklin (Chapter 1),
    Sharon Faelten (Chapters 2, 5),
    Nancy Nugent (Chapters 4, 6, 7),
    Bill Keough (Chapter 8), Marian Wolbers (Chapter 9),
    Stefan Bechtel (Chapter 10)
Research Chief: Carol Baldwin
Researchers: Christy Kohler, Holly Clemson, Susan
    Nastasee, Joann Williams, Susan Zarrow, Martha
    Capwell, Sue Ann Gursky, Carol Matthews, Pam
    Mohr, Carol Sitler, Nancy Smerkanich, Pam Uhl
Art Director: Karen A. Schell
Associate Art Director: Jerry O'Brien
Designers: Lynn Foulk, Alison Lee
Illustrators: Susan M. Blubaugh, Joe Lertola
Project Assistants: Linda Jacopetti, John Pepper,
    Nancy Wood
Director of Photography: T. L. Gettings
Photography Coordinator: Margaret Smyser Skrovanek
Photographic Stylists: Kay Seng Lichthardt, Kathryn
    E. Sommons, J. C. Vera
Photo Librarian: Shirley S. Smith
Staff Photographers: Carl Doney, T. L. Gettings,
    Mitchell T. Mandel, Margaret Smyser Skrovanek,
    Christie C. Tito, Sally Shenk Ullman
Copy Editor: Jane Sherman
Production Manager: Jacob V. Lichty
Production Coordinator: Barbara A. Herman
Composite Typesetter: Brenda J. Kline
Production Assistant: Eileen Bauder
Office Personnel: Diana M. Gottshall, Susan Lagler,
    Carol Petrakovich, Cindy Christman, Cindy Harig,
    Marge Kresley, Donna Strubeck

Rodale Books, Inc.
Editorial Director: Carol H. Stoner
Managing Editor: William H. Hylton
Copy Manager: Ann Snyder
Publisher: Richard M. Huttner
Director of Marketing: Eller Rama
Business Manager: Ellen J. Greene
Continuity Marketing Manager: John Taylor

Rodale Press, Inc.
Chairman of the Board: Robert Rodale
President: Robert Teufel
Executive Vice President: Marshall Ackerman
Group Vice Presidents: Sanford Beldon
                        Mark Bricklin
Senior Vice President: John Haberern
Vice Presidents: John Griffin
                 Richard M. Huttner
                 James C. McCullagh
                 Carol H. Stoner
                 David Widenmyer
Secretary: Anna Rodale

NOTICE

This book is intended as a reference volume only, not as a medical manual or guide to self-treatment. If you suspect that you have a medical problem, we urge you to seek competent medical help. Keep in mind that nutritional needs vary from person to person, depending on age, sex, health status and total diet. The information here is intended to help you make informed decisions about your diet, not as a substitute for any treatment that may have been prescribed by your doctor.

Contents

Preface

The Challenge of the New Cornucopia

Choosing. It's what life today is all about. What makes it so difficult, so exhilarating.

Great-Grandfather ate his oatmeal, his black bread, his barley soup, his cabbage and potatoes and carrots and onions, and if he could only get enough, he couldn't go too far wrong.

Today's food shopper is confronted by literally thousands of choices, a cornucopia that would have beggared the imagination of yesterday's czars. But with this new, unprecedented freedom of dietary choice have come unprecedented responsibilities.

A new understanding of human diet that we call the nutrition revolution is teaching us that many foods in that cornucopia can deceive us. Potatoes, which for years have supplied most of our vitamin C, may be served up fluffier and fresher looking than ever—but entirely devoid of vitamin C. Garden vegetables may reach the modern table stripped of major vitamins *and* minerals—and impregnated with harmful amounts of sodium that our modern palates can barely taste. Beverages that look like fruit drinks may be concocted from sugar, caffeine and chemicals—with not a molecule of fruit to the gallon. People worry about "junk foods," so sugary confections are disguised as "energy bars" and "granola" products. Would you put 6 teaspoons of sugar in a cup of milk? In the modern dairy department, they call it "low-fat" fruit yogurt.

The nutrition revolution teaches us more. It explains that there is a powerful link between overprocessed foods such as these and many of the most common health complaints today. Easy fatigue, unexplained nervousness, chronic aches and pains, high blood pressure, overweight, heart trouble and more have all been traced back—in large part—to poor food choices in an age of dangerous plenty.

But knowledge is power. In this book you will gain power that will give you new control over the way you feel, the way you look, the way you perform. You'll learn not only to avoid the hidden traps in modern foods, but also how to find the hidden *benefits*—the top-drawer nutrition, bargain-basement calories, foods that help our bodies resist illness and achieve maximum vitality.

Whatever else you plan to do with your life, plan on good health. To that end, The Prevention Total Health System™ presents this volume on *Food and Nutrition*.

Executive Editor, **Prevention**® Magazine

The Nutrition Revolution

Medicine, say the experts, is not our best hope for future health. It's diet that will define our destiny.

This book is a child of the nutrition revolution. In it, we present a perspective on food and nutrition that has come into focus only within recent years. That new view sees diet not as a simple necessity, like the air we breathe, but rather as a symphony of energy that we take from the environment around us and make part of our own beings. And, says the nutrition revolution, we are exquisitely sensitive to every note of this incoming energy. It conditions the way we feel, the way we look, how we grow, how we age, how we think, how we love. While it is certainly not the only important influence on our lives, the sweep of that influence is far greater than most of us realize. Diet, says the nutrition revolution, is destiny.

But how did we get to this new point of view? How do we *know* that nutrition is so important? Is it not more important, for instance, to have your blood pressure checked regularly than it is to worry about what's in your bowl of breakfast cereal? Wouldn't we be better off building bigger and better hospitals and brain scanners than bothering ourselves about the shortcomings of white bread? Wouldn't all of us, to be perfectly honest, feel just a little prouder introducing "my daughter, the doctor," than we would "my daughter, the nutrition expert"?

One man who wouldn't is an Englishman named Thomas McKeown. Not that McKeown doesn't think medical doctors are good and valuable people. He's one himself. He holds a further doctoral degree in biological sciences, and yet another in biochemistry. Over a period of nearly 40 years, Dr. McKeown has earned a reputation as a leading authority on the causes of disease and the relationship of medicine and social conditions to health. Central to McKeown's vision is the view that modern medicine "is not nearly as effective as most people believe," and that its contribution to the increase in life expectancy is also "much smaller than most people believe." Rather, he maintains, the enormous progress we've made over the last few hundred years in health and longevity can be ascribed in largest part to improvements in our environment, particularly improved nutrition.

Fiber: The Nutritional Missing Link

Dr. Denis Burkitt, who has practiced medicine in both England and Africa, has concluded that just *one* dietary ingredient accounts for "civilized" diseases like gallstones and heart attacks.

Fiber.

Dr. Burkitt's African patients—almost totally free of "civilized" illnesses—eat a natural, plant-dominated diet that contains lots of fiber. His British patients eat just what many of us do—the overrefined foods of the industrial world: the white flour, the mounds of sugar, the fat-laden red meat.

People who eat modern fare suffer a complaint that primitive people do not—constipation—and that is the start of their troubles. Modern man eliminates less frequently; his stools are meager and hard when he does; and as he strains to alleviate the condition, he increases the pressure inside his body, producing conditions like hernia, hemorrhoids, varicose veins and diverticulitis.

Going a step further, because elimination is a problem, certain cancer-causing substances are trapped in his colon, where they become threats to his health.

Finally, in a mechanism still poorly understood, the low fiber content of the modern diet disrupts the body's ability to process cholesterol and so opens the door to many heart conditions and gallbladder disease.

WHY THE EPIDEMICS FADED

Several hundred years ago, McKeown explains, the primary causes of illness and death were infectious diseases such as tuberculosis, typhus, smallpox, infectious diarrhea, scarlet fever and other scourges. Life expectancy was decades less than it is today, largely because of the terrible toll these infectious diseases took among children. Social conditions in the 17th and 18th centuries, as you may know from reading novels, were not exactly terrific. But as the 19th century began, they became even worse. Many thousands of people moved from the countryside into industrialized cities, working long hours in factories and living in crowded, unsanitary conditions. But a funny thing happened. The death toll from those infectious diseases went down instead of up. And as the years ticked by, the death rates went lower, notch by notch. Clearly, this was no temporary remission, but a real trend.

But why? For the most part, improvements in sanitation did not begin to take hold until the second half of the 19th century. Medical care, what there was of it, was wretched, probably causing more harm than good.

The answer, says McKeown, is simply better nutrition. Or even more simply, more food, food that supplied the calories, protein, vitamins and minerals that are required to build resistance against disease. It's a mistake, McKeown points out, to assume that just because a population does not exhibit specific signs of nutritional deficiency, such as beriberi from B vitamin deficiency, their nutritional status is adequate. Even today, he reminds us, millions of people in emerging Third World nations suffer from this kind of subclinical nutritional deficiency, rendering them far more vulnerable to infections. The tragically high infant death rate from infection in such countries, he asserts, is only the final stage of what is fundamentally inadequate nutrition.

The additional food made available to people by the beginning of the 19th century, McKeown explains,

e attributed to important
ges in agricultural practice.
and potatoes were introduced
urope from the New World, and
crops proved very productive.
toes, particularly, because they
well, could supply lots of good
ition during the winter. Crop
tion, manuring of soils, commer-
seed production, better farm
ements and better transportation
odstuffs from production areas to
s, largely by means of new canals,
id their part. In fact, the greater
lability of food not only reduced
ss, but permitted the population
urope to increase tremendously.
Such advances in farming prac-
resulting in a greater and more
ed supply of food, might be
sidered Phase One of the major
ges that have taken us to the
ent-day situation in health.
Phase Two extended from roughly
middle of the 19th century to the
y part of the 20th century. You
ht think that the notable feature
is next phase was the introduc-
of effective medical care, but
isn't the case. Hospitals remained
holes of infection; sad legions of
nen, who at the urging of their
tors went there to give birth, died
hildbed fever. With the exception
mallpox vaccination, there was
her prevention nor cure for any of
major killer infections like tuber-
sis that rampaged through Europe
North America.
Yet—once again—a strange thing
arred. The death rate from nearly
hese infections dropped steadily
dramatically throughout this
od. That occurred, says Dr.
Keown, as the direct result of vast
provements in public hygiene:
ification of water supplies, the
espread installation of effective
erage systems and the pasteur-
ion of milk. Meanwhile, the
ount and variety of available food
tinued to improve. This combina-
a of nutritionally conditioned
stance to disease and less expo-
e to disease organisms thanks to
olic sanitation brought about
provements in health of a magni-
e that is not appreciated today.
If we think, for instance, of such
ious infections as tuberculosis,
umonia, whooping cough, mea-

sles and scarlet fever, we moderns
almost automatically attribute their
rarity today to medical advances.
Dr. McKeown opens our eyes.
Streptomycin, the first effective
treatment for tuberculosis, was not
developed until 1947. But by then,
deaths from TB had *already* fallen to
a small fraction of what they had
been in the 19th century, when
statistics about the disease were first
registered. In fact, McKeown says,
the amount of decrease in the death
rate from tuberculosis since the early
19th century that is attributable to
drug therapy is only about 3 percent.
All the rest came from better nutrition, primarily, and secondarily, from
improvements in public hygiene and
living conditions. Pneumonia followed
a similar course, with the death rate
falling dramatically and steadily for
many years before the first effective
drug treatment was developed in
1938. Whooping cough, that terrible
killer of children? "Clearly almost the
whole of the decline of mortality from
whooping cough," says McKeown,
"occurred before the introduction of
an effective medical measure." Mea-
sles? Eighty-two percent of the
decrease in deaths from this disease
occurred before effective drug treatment was introduced in 1935. Scarlet
fever? Some 90 percent of the
improvement in the death rate occurred
before the discovery of effective
drugs. In short, most but not all of
the major causes of premature death
that had plagued mankind for so
long were brought under control, so
to speak, before the widespread use of
either vaccinations or drug therapy.

HEALTH IN THE MODERN ERA

Phase Three of the modern improvement in health may be said to have
begun about 1940. Then, for the first
time, modern medicine became truly
effective, largely thanks to the discovery of antibiotics and other drugs.
Immunization programs all but wiped
out diphtheria and polio, whose
incidence had not been greatly
lowered by improvements in nutrition and the standard of living. The
combination of new drugs and

immunization brought about the rapid lowering of death rates from other infections, too, even though most of them had already been reduced by nonmedical factors. Improved hospital sanitation, new surgical techniques, various new kinds of technology and perhaps simply an increase in the number of physicians resulted in still lower death rates, particularly among younger people.

By about 1980, however, perceptive health authorities like Dr. McKeown began to realize that the conquests of Phase Three would not go on forever. In truth, they seemed to be rapidly tapering off. Modern medicine, it seems, had been phenomenally effective in crushing the last remnants of infectious disease that had not been controlled by better diet and living conditions. But while TB and other infectious diseases were disappearing, a whole new set of diseases was taking their place. These were the chronic, degenerative diseases, notably heart disease and cancer. Along with them came diabetes, high blood pressure, and a host of other diseases, which, although perhaps not as lethal, caused great suffering and disability: diverticular disease of the colon, ulcers, gallstones, kidney stones, osteoporosis (thinning of the skeleton), and others. Huge amounts of money and research time did achieve certain improvements in the treatment of these disorders, but by and large, few if any real cures have been discovered and no immunizations or other techniques have been developed to prevent them.

Enter Phase Four. In 1979, United States Surgeon General Julius M. Richmond, M.D., announced that the next great breakthrough in health would not be a medical discovery, but would rather be millions of individual breakthroughs, as people learned to lead healthier lifestyles. Hundreds of other physicians had the same idea at just about the same time. The consensus was that the dimensions of this healthier lifestyle included better nutrition, not smoking, avoiding excess alcohol, exercise and control of psychological stress. The critical importance of diet in controlling heart disease —

the number one killer in modern society — had already become evid But in 1982, the National Acaden of Sciences of the United States proclaimed that cancer, too, migh very substantially reduced if peo ate more wisely.

The nutrition revolution is, therefore, an integral part of wha call Phase Four of modern health improvement. And there are plen of ironies to go along with that fa Whereas lack of food was once the major underlying cause of illness death, an excess of food — certain kinds, anyway — is now considere major contributing factor to hear disease, cancer and many other diseases. In Phase One, we might say, the gift to health was the gre availability of milk. During Phas Two, that milk was made safer to drink by pasteurization. During Phase Three, however, we got too much of a good thing, when the n turned into ice cream and cheesecake. In Phase Four, we are puttir ourselves on a diet.

Another irony to emerge fror the new food consciousness is the understanding that yesteryear's "I man's foods" — the coarse brown br the barley and oats, the beans and potatoes — are exactly what we to need to be eating *more* of. Eviden there is something in them that tl heart likes, and cancer doesn't.

The progress of food technolc it seems, took us just a mite furth than was good for us.

THE CAVEMAN DIET AND MODERN-DAY HEALTH

The nutrition revolution, sometin seems to have a kind of smarty-pa attitude. First, you hear that too much dairy, too much steak, too many eggs — all foods we were brou up to respect as bulwarks of good nutrition — can be bad for us. The you hear that beans and potatoes once sneered at as "starch" foods — in reality good for us. Is the nutri revolution perhaps nothing more than a new fad? And even if it's based on scientific research, how we know that everything it's tellir us isn't going to be disproven by

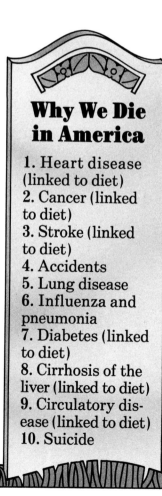

Why We Die in America

1. Heart disease (linked to diet)
2. Cancer (linked to diet)
3. Stroke (linked to diet)
4. Accidents
5. Lung disease
6. Influenza and pneumonia
7. Diabetes (linked to diet)
8. Cirrhosis of the liver (linked to diet)
9. Circulatory disease (linked to diet)
10. Suicide

tomorrow's scientific discoveries?

Yes, the new information that we have today about food and that you will read throughout this book is based upon good scientific research. But there is more here than just an assemblage of recently discovered facts. There is also a new appreciation of how the human body functions, and how that functioning relates to the different kinds of food man has eaten since his earliest history on earth.

A quick and easy way to get into trouble is to make generalizations about nutritional requirements. But one thing we can say without too much fear of contradiction is that all creatures, great and small, seem to be designed to thrive on a certain diet. Some animals have extremely specific dietary needs. Take the koala out of his eucalyptus tree, which serves both as his home and as his breakfast, lunch and dinner, and in a couple of hours he will be on the road to serious malnutrition. The Everglades kite will dine only on escargot—snails, minus the garlic and butter. Most animals, though, aren't quite so choosy. The lion, for instance, will enjoyably dine on any warm-blooded animal from a mouse on up. But put the lion on a farm full of grain, vegetables and fruits, and he will not long survive.

Which brings us to . . . ourselves. At least, ourselves some 250,000 years ago, maybe even earlier. It was during that long-ago time, long before there were supermarkets or even unsupermarkets, long before there was even the simplest form of agriculture, and long before the domestication of the first good-natured goat, that man and his environment reached a nutritional agreement. And for several hundred thousand years, it's believed, the terms of that agreement were respected by both parties.

Profound changes in the kinds of food we eat, in the very nature of those foods, did not occur until roughly 125 years ago. Only then did average people in Europe and North America begin to eat substantial quantities of refined grains, refined sugar, refined fats and canned foods. Changes in the diet that had occurred before then are considered relatively trivial in importance. Which means that for approximately 249,900 years of the 250,000 years or so that *Homo sapiens* have been eating dinner, the menu—*and the food to which our bodies had become adapted*—was substantially different from what we eat today. So brief in the historical perspective is our experience with processed foods that some have even called our modern diet a kind of experiment, an experiment that evidently is having some negative results. But we're getting ahead of ourselves. What we want to look at now is what that "original" diet actually was.

It is generally agreed that earliest man was pretty much of a nomad, dependent on hunting, fishing and gathering whatever edible fruits, seeds, vegetables and roots he could find. And his hunting was not confined to the likes of zebras and antelope, but, judging from the habits of some recently discovered "Stone Age" tribes, also included frogs, lizards, snakes and a good many insects (which are quite high in nutritional value, it turns out).

Quite a smorgasbord, it seems. We might even say that until very recently, people pretty much ate anything they could get their hands on, anything that didn't taste awful or eat them first. Yet, this doesn't mean we ate *anything*, because there were a lot of things we couldn't get our hands on.

THE LOW-FAT OF THE LAND

We did not, for instance, eat a high-fat diet. This can be said with confidence because it is nearly impossible to eat a high-fat diet without the existence of agriculture. Even a group of people that was very successful in hunting big juicy gnus and zebras would be eating a low-fat diet, because free-living ruminants are, in fact, not very juicy at all, having much less body fat than modern animals fattened in pens. Nearly all fish and shellfish are also very low in fat. Most vegetable-source foods are even lower in fat, with the exception of nuts and seeds. So limited in fat was the original diet of man that it's likely we actually

A Stone Age Menu

- Water lilies
- Wild grapes
- Figs
- Nuts and seeds
- Tender shoots
- Honey
- Tree sap or gum
- Fish and shellfish
- Turtles and tortoises
- Lizards
- Opossums
- Water snakes
- Pelicans
- Geese and ducks (and their eggs)

A Modern Menu

- Hungry Man (for the hearty appetite) Turkey Dinner with gravy and dressing and whipped potatoes
- A Harvest Get-Together—Broccoli Fanfare (with broccoli, shell macaroni, peas, corn, and red peppers in a butter sauce)
- Heat 'n' Eat Biscuits
- Thaw and Serve Pecan Pie
- Cool Whip topping
- Mellow Roast ground coffee, Sweet 'n' Low Poly Rich non-dairy creamer

needed an occasional shot of extra fat to help tide us over times when food was in short supply—times which came along pretty often. We might even hypothesize that part of our biological inheritance includes a *craving* for fats. Occasionally pigging out on nuts and seeds, the eggs of wild birds, or whatever fat could be derived from the carcass of a fresh-killed animal would no doubt have been a very important protective instinct for surviving droughts, floods, long cold winters and tribal migrations.

Speculation aside, one thing we know for sure about fat is that our bodies are all too ready, willing and able to go along with this scenario. Fat, as we all know, is easily stored by the body in a number of curiously expandable warehouses. When needed—because of a shortfall in daily calories—the fat can be combusted to create the energy we need to keep us going.

The key words there are "when needed." The reason we apparently enjoy a bit of fat in our diets, and store it so readily, is that the conditions under which we have lived for 99.95 percent of our sojourn on earth *demanded* such a system. Early humans whose fat eating and storing mechanisms didn't work very well would presumably be the first ones to die off during hard times. As years and ages went by, bringing

with them uncountable periods of scarcity, those who *did* have such instincts and abilities would have been preferentially spared, passing on their coping mechanisms to generations that followed.

Today, these highly adaptive survival mechanisms have turned into mechanisms of destruction. Our taste for fat, and our infinite ability to store it in every nook and cranny of our bodies, including the linings of our arteries, has betrayed us in these times of unmitigated plenty. And the trouble-makers are more numerous than those familiar nuts and seeds that our forebears cherished. Our modern beef cattle are marbled with far more fat than ever infiltrated the muscles of their wild ancestors. Butter and cream, once rarely eaten by humans, and later considered luxuries, have become abundant and cheap. We make our cookies and cakes and croissants and doughnuts and even our saltines with fat. We smear it on our toast, rub it on corn on the cob, and dip our lobster in it. Both halves of fish 'n' chips are cooked in it. We pop a pat or two into our morning oatmeal and plop a fluffy pile of it on our Irish coffee.

When the nutrition revolution tells us that we are eating two to four times as much fat as our bodies have been equipped by adaptation to handle, we can now understand why. And when we learn that these high levels of fat cause atherosclerotic heart disease, promote cancer, aggravate diabetes and much more, we shouldn't be surprised. Even a far less sensitive mechanism than the human body, like the internal combustion engine, will become gummed up and malfunction if its fuel mixture is not very close to what it was designed to handle.

Health philosopher Robert Rodale, the editor of *Prevention* magazine, has used the phrase "mankind's nutritional programming" to describe the relationship between our bodies and our diet. As our diet strays away from the programming embedded in our tissues over hundreds of thousands of years, things begin to go wrong. When the error is in the direction of far too much fat, our bodily mechanisms become *literally* gummed up.

Since 1910, the number of calories in our diet hasn't changed much, but how we *get* those calories sure has. Fat intake has soared by 25 percent, pushing the same amount of carbohydrate out of the diet and also pushing us close to the edge of a collective health disaster. Simply put, more fat means more disease.

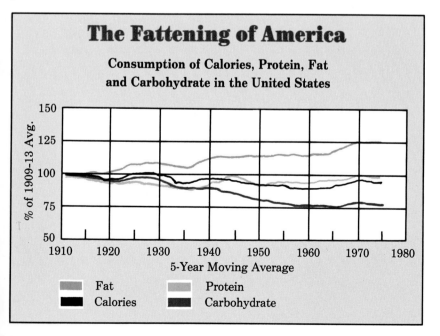

The Fattening of America

Consumption of Calories, Protein, Fat and Carbohydrate in the United States

% of 1909-13 Avg.

150 / 125 / 100 / 75 / 50

1910 / 1920 / 1930 / 1940 / 1950 / 1960 / 1970 / 1980

5-Year Moving Average

Fat Protein
Calories Carbohydrate

SWEET DREAMS AND BITTER REALITIES

The sweetest girl in the world . . . a honey of a deal . . . what a sweet thing to do . . . home, sweet home . . . good night, sweet prince . . . swing low, sweet chariot . . . sweet dreams, sweetie pie.

If there is something about fat that suits our desire for a certain mouthfeel, it's nothing compared to our craving and appreciation of sweetness. But how did this come about? Were there candy trees back in caveman days? No, not exactly. But there were melons, berries and other fruits that were ripe for the picking at certain times of the year. The sugar in these sweet fruits gave our ancestors a few extra calories that they could probably use. These are only seasonal treats, remember, and the normal diet in those days was limited in calories. We made further good use of these occasional sweet treats by learning how to convert their sugar into fat, which could be stored against the time when fruits and other foods would be scarce.

Besides being sweet, fruits are also excellent sources of vitamin C, a nutrient of critical importance in maintaining health, resisting infection and healing injuries. Delighting in the sensation of sweetness, then, would have been an invaluable survival mechanism for our ancestors, leading them to the best available sources of vitamin C.

It's easy to imagine that individuals who did not have this instinctual love of sweetness would be getting less vitamin C in their diet, and would therefore be far more vulnerable to disease. And, just like individuals who were not able to store fat, they would have gradually died off, leaving the human gene pool much as we find it today—full of chocolate lovers.

Paralleling the history of dietary fat, sugar in its pure form did not become available for human consumption until very recently in our history, and long, long after our bodies had become adapted to a diet of natural foods. By the mid-19th century, sugar, like dietary fat, had become both abundant and cheap. Sugar found its way into hundreds and eventually thousands of food products. And we needed little sweet talk to convince us that the stuff tasted good. Currently, the average American adult consumes on the order of 120 pounds of sugar a year. Some 20 to 25 percent of all the calories we consume, in fact, comes from sugar, and that's not including the sugar naturally found in fruits and other foods. Now, if you picture what 120 pounds of sugar looks like—you could fill a small sandbox with it—you might not think you eat that much. But much of the sugar we consume is invisible. A typical soft drink, for instance, contains about 8 teaspoons of sugar suspended in the liquid. More sugar is mixed into the countless confections we eat, the cakes and pies, the gelatin desserts and ice cream, the imitation fruit drinks and even fruit-flavored yogurt—which typically contains 6 or 7 teaspoons of added sugar.

Once again, our dietary instincts—designed to operate in a world of natural foods—have betrayed us in this new world of food *products*. And, says the nutrition revolution, the price we pay for feeding these instincts run amok is steep. Rampant tooth decay, a condition virtually unknown in societies that eat only natural foods. Obesity, a condition that not only looks bad, but also greatly aggravates any circulatory problems (such as those caused by eating excessive fat). Maturity-onset diabetes, a condition dangerous in itself and especially dangerous to those with heart problems. And, as all those calories from sugar satisfy our hunger but fail to provide any vitamins or minerals or protein or fiber, the stage is set for any one of a host of nutritional deficiency symptoms to make an appearance.

We've got to clean up our act, says the nutrition revolution.

SALT, HUMAN HISTORY AND HIGH BLOOD PRESSURE

There is at least one other important dietary element that was very hard to get in days gone by, but is hard to

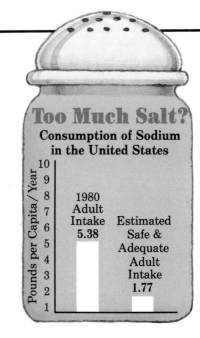

Modern Americans consume more than 5 pounds of salt a year, or 3 times the amount considered safe. Much of it is hidden in commercially processed food. And while the consumption of sugar products has dropped in recent years, it still amounts to more than 125 pounds a year.

escape in our own era. Salt.

A small amount of salt, like a small amount of fat, is required to maintain health and life. Yet, salt (sodium, to be more accurate) is not very abundant in natural foods; much less abundant, in fact, than most other nutrients. The daily requirement of sodium isn't known for sure, but it is believed to be approximately 400 to 500 milligrams a day. To get some idea of how difficult it was to obtain that much sodium in a natural environment, let's imagine we're watching a person who lived a few thousand years ago eat her way through one day. She wakes up with a big appetite, and breakfasts on a half pound of meat left over from yesterday's kill and an orange. For lunch, she puts away a whole pound of cooked beans and a pound of corn. At dinnertime, she gets serious. She begins by going down to the ocean and harvesting a dozen plump oysters from the salt water. Then she bakes herself a handful of wheat kernels, a couple of potatoes, and one or two onions for flavor. For a midnight snack, she has a couple of apples. With all that food, even with oysters from the sea, she has fallen just short of the 400-milligram mark for sodium: probably enough, but *just* enough. Had she not eaten the oysters, her sodium intake for the day would have been a mere 215 milligrams, which is below even the most conservative estimates of dietary requirement.

If it's so difficult to get sodium from natural foods, how did we manage to survive all these years? For that, we can thank adaptation, the same wonderful process that taught us how to store fat in times of plenty. What happened is that our bodies learned how to conserve salt. While many other dietary elements are freely expelled from the body in one form or another, salt is very nicely retained by the fluids of our bodies. Today's sodium shortfall can easily be taken care of by the extra bit of sodium we may have had last week from some of the relatively few natural foods that, like meat and oysters, contain meaningful amounts of sodium; spinach, carrots, celery and milk are good examples.

In time, however, we made two

discoveries about salt. The first was that when liberal amounts of salt are added to certain foods, notably meat and fish, it can prevent them from spoiling. Second, we discovered that adding salt seems to zip up the flavor of food that is bland, canned or overcooked.

The result is that instead of taking in around 500 milligrams of sodium a day, Americans on the average consume between 8,000 and 15,000 milligrams a day, or roughly

20 times the amount we need.

That's the arithmetical result. The medical result is that 16 percent of the adult American population has high blood pressure, with the rate ranging up to 40 percent in older age groups. Based on research showing that hypertension is rare in primitive societies that do not consume purified salt, and that blood pressure among these people does not increase with age as it does in our own society, most of this plague of high blood pressure has been attributed to the huge amount of salt in our modern diet. Significantly, like sugar, much of the salt we consume is "hidden"—in everything from canned vegetables and bread to dairy shakes—which may contain almost 300 milligrams of sodium—served at fast food restaurants.

While our bodies were learning how to conserve sodium—hardly suspecting that someday we would be eating at fast food restaurants—

Ice cream epitomizes how our diet has evolved as civilization has progressed—it contains lots of sugar and fat. And although we all enjoy our ice cream from time to time, scientists say that if we overindulge in it and other sugary, fatty foods like pastry, cakes and cookies, we might set ourselves up for heart disease, high blood pressure and diabetes.

Although the key factor in understanding health and disease, nutrition is rarely a required course in leading medical schools.

they didn't bother to do the same for another important dietary mineral, potassium. Potassium is so plentiful in natural foods, particularly plant foods, that there is apparently no advantage to conserving it. But what has potassium got to do with sodium? Until recently dieticians and doctors would have said "not much." But the nutrition revolution tells us that the relationship has major consequences for public health. Potassium, it turns out, helps counteract the harmful effects of excess sodium. And once again—you can almost depend on it—modern food processing plays havoc with human physiology. While it increases sodium, it actually

depletes potassium. A serving of fresh peas, for instance, contains a scant 1 milligram of sodium and 380 milligrams of protective potassium. The same serving of commercially frozen peas has 100 milligrams of sodium and only 160 milligrams of potassium. Canned peas are worse yet, with 230 milligrams of sodium and 180 milligrams of potassium.

FIBER, THE FORGOTTEN HEALTH FACTOR

So far, we've seen why there have been large increases in our dietary fat, sugar and salt, and why our

Med School Fare: Undernourished
MEDICAL SCHOOL CURRICULUM

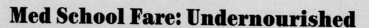

Hourly Comparison—First and Second Years

School	Subject	Hours	Subject	Hours	Subject	Hours	Subject	Hours
Duke University School of Medicine	Introduction to Clinical Medicine	196	Genetics	38	Pathology	210	Nutrition	0
University of North Carolina School of Medicine	Introduction to Medicine	50	Genetics	25	General Pathology	110	Nutrition	25
University of California, Los Angeles, School of Medicine	Psycho-pathology	4	Social Medicine	10	Pathology	140	Nutrition	0
University of Hawaii, John A. Burns School of Medicine	Introduction to Human Behavior	36	Community Health Problems	18	Human Pathology	202	Nutrition in Health and Disease	12
University of Pennsylvania School of Medicine	Neuro-biology	144	Statistics	10	Pathology	136	Nutrition	0
Columbia University College of Physicians & Surgeons	Neural Sciences	104	Biostatistics	10	Pathology	43	Nutrition	0
Ohio State University College of Medicine	Neuro-anatomy	63	Embryology	25	Pathology	165	Nutrition	0
University of Illinois College of Medicine at Urbana-Champaign	Neuro-science	25	Embryology	31	General Pathology	20	Nutrition	11

chemistry dictates that we ⸱ pay for these recent acquisi- ⸱ with our health. The final ⸱r dietary change we'll present in ⸱ chapter is a subtraction. And ⸱usly, almost no one noticed that ⸱s missing until as recently as ⸱1970s.

"Nonnutritive fiber," they used ⸱ll it. What they meant was the ⸱ that the digestive processes ⸱dn't break down and absorb. No ⸱ paid much attention to fiber, ⸱pt in a negative way. People with ⸱able bowel problems were told to ⸱ away from fiber (roughage) ⸱use it would only irritate ⸱r systems.

As we explain in "Fiber: The ⸱ritional Missing Link," all that ⸱ged when a British surgeon began ⸱ublicize the discoveries he had made ⸱r extensive research in Africa.

The nutrition revolution was ⸱k to pick up on the work of Denis ⸱kitt, M.D., and other physicians. ⸱hin ten years, they had amassed a ⸱lth of information strongly sug- ⸱ting that although fiber contains ⸱nown nutrients, you can never- ⸱ess develop symptoms of a fiber ⸱ciency. Some of those deficiency ⸱ptoms, the new nutrition revolu- ⸱ believes, include heart and ⸱ulatory problems, blood sugar ⸱urbances, obesity, ulcers, hemor- ⸱ds, varicose veins and the irrita- ⸱ bowel syndrome—the very prob- ⸱ that was previously believed to be ⸱d reason for avoiding fiber. Even ⸱cer of the lower bowel has been ⸱ed to insufficient dietary fiber.

Taking the historical perspec- ⸱e, it's easy to see that mankind ⸱ame adapted to a high-fiber diet ⸱ny years ago. Grains, legumes, ⸱ny crops, vegetables, fruits—virtually ⸱the traditional dietary staples—are ⸱ sources of fiber.

Dietary fiber took the big plunge ⸱ust about the same time that we ⸱ an to load up on fat and sugar. In ⸱ latter part of the 19th century, ⸱ite flour made its appearance in ⸱cery stores and was an immediate ⸱, because—bereft of its oily germ ⸱tion—it kept much longer with- ⸱ becoming rancid. Bread made ⸱h white flour was softer and ⸱fier, and was considered a luxury ⸱w available to the common man.

Although a handful of people, even in those early days, were warning that this new kind of flour was not as healthful as the old, no one paid much attention. Before long, nearly everyone was eating bread and other wheat products that contained some 60 percent less fiber than they used to get from whole wheat bread.

But that's only part of the story. New advances in agricultural technology and the general rise in prosperity soon made it possible for people to eat much more beef, pork, chicken, milk, butter and cheese than they had previously consumed. None of these foods contains any fiber whatsoever. Then there was sugar, a product that was eventually to satisfy close to one fourth of all caloric needs, and do so without providing a trace of fiber. As these new foods became a part of the common diet, they tended to replace grains and beans and other fiber-rich staples. Today, we can reasonably estimate, people consume on the average only about one-third as much fiber as we did for the quarter of a million years that preceded the emergence of Wonder Loaf. Our new low-fiber, high-fat diet is particularly unfortunate, we know now, because fiber protects against excess fats the way potassium protects against excess sodium.

THE DIET OF A HEALTHIER FUTURE

Let's briefly summarize. Over the course of many thousands of generations, the human species adapted and fine-tuned itself to its nutritional environment. That environment was one that was low in fat, low in salt, high in potassium, rich with fiber, and completely lacking in refined sugar. Among the adaptations we made to permit us to thrive in such an environment were the abilities to store fat, conserve sodium and easily excrete potassium. Because food was often scarce, we also developed the ability to convert sugar into fat, which can be stored in limitless amounts. To further facilitate survival during hard times, we apparently developed a liking for fat and a

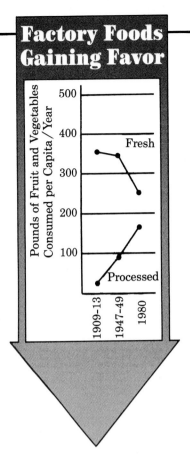

Factory Foods Gaining Favor

Back in Grandma's day, foods were eaten fresh. With the advent of refrigeration and home freezers after World War II, commercially processed foods became an attractive alternative to daily shopping. By 1980, the large numbers of women holding down full-time jobs had little time to prepare meals from scratch. As a result, the fruits and vegetables carried into the house came in cans and frosty cartons rather than a garden basket.

craving for sugar. But little more than a hundred years ago, our nutritional environment changed radically, although our body chemistry didn't. Suddenly we were eating a lot of fat, which our bodies — programmed to suspect a famine around every corner — gratefully stored. Suddenly we were eating a lot of salt, and our bodies salted it away. Suddenly we were eating less potassium and our spendthrift kidneys literally peed it away. We began eating so much sugar that we go mouthful of cavities and the tast buds sitting next to them said, w this is wonderful, feed us more!

The effects of this maladapt tion were not immediately obvio We were so enchanted with the r disappearance of infectious disea that we paid little attention to th emergence of the chronic disorde And, because chronic conditions

Four-Star Menus: A Day in the Life of a Perfect Meal Plan

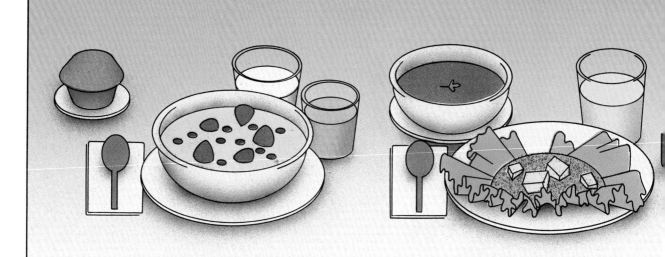

Breakfast

This is about as close to a perfect breakfast as you can get. The bran muffin and oatmeal with strawberries and raisins provide six times as much food fiber as a run-of-the-mill plate of bacon and eggs with buttered toast and coffee. With orange juice on the side, our breakfast gives you 120 milligrams of vitamin C — well over twice the government's Recommended Dietary Allowance for that vitamin. And with skim milk, this is a *lean* way to start the day, supplying less than 20 percent of the fat of the bacon-and-egg breakfast.

Lunch

A light and lively salad of tuna and tabbouleh on endive, with cream of toma soup and a "fruit smoothie" (a blend of yogurt and banana) supplies a whopping total of 46.6 grams of protein. That's nea as much as most adults need for the whol day. By comparison, a bologna sandwich on white bread, with brownies, would contain 60 percent less protein. And all th foods shown supply fair amounts of vitamin A, several B vitamins, potassium calcium, selenium and other health-buildi vitamins and minerals.

heart disease and maturity-onset diabetes usually do not become symptomatic until the fifth or sixth decade of life, they were often attributed to old age. Now we know them for what they are: diseases of maladaptation.

Unlike the dinosaurs that perished millions of years ago, we *can* adapt. Remember the day's menu of the imaginary primitive woman, eating her high-fiber diet? Every-thing in this menu is still available today in any supermarket: the meat, the oysters, the beans and corn, apples and oranges, potatoes and onions. This diet is not only rich with fiber, but is also low in fat, low in salt, high in potassium and has copious amounts of vitamins to boot. Each of us today can create our *own* nutritional environment, and in so doing, cooperate with our bodies instead of fighting them.

Dinner

A nutritional banquet of oven-baked chicken casserole, complete with carrots, potatoes, sweet potatoes and cranberry sauce, gives you ample potassium and vitamin A, plus fair amounts of magnesium, a hard-to-get mineral. The spinach salad and chicken total up to 3 valuable milligrams of iron. Dessert is no empty-calorie treat, either. Pumpkin pie provides a respectable 2,810 International Units (I.U.) of vitamin A. And an occasional glass of white wine with your meal can do your heart some good, because small amounts raise blood levels of high-density lipoproteins, factors that protect against heart attacks.

Snacks

Any time of the day or evening, well-chosen snacks contribute their fair share of nutrients and fiber to your diet. The trick is to select foods that are as close to nature as possible. Goodies like grapes, apples, peanuts, sunflower seeds and whole grain oatmeal cookies can deliver plenty of fiber, B vitamins and trace minerals and are low in salt and sugar—unlike customary munch-ies like chips, pretzels and candy, which offer no such nutritional bonuses and far too much salt and sugar. Cheese and eggs are wholesome sources of ready-to-use protein, plus concentrated sources of calcium, which is vital to bones, teeth, heart and muscles.

A-Plus Nutrition All Your Life

If you want to eat birthday cake at 90, it helps to eat a little better before.

Your body is never quite the same from week to week and year to year. From one stage of life to the next, it changes dramatically—and so do your nutritional needs. As a child, you grow faster than at any other time in your life. During adolescence, hormone surges prepare you for reproduction. In early adulthood, a quicksand of responsibilities puts extraordinary demands on your time and energy. And as the body begins to slow down after five or six decades, you need to compensate for the effects of wear and tear on various organs.

Each stage of life calls for a special mix of nutrients. After all, dog food manufacturers formulate different chow for puppies, mature dogs and aging dogs—you deserve at least as much consideration. Choosing the best diet for each stage of life will help you withstand stress, illness, infections and pollution-induced damage. And if that isn't enough, it will also help you dodge disorders with a genetic component, like diabetes or high blood pressure. For example, the child who's weaned on candy and soda may be more likely to grow into an insulin-dependent diabetic than one who's encouraged not to eat sweets. And the youngster who's not accustomed to salting his or her food may have a better chance of maintaining normal blood pressure for life. In fact, the need to eat more of certain healthy foods—and less of those that aren't so good for us—begins in infancy.

Breast milk—produced and packaged by Mother Nature—is the perfect food for babies. It had better be: Newborns triple in weight by their first birthday. But isn't formula—produced and

Programming Kids for a Poor Diet

It's prime time: Do you know what your children are eating? Chances are, it's candy-coated cereal, soda or other heavily advertised junk foods, according to a study of the effect of TV commercials on the eating habits of 96 children, aged 4 to 9.

When kids watched commercials for candy bars, cookies and other low-nutrition foods, the boys in the group sought those same foods when hungry. Yet TV ads for wholesome foods like cheese and apples had no effect on either boys or girls.

It seems the junk food messages TV aims at children come through loud and clear — a fact nutrition-conscious parents should know.

packaged by super-smart scientists — just as good? Not by a long shot.

WHY BREAST MILK IS BETTER THAN FORMULA

Breast milk contains nearly 2½ times more vitamin C and 1½ times more vitamin A than cow's milk.

The availability of iron in breast milk is exceptionally high. An infant absorbs about 70 percent of the iron in breast milk, compared to 30 percent of the iron in cow's milk formulas and only *10* percent in other formulas.

Mother's milk contains a unique mix of amino acids (the building blocks of protein) tailor-made for babies and unmatched by formulas. That all-important protein is converted into muscles and skin, as well as the brain and other organs.

Breast milk contains only one-fourth as much sodium as formulas do, cutting down on a factor that may contribute to high blood pressure later in life.

Cholesterol in human milk may stimulate the production of certain cholesterol-lowering enzymes that can regulate cholesterol levels throughout life — helping to reduce a major risk factor for heart disease.

Breastfed babies usually don't overeat and are less likely to become obese teenagers and adults. Something secreted in breast milk — an increase in protein and fat that occurs after about ten minutes of nursing — signals a baby that he or she has had enough. In contrast, a mother who sees some formula left in the bottle may push her child to continue to drink, whether the baby needs it or not. That "clean plate" syndrome, continued through life, can easily lead to extra pounds.

But mother's milk provides more than nutrients and calories. The nutrients in breast milk are easier to absorb than those in cow's milk or even most formulas, sparing babies the agony of diarrhea and other intestinal upsets that make life miserable for so many bottle-fed infants. And breast milk contains many unique factors such as antibodies to keep infants free of bacterial and viral infections. Cow's milk provides few of those immune factors that

are passed from mother to child in breast milk.

As a result of those factors, breast-fed babies are generally healthier. A doctor at the Mary Imogene Bassett Hospital in Cooperstown, New York, reports that of the children studied there, breastfed youngsters had fewer bouts of vomiting and diarrhea than did bottle-fed infants.

Breastfed babies tend to have fewer allergies, too. Overwhelming evidence shows that the longer babies are breastfed, the less likely they are to develop hives, eczema, hay fever, asthma and other problems either commonly caused or worsened by food allergies.

"No other way of feeding infants has produced better growth or health than breastfeeding," writes Calvin W. Woodruff, M.D., a professor at the University of Missouri School of Medicine, Columbia, in the *Journal of the American Medical Association.*

WEANING TO WHOLE FOODS

Mother's milk is all a child needs for the first six months. During the next six months, parents can add table foods gradually, starting with treats like strained bananas and working up to strained vegetables and minced bits of meat. As infants sprout into toddlers, they grow more slowly but still require solid nutrition. Between the ages of 2 and 12, their teeth, muscles and bones continue to grow rapidly — a job that calls for food packed with protein, vitamins and minerals. Clearly, there's not much room for nutrient-empty foods like soda, candy bars and other sweets.

In fact, sweets are about the worst source of calories you can feed a child. The link between dental cavities and sugar is inescapable: Sweets react with bacteria in the mouth to form an acid that dissolves tooth enamel, producing cavities. And children's teeth are particularly susceptible to cavities because they have more fissures and pits than adults' teeth do — handy niches for bacteria to invade.

As it stands now, the average sweet-eating child will have five decayed teeth by age 5. By age 15, one-third of the child's teeth will be decayed, filled or missing—hardly the equipment with which to enter adulthood. Take away the sweets (provided the child also brushes and flosses), and he or she will have almost *no* tooth decay. In place of sweet snacks, try fresh vegetables, popcorn and nuts.

Childhood is also the time to start *preventing* the diseases we usually think of as problems of middle age—high blood pressure, heart disease, diabetes and cancer. They each seem to have a *long* incubation period. Even little kids can be old before their time.

To begin with, for many people too much salt in childhood can lead to high blood pressure later. A study published in the *American Journal of Public Health* measured the sodium intake of a large group of third-graders in each of two communities— one with high-sodium drinking water and one with low-sodium drinking water. It found that blood pressure averaged two to four points higher in children living in the town with more sodium in the water.

That same blood pressure boost probably occurs when children get extra salt in their diets. One way to prevent that is to feed your *infant* less salt. Parents who salt their babies' food or let them eat high-salt canned food are starting a habit that's hard to break. The baby won't miss the salt—he or she can't even taste it. (Salt-sensing taste buds don't form until a child is over a year old.)

Too much fat in a child's diet is just as harmful as too much salt. A study of 800 girls aged 9, 10 and 11 found that 1 percent had high cholesterol and 3 percent had high triglycerides—two types of blood fats related to heart disease. Even more alarmingly, doctors have discovered fatty streaks in the coronary arteries of *infants*. If a child with those early signs of heart disease continues to eat foods high in saturated fats, those streaks and blood fats may eventually form artery-choking plaque that can climax in a heart attack or a stroke when the child grows up. But if such a child eats little saturated fat, the blood fats most likely will return to normal and the fatty streaks will fade away.

Charting Your Kids on a Healthy Course

4 years — Height: 37–42 in. Weight: 28–45 lb.

7 years — Height: 44–51 in. Weight: 42–65 lb.

9 years — Height: 48–56 in. Weight: 48–90 lb.

12 years — Height: 54–64 in. Weight: 66–128 lb.

FOOD TO GROW ON

At adolescence, growth and sexual development take off. Boys often grow 4 to 6 inches and put on 20 or 30 pounds in a year—most of it lean muscle. Girls grow less dramatically. For both, however, that growth spurt demands more calories than at any other time of life.

To meet that demand, teenagers can easily wolf down three full meals a day, plus afternoon and evening snacks. Nutritional problems arise because teenagers like food that can be prepared and eaten quickly, without plates or silverware. They like food that can be eaten whenever they feel like it, when they are in a hurry, or when they are with their friends. So they customarily reach for snack foods, sweets, baked goods and fast food meals.

Those kinds of foods add up to poor nutrition—for several reasons. First, they tend to contain loads of fat, salt and sugar. The same researchers who linked high-sodium drinking water to elevated blood

When children eat right, they stand straight, play energetically, get along with family and friends—and sidestep the road to serious disease later on. Diet during these tender years calls for concentrated sources of protein, vitamins, minerals and fiber—and a minimum of sweets and junk food.

Teen Untouchables

Liver
Fish
Squash
Clams
Spinach
Cabbage
Beets
Salads
Casseroles
Peas
Beans

Teen Fill-Me-Ups

Soft drinks
Pie, cake, cookies
Hamburgers
Pizza
Fried chicken
French fries
Ice cream
Spaghetti
Candy
Milk
Orange juice
Steak
Hot dogs

pressure in third-graders, for instance, found the same link in teenagers in the same town. Also, as much as teens need plenty of calories, eating refined, high-fat food can lead to overweight. And overweight teens are headed for a lifetime of weight-related health risks—including cancer, diabetes, heart and gallbladder disease. In fact, evidence strongly suggests that a woman who eats a high-fat diet from adolescence onward is more likely than others to develop cancer of the breast or uterus.

Haphazard eating habits during the teen years also may lead to shortages of key nutrients that teens need for good health. Some people believe that teens are bound to get all the vitamins and minerals they need because of the sheer volume of food that they eat. But that's not true.

"The 13- to 16-year-old group is one of the more [nutritionally] vulnerable segments of the entire population, second only to the preschool child," says William McGanity, M.D., professor and chairman of the department of obstetrics and gynecology at the University of Texas Medical Branch, Galveston. Study after study has shown that teens tend to be low in iron, thiamine, magnesium, calcium and vitamins A and C, among others. If those deficiencies drag on for several months or years, they can cause a host of health problems.

Iron deficiency, for example, is a common cause of chronic tiredness, lack of concentration and clumsy athletic performance in teens. Both young men and women need adequate iron—men for lean muscle growth and women to replace menstrual losses. So they should eat lean meat or fish, eggs, whole grains, peas and beans—and liver, if they like it.

Teens who exercise need more thiamine, to make up for large amounts of the B vitamin used up during exertion. But refined carbohydrate foods—soda and other sources of so-called "quick energy"—are abysmally low in thiamine.

Energy and endurance to play hard require still other key nutrients. A study of work habits of adolescents aged 12 to 16 showed that those who got too little vitamin C, riboflavin and vitamin B_6 had lower levels of energy and endurance than

well-nourished teenagers.

As for the effect of nutrition on teenage behavior, one study showed that a group of girls aged 11 to 15 were quarrelsome, aggressive, listless and lazy when they ate a diet dominated by foods made from sugar and white flour, which are low in protein and vitamins. The girls gradually became happy, polite and well-adjusted when they ate more fresh fruit and vegetables, dairy products and fresh meats.

Teens *can* get into trouble nutritionally. Or they can eat the good stuff: lean meat, fish, poultry, fresh fruit and vegetables, whole grain bread and cereals, nuts and seeds and low-fat dairy products. It's all in how you package it. Since snacking is unavoidable, you can help the teenagers in your household to eat better by stocking up on handy foods like single-serving containers of assorted fruit juices and yogurt, whole grain crackers, dried fruit, seeds, nuts, popcorn, low-fat cheese and leftover chicken drumsticks. That way, teens will be less inclined to look for chips, soda, cakes and other disaster foods.

EATING FOR TWO

Becoming pregnant can be the most important biological event of adulthood for a woman. Carrying and nurturing a child calls for extraordinary nutritional supplies. If a woman is eating a diet of whole, unrefined, vitamin- and mineral-packed foods when she becomes pregnant, her baby has a head start in life. But if her diet is cluttered with overprocessed or snack foods, pregnancy may be the best time to improve it. Many of the problems that can complicate pregnancy—toxemia (a buildup of poisons in the body), extreme overweight, diabetes and retardation of the unborn baby's growth—are related to poor nutrition.

Complete, sensible nutrition also does good things for the baby. Well-nourished fetuses usually turn out to be bigger, healthier—and *smarter*—babies. Intake of calories, protein, folate, calcium, and vitamin B_6, iron and sodium are especially critical during pregnancy. (And

Put these students at the top of their class. They're smart enough to know that good foods—like the fresh fruits, milk and other hearty items shown here—may mean good grades because eating right helps them to feel happy and alert.

breastfeeding calls for *more* than the optimum intake of many of those same nutrients.)

During pregnancy, a woman also needs an extra 300 calories a day—both to feed her growing baby and to make up for the stepped-up metabolism of pregnancy. If a pregnant woman finds herself gaining 20 or 30 pounds, she shouldn't worry. Contrary to past belief, which said that expectant mothers should gain no more than 15 to 18 pounds, a woman should gain about 4 pounds a month during the first three months of pregnancy and 1¾ to 2 pounds a month during the last six months. Half of that goes to the fetus, half to fat stores. Because the baby's brain grows most during the last three months in the womb, and the first three months after birth, the last thing a woman wants to do at that time is to cut back on food.

Not all calories are created equal, though. Each morsel Mom eats must be packed with nutrients that both she and the baby can use. A pregnant woman needs 30 extra grams of protein a day—preferably from top-notch sources like eggs, milk, yogurt, cottage cheese and other unprocessed cheeses, fish, meat and poultry. But many mothers don't get that much. One study showed that out of 50 pregnant women, 15 ate a poor diet—with too little milk, meat, fruit or vegetables.

Of all the vitamins, folate and vitamin B_6 (pyridoxine) are custom-made for ladies-in-waiting. Because pregnancy drains the body of folate, an expectant mother should double her intake. Unfortunately, up to

one-third of pregnant women in the U.S. may have folate deficiencies. And deficiencies of folate can lead to anemia for mother *and* problems for baby. That's why many obstetricians recommend folate supplements for women who are pregnant or breast-feeding. You should also look to high-folate foods like brewer's yeast, liver and other organ meats, whole grains, peas and beans, dark green leafy vegetables and beets.

In fact, if a woman is even *thinking* of becoming pregnant, she should beef up her intake of both folate and vitamin B_6, especially if she's been taking oral contraceptives. The Pill is notorious for robbing women of both those B vitamins. If a woman starts out with too little B_6 or consumes too little during pregnancy and nursing, her baby will be deficient and more likely to be irritable and cry easily or (if she's *very* low in B_6) suffer tremors and seizures. Researchers at Purdue University found that of nursing mothers they studied, most were getting far less B_6 than they and their babies needed. Since refining, processing and storage all deplete foods of B_6, the best bet is to eat plenty of B_6-rich foods like salmon, chicken, organ meats such as liver, sunflower seeds, nuts, broccoli and bananas.

During pregnancy, the need for iron—the key nutrient for robust, oxygen-rich blood—is higher than ever, even though a woman is no longer losing iron through menstruation. From conception to birth, iron is continuously shuttled to the fetus. Yet few women start out with enough iron or eat enough iron-rich food to carry them through pregnancy and childbirth. If they have closely spaced pregnancies, iron needs are higher than ever. So along with extra protein and B vitamins, a pregnant woman needs an extra 30 to 60 milligrams of iron a day.

The old days of salt restriction during pregnancy are gone. A pregnant woman actually needs at least 2 grams of sodium a day to keep up with her expanded blood volume and to nourish her child.

When it comes time to breastfeed, the content of mother's milk depends to some extent on mother's diet. So a breastfeeding woman needs:

Eating for Better, Not for Worse

"The diets of husbands and wives are generally similar," say researchers who studied the eating habits of 281 married couples and published their findings in the *American Journal of Clinical Nutrition.*

This means there's a chance of marital friction when one spouse decides to make a healthful change in the

diet—to buy whole wheat bread instead of white, to eat more fresh vegetables instead of canned, to eat less red meat and more fish and poultry.

We never heard of anyone who got a divorce over brown rice. But like any other household change, upgrading the marital diet is best approached with conviction garnished with a hefty portion of tact and patience.

Chances are, your efforts will pay off: Another study of eating patterns of spouses found that if one spouse eats more vitamin A- and vitamin C-rich fruits and vegetables and breads and cereals, the other tags along.

25 percent more calories than normal—the equivalent of one full meal above and beyond what she was eating before she became pregnant.

25 percent more vitamin E (preferably from whole foods containing unsaturated fats and oils, like soybeans, whole grains, seeds and nuts.

50 percent more vitamin A (from yellow fruits and dark green vegetables).

50 percent more calcium (from milk and milk products).

50 percent more folate and 25 percent more B₆ than before pregnancy.

eplenish fluids, both pregnant
nursing mothers need to drink at
t 2 or 3 quarts of water or other
ds every day. Incidentally, alco-
and coffee are out, because of
r potentially harmful effects on
child's nervous system.

J'RE NOT A KID ANYMORE

gnancy is only part of the chal-
e of postadolescence. By 20 you're
rown-up." That means you don't
l calories to feed physical develop-
t, and the calories you do get are
ned more slowly. So you can't eat
uch as you did when you were 14
expect to stay at the same
ght. Even if you gain a mere
unds a year, in 10 years you'll
e gained 20 pounds, and in
ears 40 pounds.

Understanding your appetite
help to control weight gain—
ecially for women, who seem to
on pounds far more easily than
. A study of menstruating women
lished in the *American Journal of*
ical Nutrition showed that they
te more food per day during the
days after they ovulated than
ing the ten days before. Appar-
ly, the increase in progesterone
decrease in estrogen after ovula-
stimulate the appetite. Knowing
t can help women control the urge
inge.

Eating well may help women
id a collection of miseries known
Premenstrual Syndrome (PMS).
one time or another, nine out of

ten menstruating women experience premenstrual breast swelling and tenderness, abdominal discomfort, water retention and weight gain, mood changes, headaches or insomnia. Many experience such symptoms regularly. One study, however, showed that women who regularly suffer PMS tend to eat a lot of refined sugar. Conversely then, cutting down on junk foods and eating more complex carbohydrates (whole grains and fresh vegetables) may remedy PMS.

The years from 20 to 40 are also apt to be the busiest of your life. Tight time schedules push breakfast off into a midmorning snack of coffee and a doughnut. Lunch may be skipped—or end up as a meat-laden, fatty, alcohol-laced spread. Dinner is often intruded upon by night school, business trips, overtime or taking the kids to baseball practice. With the logjam of obligations created by a two-paycheck household, it's easy to become indifferent to a good diet.

Singles also succumb to meals on the run. A study conducted at Auburn University in Alabama and published in *Nutrition Reports International* found that among 50 single, working women aged 22 to 33, nearly half were low in calcium, iron, vitamin A and thiamine—partly because of the poor nutrient quality of meals eaten away from home.

But single or married, healthy eating helps busy people to function and feel better. Of 266 jet crew members, nearly one out of five reported that they suffered various hunger-related symptons of ill-being if they skipped meals: faintness, sweating, palpitations, difficulty concentrating, irritability and nausea. "The meal in the middle of the working period appears to be significant, even if . . . it's a light one," say the researchers who interviewed the airline crews.

Actually, keeping your meals sensible improves your whole mental—and marital—outlook. Some psychologists and medical professionals are finding that the foods couples eat may be responsible for emotional problems in many troubled marriages. The problem, they say, can often be traced to hypoglycemia (low blood sugar) aggravated by too much sugar and other refined carbo-

"Eating on the run—little or no breakfast, too many snacks—is a big problem among people 20 to 40 years old. That's one of the reasons why they develop poor resistance, arthritis, hypoglycemia and various other metabolic problems."
—Michael Walczak, M.D., past president of the International College of Applied Nutrition.

hydrates, or erratic eating habits. Both can lead to anxiety, depression, irritability or other unstable emotions—prime ingredients in a stormy marriage.

So whether you're totally or partially responsible for food planning and preparation at your house, there are plenty of reasons to make the right food choices. One way to do that is to make a habit of shopping only from the perimeter of your supermarket and avoiding the snack and convenience food aisles. Taking one evening a week to plan meals in advance also helps tremendously, since carefully planned meals are usually more nutritious than hasty compromises.

A MIDLIFE CRISIS IN NUTRITION

The reduction of estrogen at menopause threatens many women with osteoporosis, a disease in which bones become so fragile that they can break at the slightest jostle or bump. Not only do women have less bone mass than men to begin with, but with that drop-off in estrogen production, bones lose large amounts of calcium, leaving millions of women prone to bone fractures and back pain.

Middle-aged women at special risk for osteoporosis are those who have one or more of the following risk factors:

- A low intake of dairy products
- A high intake of coffee (which steps up calcium loss)
- A sedentary lifestyle (bones, like muscles, grow stronger and denser when stimulated by regular exercise)

The way to save bones is to exercise, take a calcium supplement of at least 500 milligrams, and hold your coffee intake to a cup a day.

Two of the problems of middle-aged men—impotence and loss of sex drive—may be consequences of overweight or overindulgence in alcohol (or both). So eating and drinking moderately does more than protect men against heart disease—it can keep them as frisky at 60 as they were at 30.

The melonlike paunch that blooms on so many middle-aged men could be a telltale sign of nutritional

deficiencies—and a harbinger of health in old age. A study at the University of Rhode Island show that despite high intake of calorie overweight men between the age 35 and 65 got less than their basi requirements for calcium, vitami and the B vitamins thiamine (B_1) riboflavin (B_2)—certainly not the nutritional profile with which to your sunset years.

A RETIREMENT PLAN FOR YOUR BODY

In later life, the rate at which you burn calories slows even further, you need fewer calories. But you need *more* vitamins, minerals and other nutrients. In fact, some of t bodily imperfections that are bla on getting old—thinning hair, dr skin, loose or missing teeth, mus weakness, constipation and ment confusion—may actually be sign malnutrition. And they can be prevented—or reversed—by care attention to what you eat.

Many older people lose inter in good food because they can't t it very well. Doctors estimate tha ten million people in the United States—many of them elderly—s from "hypogeusia," or a loss of th sense of taste. To compensate for their dulled taste buds, they ofte turn to salty or sugary foods that usually nutrient poor.

But zinc, a trace mineral, is essential to a sharp sense of taste and may restore appreciation of f Robert Henkin, M.D., who runs Center for Molecular Nutrition a Sensory Disorders at Georgetow University in Washington, D.C., believes that hypogeusia is often to poor zinc absorption, and says that taste-impaired people shoul take in more zinc than others. In one study showed that older peop ability to taste sweets and salt improved after zinc supplementat which means they could be satisf with less salt and sugar. A zinc supplement is a handy way of getting more of the mineral, but should also eat more zinc-rich foo like fish, green beans, lima beans nuts and whole grain products.

Another reason many older

people don't eat right is that they wear ill-fitting dentures, making fresh foods difficult or impossible to chew. But the alternatives—soft, overprocessed foods—have lost most of their nutrients through refinement. A stronger denture adhesive isn't the answer. *Jaw bone deterioration* is a prime cause of loose dentures—and you can correct it with extra calcium.

"As the jawbone grows smaller, it becomes difficult for people to wear their dentures," says Kenneth E. Wical, D.D.S., chairman of the removable prosthodontics department at Loma Linda University's School of Dentistry in Loma Linda, California. Extra calcium, he told us, apparently slows that process. In one study, Dr. Wical and a co-worker divided 46 denture wearers into two groups. For one year, half received supplements that provided a total of 750 milligrams of calcium and 375 I.U. of vitamin D daily. ("Adequate vitamin D is absolutely essential for absorption and metabolism of calcium," he points out.) The other group received a fake, look-alike tablet.

The results were impressive. At the end of the year, the people taking calcium experienced much less jawbone loss than the others.

What older people drink is as important to their health as what they eat. Older bodies contain 5 to 10 percent less water than they did when they were 40; and by age 80, kidneys filter fluids and waste only half as efficiently as they did at 25. So you need to drink from 1 to 1½ quarts of water a day to help flush out waste and expedite other water-dependent biological jobs.

In fact, drinking plenty of water is an excellent aid against constipation, a major problem in old age. Better yet, drink water *and* eat bran, a high-fiber food that can restore normal bowel function. In a study of ten constipated nursing home residents, doctors found that bran speeded up bowel movements considerably more than did bulk laxatives.

Speaking of laxatives, older people take more drugs than any other segment of the population. The typical elderly American takes from 4 to 7 different drugs every day, and perhaps as many as 13 different drugs in a year. Many commonly

The Most Important Nutrients after Age 60

Iron. Deficiency of iron is fairly widespread among older people. Obvious signs like shortness of breath and a rundown feeling aren't always present. Eating liver, nuts, eggs and whole grain foods will reestablish iron levels.

Folate and Vitamin B$_{12}$. A lack of folate can mimic senility; too little B$_{12}$ can short out brain waves and cause fatigue. Organ meats, beans and fresh vegetables can help keep those frailties at bay.

Calcium and Vitamin D. These are absolutely necessary to avoid the thin, fragile bones of osteoporosis and osteomalacia, and they keep teeth from loosening or falling out. Milk and fish will supply both nutrients.

Protein. Protein needs are as high as ever; the nutrient counteracts the wasting of muscle that accompanies old age.

Vitamin C. This vitamin interacts with so many nutrients in so many ways that it's pivotal to all aspects of health and nutrition for the elderly. Vitamin C enhances iron absorption, lowers cholesterol, speeds wound healing, shields against stress and slows aging by protecting vitamin E from oxidation. Green peppers, citrus fruits, broccoli, brussels sprouts and cantaloupe are some of the best sources.

used drugs rob the body of vitamins and minerals. Aspirin, for instance, depletes the body of vitamin C. Diuretics can cause a loss of calcium, magnesium and zinc. Mineral oil (sometimes used as a laxative) may cause deficiencies of vitamins A, D and K. The antibiotic neomycin interferes with absorption of potassium, calcium, vitamin B$_{12}$ and iron.

And a nutritional deficiency is nothing to laugh at, particularly for older people, because it can disguise itself as senility.

"A deficiency of vitamin B$_{12}$, folic acid [folate], iron, protein or calories can affect the brain and make people demented," says Richard W. Besdine, M.D., a doctor affiliated with the Harvard Medical School.

Indifference to food—for whatever reason, at whatever age—can lead to poor health. Sooner or later, shoddy eating habits leave their mark. So of the nearly 100,000 meals of a lifetime, plan each as if your life depended on it. Because it does.

3

Catering to Your Own Style

Going your own way doesn't have to mean losing touch with your nutritional needs.

The nuclear family has had a meltdown. Mom is out of the kitchen and in the office. Sis is a vegetarian. John is a high school jock, and wolfs down 4,000 calories a day. And executive Dad eats more meals on the road than in his own dining room.

But different lifestyles don't have to mean indifferent eating habits. Mom could rely on processed foods—or learn how to prepare nutritious meals in less than 20 minutes. Sis could develop anemia—or adopt a meatless meal plan that meshes with her family's main courses. John could live on milk shakes and burgers—or cut down on fats and focus on hearty carbohydrates. Dad could become menu myopic and order nothing but well-done steaks and love-handle desserts—or turn into a health gourmet.

In short, we can choose how we live *and* how we eat. There's a way to cater to your own style and not have the caterer charge you an arm, a leg and the rest of your healthy body. You can be single . . . a couple . . . a family with lots of kids. You can travel . . . be into super-fitness . . . love throwing parties. This chapter will give you the info you need to do it well and *feel* well, too. But let's look at those lifestyles one by one. That means starting with single people.

Eating alone is often no fun, but the worst thing about it—worse than the loneliness or the boredom—may be the bad nutrition that often comes with it. Because it is no fun, when dining alone we frequently rush the issue and end up consuming too little good food or too much junk. We eat whatever happens to be in the refrigerator or we grab a bunch of munchies and a beer and plop down in front of the TV for an endless string of early evening news reports.

Well, we'd like to propose a simple remedy for the I-hate-to-eat-alone syndrome. Pretend that you're *not* alone. Pretend that you have a guest and that that guest is *you*.

INVITE YOURSELF TO DINNER

This little deception will bring about a number of desirable changes in your lonely and hurried eating habits.

First (and most important), it will mean that you will cook a full and nutritious meal for your guest—some protein, a vegetable, maybe a potato and a salad, and even a sensible dessert. And perhaps, in going to this added trouble, you'll discover that cooking is an enjoyable act, a satisfying pastime that makes those first few moments at home seem not quite as empty as they used to. But even if you don't reach this stage of consciousness, don't worry; you won't have to cook *every* night. Preparing a full meal for yourself will produce lots of delicious leftovers, and you can freeze them and give yourself a night off now and then. Which brings up another point: Don't try to "cook for one." That's an impossible and self-defeating task. Use normal recipes and prepare normal amounts of food. You'll be better off for the leftovers and a well-stocked refrigerator.

Second, our deception will mean that you'll set the table for your guest and that you will flatter "him" with all the attention to detail and comfort that you normally deny yourself. But one thing you shouldn't include in this pampering—at least at first—is the TV, the paper, or a book, even a good one. Reading while we eat usually means forgetting what we are eating, and *that* always means eating too much.

Finally, to avoid this unconscious gobbling—either as solace or a substitute for companionship—*don't* put the whole pot on the table. Give yourself measured portions of everything while you have your wits about you, and stick to them. Don't go back for seconds. Along with the many small courses in your complete "party" meal, these controlled portions will keep both your senses and your mind occupied. And with their built-in check on your eating, you may even be able—eventually—to watch TV or read at the table.

COOKING FOR TWO

Cooking for two people may be thought of as a case of simple arithmetic: It can be half as expensive, doubly delicious and twice as much fun. The pleasures of dining

---

Recipe for One: Crab Imperial

Makes 1 serving

- 1 tablespoon butter or margarine
- 3 tablespoons finely chopped green pepper (about ¼ of a pepper)
- 1 tablespoon finely chopped mushrooms
- 2 teaspoons whole wheat pastry flour
- ¼ cup half-and-half

- 1 tablespoon minced onion
- ¼ teaspoon Worcestershire sauce
- ¼ teaspoon Dijon-style mustard
- 2 ounces lump crab meat, cleaned of shells and cartilage
- 1 tablespoon shredded sharp cheddar cheese

Melt butter or margarine in a small saucepan or skillet. Saute green pepper and mushrooms until softened. Add flour and cook 1 minute while stirring. Add the half-and-half and cook and stir until slightly thickened. Add onion, Worcestershire sauce, mustard and crab meat. Combine well and pour into a custard cup.

Cover crab mixture with the shredded cheese and bake at 400°F for 10 to 15 minutes, or until cheese is melted and mixture is bubbly.

with just one other person are legendary. Whether it's an elegant tea for two or a simple loaf and thou, two people breaking bread together take part in a ritual that is somehow more intimate than that experienced by a larger group.

But no matter how enjoyable the act of dining with someone else may be, it has to be said that cooking for two can sometimes be a baffling experience. Not just young couples setting up housekeeping for the first time, but parents, too, whose grown children have left home, are frequently faced with some perplexing problems in the kitchen.

Pots and pans often prove too big for the quantity of ingredients used. Meats and vegetables are often sold only in family-size amounts. Standard recipes generally serve four to six people and are not always easy to reduce proportionately—pity the ambitious cook trying to modify a beef Wellington to serve two!

But there are practical solutions to these problems. For example, you can prepare individual chops instead of a roast, or chicken breasts instead of a whole bird. The price per pound may be higher, but the immediate cash outlay for two is less, and you'll be gaining a more interesting and varied diet besides.

When those really unavoidable occasions arrive and too-large portions present themselves, a certain familiarity with the sort of recipe that transforms them into new dishes is very useful. When making rice, for example, you've probably found that it seems to turn out better when a full recipe is made (about 3 cups of cooked rice). Whatever portion can't be finished by two people makes a satisfying base for another meal—mixed cold into a salad with mayonnaise and chopped vegetables, or popped into green peppers and baked. Though one bunch of broccoli is usually too much for two to finish at a sitting, it yields just enough left over to be whizzed in a blender the next day with some buttermilk for a cool, refreshing soup, or you can turn it into tasty little timbales for two.

A modest investment in kitchen equipment is a boon to the person cooking for two. A sturdy skillet measuring 6 to 8 inches across the bottom is useful for tasks such as scrambling a couple of eggs, poaching two fish fillets, or sautéing a pair of chicken breasts. A well-made heavy saucepan that holds 3 to 4 cups of liquid comes in handy for cooking small amounts of vegetables or simmering sauces for two. And a couple of custard cups or ramekins are very practical for baking and serving any number of things in small portions: little meat loaves, puddings, timbales and the like.

Once you've become adept at thinking in terms of two, the many advantages of this sort of cookery are soon apparent. For one thing, the simpler needs of two people require less cooking and cleanup time. Occasional little treats, which seemed too costly when a whole family had to be fed, are now more affordable—a chunk of fancy cheese, perhaps, or two fillets of expensive, fresh sole. You could even succumb once or twice to moments of luxury that you would never have considered when there were more mouths to feed at home.

FEEDING THE KIDS RIGHT (TRYING, ANYWAY)

If you have been trying to introduce your family to good nutrition, as so many of us have, you know that the results are indeed rewarding. You have also found that the venture itself can be mighty frustrating.

"How do I get my children to eat the foods that are good for them?" is a question we hear frequently.

Many children are being seduced into the sugar blues by peer pressure and by thousands of TV commercials extolling foods that are over-sweetened, oversalted, loaded with additives and very low in the nutrients essential for health and vitality.

Since there is increasing evidence pointing to poor nutrition as the root cause not only of many physical ailments, but also of mental and behavioral problems, getting kids to eat right becomes a top-priority issue worthy of our best efforts and most creative manipulation.

And one of the meals that's easiest to steer in the direction of health is breakfast, particularly when tiny tots are allowed to help themselves, grown-up style.

Put out attractive bowls of wheat germ, sunflower seeds, sesame seeds, raisins, sprouts and perhaps dried or sliced bananas. Put the milk in a small pitcher. Let the children pour their own and don't fret about the mess.

Eggs are a good food for breakfast, high in protein that sticks to your ribs. Most children enjoy soft-cooked egg with whole wheat toast broken into it.

Many children who refuse eggs

adore french toast. Use whole wheat bread and try a little honey in the egg and milk mixture. Then dip the bread in a mixture of wheat germ and sesame seeds. Serve with yogurt or applesauce; avoid pancake syrups. Use unsweetened applesauce, now available commercially, or better yet make your own, using apple juice or pineapple juice as the liquid in which you stew the apples.

Children love anything on a stick they can lick. Keep a supply of homemade Popsicles in the freezer and pull them out when you hear the siren song of the Good Humor man. Pure orange juice is often a favorite for these treats. Kids also love the swirly effect of yogurt and fruit in layers. Plain yogurt layered with pure grape juice is especially nice to look at and to lick.

Another favorite is frozen carob bananas on a stick. Make a paste of ¼ cup of carob powder and about 2 tablespoons of water. Cut bananas in halves or thirds. Roll them in the carob paste and then in coconut or chopped nuts. Insert a flat stick in one end of each and freeze.

To break a chewing gum habit, offer good chewy substitutes like dried apples, dried apricots, dried banana slices or dried fruit leather, which is a real treat. Line a cookie sheet with parchment paper or plastic wrap. Spread unsweetened apple butter thinly over the paper or plastic and place the cookie sheet in the oven, set at a very low temperature. The pilot light of a gas oven or the lowest possible setting on an electric oven provides enough heat. It might take 40 hours or more for the fruit to dry out. When it does, peel it off and roll it up. The leather can be frozen and then broken off in chunks. You can make fruit leather from any kind of presoaked dried fruit that is blended in a blender. Sure beats chewing gum for taste and nutrition.

Will your child feel deprived because he is not allowed empty-calorie sweets? Not at all. He may gripe about it, but inwardly he will feel very secure that you care enough about him to care what he eats. Recent research reveals that children are happier and more secure when they are given an imposed code of

Recipe for Two: Pasta with Gorgonzola

Makes 2 servings

½ pound spinach or whole wheat spaghetti or fettuccine

¼ cup sunflower seeds
½ cup milk
½ pound Gorgonzola cheese, crumbled

Cook pasta according to package directions. Meanwhile, toast sunflower seeds by placing them in a small skillet and cooking over medium heat, stirring constantly (they burn easily!) until golden brown.

When pasta is done, drain it thoroughly. Pour milk into the pot used to cook the pasta and heat until bubbling. Turn off heat, add cooked pasta and toss. Add Gorgonzola to pasta and toss again. Serve immediately, topping each portion with toasted sunflower seeds.

conduct and know what the rules are.

The rewards? More than you can count. "A program of good nutrition," says famed pediatrician Lendon Smith, M.D., "has its reward in a calm, cheerful, nonallergic child who, because he feels better, will eat better.

"A meal should be a fun, social event. Give the hungry house apes and the depressed, surly, low blood sugar types some raw items or a salad about an hour before mealtime. They should be cheerful and calm when they come to the table," says Dr. Smith. "And because they feel better, they should be more accepting of the good foods you set before them."

Or you could try having your kids cook their own food.

IS YOUR KID A JULIA CHILD?

"Let my kids cook? Are you kidding? I'd rather do it myself! When they're in the kitchen, there's more mess, less food, and always an impending need for the emergency squad." Nobody really said that, but most people *think* it when the subject of kids in the kitchen comes up. Still, we think you should reconsider the idea by *rethinking* it. Kids will never gain the notion that cooking is a pleasurable activity if their first day in the kitchen is also their first day on their own; cooking will always seem an unpleasant obligation to them, one that comes somewhere between walking the dog and taking out the garbage. So get your youngsters started early and then only on a wouldn't-it-be-neat basis.

And reconsider also that their problems with mess and yours with fuss may be simply snafus in planning. Don't leave kids alone in the kitchen, and don't expect them to do veal Orloff or a gossamer souffle from start to finish. But, on the other hand, don't choose *only* those recipes that children can do all by themselves, because if you do, you'll be stuck with cornflakes with white sauce and peanut butter au jelly. Instead, choose something *you* enjoy making (and eating) and divide the labor: Let them do the things they can safely manage, and you do the rest. Making yeast bread or Oriental

stir-frying are two good places to begin. And so are man-size tee shirts for each mini-chef. They cover more than aprons do, and with them, little boys won't think they're being made to dress up like Mrs. Brady on TV.

If you're trying yeast bread, add these steps to your usual procedure. Kids can do well with the beginning stages of mixing, but you should take over as the flour mounts and the dough stiffens. From there on, however, they can step in again. Most children like to knead a good, elastic dough, and, if you have chosen a recipe calling for free-form, sheet-baked loaves, they can deal with the final loaf-shaping step, too. You should, of course, maneuver the bread in and out of the oven for them.

Stir-frying is fun for kids, too. Obviously, they can't do all the cutting that's required, but they do like the actual wok-flipping and can negotiate it safely. That's because woks don't spatter and the traditional stir-frying tool has a long, easy-to-hold handle. What's more, most Oriental recipes have simple dump-it-in-the-pan sauces that youngsters can handle, and short cooking times. There is no time in chicken with mixed vegetables for even a six-year-old to get bored or

Baking, whether it's bread or carob brownies, isn't for adults only. Every kitchen is big enough to include the kids in preparing family meals. A man-size tee shirt is the perfect apron to protect pint-size helpers against spills or slips. Parents should start with simpler recipes before moving on to more elaborate dishes. But no matter the recipe, a team effort between parent and child can make for happy times around the kitchen counter.

Better Lunches for Kids

What's for lunch? At most schools it's "mystery meat" and vegetable debris hiding in gelatin salad. But in the New York City schools, the selections below greeted students after Liz Cagan, the school system's food services administrator, brought in nutrition consultant Barbara Friedlander Meyer.

Tomato
Lettuce
Green pepper
Cucumber
Carrots
Celery
Onions
Potato salad
Macaroni salad
Tuna fish salad
Fresh apple with raisins

And these were just the raw materials for the do-it-yourself lunchers. The list doesn't include the daily entrees, which contained, by the way, no artificial flavors or colors, no MSG, no nonbeneficial additives at all and reduced amounts of salt, sugar and fat.

remember that Huckleberry Hound has a prior claim on his attention.

HOW TO FIND GOOD FOOD IN A STRANGE TOWN

How does the road-worn traveler find restaurants serving good, wholesome food? We turned to a number of people who travel extensively to find out.

If anyone could be an authority on the subject, it must be Michael Stern, coauthor with his wife, Jane, of the book *Roadfood* (Random House, 1980). The Sterns traveled several hundred thousand miles and wore out four or five cars while writing *Roadfood,* which is a guide to more than 400 inexpensive regional restaurants.

"We considered ourselves guinea pigs," quips Michael. "We ate at every place in the book and actually lived to tell about it."

Eventually the Sterns were able to compile a list of certain guidelines they followed when looking for a place.

"Avoid places that have big billboards on the highway or big display ads in the Yellow Pages of phone books," Michael advises. "Never eat at restaurants that spin on top of a needle and never ask motel clerks, people at official tourist welcome stations or the local chamber of commerce where to get a good meal. They will almost always send you to the pretentious French restaurant in town — the 'duck and orange sauce' place — or a very expensive hotel. Also avoid restaurants where you see a lot of out-of-state license plates."

Travelers should observe a restaurant's parking lot. It is said that travelers should eat where truck drivers do, but Michael disagrees. "I think truck drivers eat probably some of the worst food in the world," he says. "That old cliché probably grew up before the interstates when truckers were more like pioneers who had to find a good place to eat and to stay. But now truckers are captives of the interstate, and the truck stops along these highways are generally the worst places to find good food."

Pickup trucks can be a good sign, however. "When you're driving in the early morning in the South and Southwest, look for places with pickup trucks in the yard," Michael

The food of the future in schools, colleges, hospitals and office cafeterias will be a far cry from the bland, lifeless fare served in most institutions today. For example, Cornish game hen flanked by steamed vegetables, a crisp salad, whole wheat bread, fresh blueberries and a tall glass of milk is a meal brimming with just about every vitamin and mineral your body needs — thanks to light cooking and the use of whole grains and vegetables and lean meat.

Mixed Mates

You're a vegetarian, your mate is a meat eater. How do you avoid arguing over every meal? Well, one way is to cook meatless dishes that still have a hearty meat flavor. That means when you subtract meat, add something to fill in the gap.

And *that* means much more than simply plugging in a vegetable protein for the animal variety in the original recipe. It means adding strong and savory tastes to replace those that left with the meat.

For instance, try a lasagna that replaces ground meat with the firm and tasty pleasures of eggplant. A chili that uses the flavors of tamari soy sauce and blackstrap molasses in place of spicy meats. And a whimsical "Beans Stroganoff" that substitutes 2 kinds of beans and chopped walnuts (plus some more tamari) for the beef cubes of the classic recipe.

says. "You'll find a good breakfast with homemade biscuits or rolls."

Restaurants that have been operating for a long time in a small town often are good bets. "It also helps to talk to the locals," says Michael, "but don't just walk up to anyone. He or she may assume you mean something expensive and expensive does not necessarily mean good. Walk up to a postal worker or a police officer and ask, 'Where do *you* eat when you eat out?' Shadow them to a lunch counter and you'll probably find good food."

One problem is that good food means different things to different people—even to restaurant operators. "We ran into a lot of restaurant owners serving fresh, native produce and homemade breads who modestly dismissed their menus, saying, 'Well, this isn't really *good* food, but we do our best.' Even to the restaurant owners, 'good food' was something you put on a tie and jacket to eat. But we found ordinary food infinitely better than tie-and-jacket cuisine."

Boardinghouses in the South provided the Sterns with some of their more memorable meals. "At one boardinghouse in Texas, you pay $4 or $5 for a meal that just keeps coming—ham, chicken, turkey, biscuits, fresh vegetables. By the time we arrived at dessert, we were stuffed. The manager said, 'You don't have any more room right now, so why don't you just go upstairs and rest awhile? When you come back down, the desserts will be here for you.'" The Sterns were not registered as guests but welcomed the invitation for a brief respite. When they returned to the table, platters brimming with homemade desserts awaited them as promised.

The Sterns discovered their food bills ran amazingly low when they ate in regional establishments. "In so many towns, the best food is the cheapest, too," Michael says. "The most expensive place is serving food that has been shipped from Godknows-where and turned into Cordon Bleu in a microwave oven."

The Sterns' travels were not restricted by lack of a car, but not all travelers are fortunate enough to locate their meals on wheels. With a growing national emphasis on energy

You don't need meat to greet the holidays. Vegetarian dishes are a healthy toast to the New Year, Thanksgiving or any festive occasion. Here the meal starts with an appetizer of Brie cheese topped with egg white and poppy seeds. The entree is broccoli bake with pasta, with a side dish of acorn squash. The bread is potato rolls; the salad, a delightful mixture of fruit and sprouts; and the dessert, maple chiffon pie.

Runners completing the annual Prevention Marathon in Northampton County, Pennsylvania, celebrate the end of their 26-mile run with a hot meal. Provided by the race's sponsor, lunch features a salad bar that's heavy on muscle-mending protein supplied by beans rather than meat. The meal also includes hot soup and a carbohydrate-rich baked potato. Marathon champ Lou Gunderman rounds off his meal with his "just desserts"—a full assortment of fresh fruit and lots of replacement fluids.

conservation, many people may choose buses and trains for transport, which often leave passengers to fend for themselves in the downtown areas of cities.

When Bonnie Prudden hits the trail every weekend, all roads must lead to good nutrition. Founder of the Institute for Physical Fitness in Stockbridge, Massachusetts, Ms. Prudden struggles to maintain a well-balanced diet wherever she is.

"We travel so much and so fast that we've had to just choose well wherever we are—which isn't always easy, you know," she sighs. "We *never* order the dish of the day, soups, desserts or anything au gratin. We just order something they can't possibly destroy, like broiled fish and a salad."

Ms. Prudden does warn travelers to "get *nothing* with a sauce. You have no idea what's in it, and you have no idea what goes on in the kitchen."

She adds that asking for recommendations at the nearest gas station occasionally works. "Every man in town knows where the best steak is," she muses, "and where the best steaks are, you're apt to find the best food."

Travelers on restricted diets due to religious tenets, health, career or personal reasons may face additional roadblocks to good food. But they can turn that challenge into a real opportunity if they handle it right.

"I eat kosher, so I have to find other Jews who also eat kosher when I travel," says Robert Mendelsohn, M.D., of Evanston, Illinois.

"If you belong to any religion that has stringent food regulations, then you have a built-in network of people, not only nationally but internationally, who observe the same kind of eating patterns you do. All you have to do is take advantage of that network."

Dr. Mendelsohn says that observant Jews share at least one advantage since the network experience "affords them not only kosher food but new friends and a pleasant social environment."

Michael Mahoney, Ph.D., professor of psychology at Pennsylvania State University, is a lacto-ovo vegetarian who has learned to plan ahead when he travels.

"If I'm flying, I'll call the

Food to Go

To meet the executive stress of missed planes, long days, overheated hotel rooms and wily competitors, you need all the *good* nutrition you can get. One way is to bring along a "CARE package" from home.

Try the crunchy-sweet mixture of nuts, seeds and dried fruits that camping aficionados call "Trail Mix." Or how about a selection of cheeses and a variety of fresh fruits? The beauty of most of these foods is that they store well without refrigeration (briefly) and can be eaten without utensils.

airlines in advance and request a vegetarian meal. Anyone who is interested in good nutrition can do this," he says. "On coast-to-coast flights, I'm also careful to avoid the dehydration effects of flying at high altitudes. I drink lots of fluids and refrain from alcohol, which acts as a diuretic."

When he's grounded, Dr.

Recipe for a Busy Cook: Carrots, Cauliflower and Pumpkin Seeds

Makes 4 servings

1 tablespoon corn oil
1 medium onion, sliced
     into thin rings
2 cups cauliflower florets

2 medium carrots, sliced
     diagonally
1 tablespoon minced
     fresh parsley
¼ cup pumpkin seeds

In a large skillet, warm oil, then add onion rings. Cook over medium heat for a minute or two.

Break cauliflower florets into bite-size pieces and add them to skillet along with carrots. Stir with onions, then cover, adding a few spoonfuls of water so that the vegetables will steam.

Stir vegetables occasionally, adding a little more water, if necessary, and steam until tender, about 15 minutes.

Toss vegetables with parsley and pumpkin seeds. Serve hot.

Mahoney occasionally asks to see the menu prior to entering a restaurant.

"I also have found that many restaurants within a hotel have special dishes which are not even on the menu. I've obtained 'unlisted meals' several times this way, and they were great!"

If travelers let their fingers do the walking through the Yellow Pages of a phone directory, they may find other great meals listed under "C." Not for cuisine, of course, but for clubs. Organizations like the American Legion, the Lions Club, the Elks Club and La Leche League International have chapters located around the country. For members and non-members alike, a phone call to one of these groups may lead to a great meal.

La Leche League president Marian Tompson says her groups would be glad to recommend good dining facilities for travelers. The league is an organization of mothers located around the United States and abroad who give each other advice and assistance on breastfeeding.

"La Leche people would know where the good places in town are because they really care about good nutrition," she says.

EAT YOUR WAY TO A HAPPY HOLIDAY

The holidays. The mere thought is enough to tingle the taste buds. Great food, big parties, good times, old friends—the proverbial eat, drink and be merry season.

Just how in the world are you going to resist it all? Well, you really don't have to—if you're a normal, healthy person and if you know when enough is enough.

"Eating and the holidays go together, and I see nothing wrong with giving in to a rare burst of overeating on a special occasion," David A. Levitsky, Ph.D., a nutritional scientist at Cornell University, told us. "Overeating in a convivial, holiday atmosphere is very natural and traditional. The positive social and psychological effects of occasional holiday indulgence far outweigh any possible nutritional hazard."

The body was made to withstand a lot of insult, notes Dr.

Levitsky. And if you're already a person in good health and have enough sense to return to your routine of sensible eating habits immediately afterward, the good time from the night before should have no lasting effect on your body.

The point is that indulgence can be okay—once in a while. But *over*indulgence can literally knock the spirit of the season right out of you, both physically and mentally. The malady is commonly known as the "holiday blues."

"There's been a lot of talk about the holiday blues being a psychological problem, and I'm sure it is to some degree," says Warren M. Levin, M.D., director of the World Health Medical Group in New York City. "But we feel there is an altogether different cause, and it has to do with the sudden change to a poor kind of diet.

"People's lifestyles change during the holidays, and they have a tendency to overindulge. It's not just excess refined sugar and alcohol that cause problems. People also eat too many fats and too many things like cakes made with white flour."

The results: anxiety, crankiness, fatigue and even depression—classic symptoms of low blood sugar. "Eating a big meal with a lot of fat, even if you're not taking in sugar and alcohol, can also give you a negative effect," Dr. Levin told us. "Increased fat causes the stomach to empty slowly. It gives you a full feeling, makes you bloated and feel logy."

But feeling uncomfortable isn't the only side effect of too much sugar and alcohol. They also rob our bodies of the precious vitamins and minerals we need to stay in good health. And it doesn't take an awful lot of eating and drinking for this to happen. Thiamine, riboflavin, niacin, folate, choline and vitamin C are all depleted by alcohol. Sugar also depletes thiamine, niacin and choline.

So, how much indulgence is too much? For alcohol, the answer is relatively simple. If you feel intoxicated, you know you've had too much. As for overloading on food, Dr. Levitsky says one feast or maybe even two should be the limit over a two-week stretch.

Knowing where to draw the line on things like sugars, fats, processed cakes and snacks is more complex. The best course would be to avoid them altogether. Second best is to eat as little as possible.

"Every person has a different tolerance for such foods," says Dr. Levin. "The healthier the person, the worse his tolerance for unhealthy food. You must pay attention to what your body is telling you."

But there are ways to eat sensibly and have a good time, too. The best advice is that whatever you do, do it in moderation.

Yet the effects of overeating can be small compared to the results of overuse of alcohol during the holidays—especially for the occasional drinker.

"People who drink every day will probably not drink any differently during the holidays," notes Boris Tabakoff, Ph.D., director of the Alcoholism and Drug Abuse Research and Training Program at the Univer-

The Luxurious Lunch Box

Peanut butter and jelly. Or last night's meat loaf. That's the typical brown bag lunch. For a change, try these variations.

For a better butter, whiz 1 cup of peanuts in a blender or food processor until finely ground. Add 1 tablespoon of tahini (sesame butter) and ¼ teaspoon of cinnamon.

Spread the butter on bread and, instead of jelly, add grated carrot and seedless raisins, or wheat germ and banana slices, or apple butter and coconut flakes.

Or try one of these sandwich combinations:

1. Cream cheese and walnuts on whole wheat raisin bread
2. Lightly steamed string beans chopped with hard-cooked egg and walnuts
3. Tuna mixed with grated carrot, a touch of mayonnaise and lemon juice

Guilt-Free Party Foods

- Fresh fruit punch, herb teas or hot or cold apple cider *instead of* caffeine-filled cola, sugary sodas and cholesterol-laden eggnog
- Frozen yogurt *instead of* ice cream
- Crudités (fresh raw vegetables) *instead of* commercial cheese puffs and pretzels
- A yogurt and fresh clam dip *instead of* processed dips
- Stuffed fresh mushrooms *instead of* caviar
- Chilled shrimp on toothpicks *instead of* salt-heavy smoked salmon or anchovies
- Carrot cake or carob brownies *instead of* white flour pastries
- Dried fruits *instead of* candy

sity of Illinois Medical Center in Chicago. "But for the occasional drinker who hasn't a tolerence for alcohol, it could be a problem. Also, some liquors, especially less expensive brands of whiskey, are contaminated with toxic chemicals—oils and aldehydes—that can make a person sick."

And while red wine may have the same amount of alcohol as white wine, red wine has more such toxins. Thus, says Dr. Tabakoff, white wine is probably better than red wine, and vodka is preferable to whiskey for the occasional drinker.

"Alcohol also depletes the system of vitamins very fast," Dr. Tabakoff told us. Anytime you have been drinking, no matter to what extent, the drinking episode should be followed by a healthy, balanced meal. He also recommends a B complex vitamin supplement.

However, at some time during the holidays, many people are bound to have a little too much of something that's just not too good for them. What happens then? In most cases, they should be able to bounce back from a little excess fairly easily.

For an upset stomach from too much food, Dr. Levin recommends taking 2 to 3 teaspoons of vitamin C powder with 1 teaspoon of sodium bicarbonate powder mixed in 8 ounces of water.

As for the wrath of excess drink—the hangover—there's no known cure, except maybe time and replenishing the system.

"Some people recommend vitamins for a hangover, but I think they should be taken at the time of error in judgment," says Dr. Levin.

Before going to a cocktail party, Dr. Levin suggests supplementing the body with up to 3,000 milligrams of vitamin C, 500 milligrams of niacin, 100 milligrams of vitamin B_6, 200 milligrams of thiamine, 100 milligrams of pantothenate, 15 to 20 milligrams of zinc and 500 milligrams of magnesium.

Yes, the holiday season is a time to enjoy. Just remember to use your head. As Dr. Levitsky says:

"Eating too much once in a while can't hurt the average person. You just have to remember if you do it today, you can't do it tomorrow, too. Or even the next day."

Too late for breakfast and too early for lunch—that's brunch. Sunday is the traditional day for brunching, a day to lounge about and catch up with the rest of the family. Saturdays are good, too, and a holiday brunch is a wonderful way to gather with special friends. Brunch doesn't have to be butter-laden eggs, bacon and sticky buns that leave you with a heavy stomach from the fat load and a bad case of sugar shock. As if that weren't enough, the 2 or 3 cups of coffee you have get you all wired up with no place to go. Make brunch a delicious affair. Make it creative, since you've got more time to put into it. But most of all, make it a good way to start off your day by making it healthful. This delightful spread features a golden cornmeal muffin and lightweight buckwheat crepes filled with cheese and fruit. An appealing ambrosia salad (for the gods and you) has orange and grapefruit sections nestled in half a grapefruit, with grated coconut sprinkled on top. The drink is a luscious strawberry-orange eggnog. And that's just a sampling of the many, many wholesome foods that can grace your brunch.

4

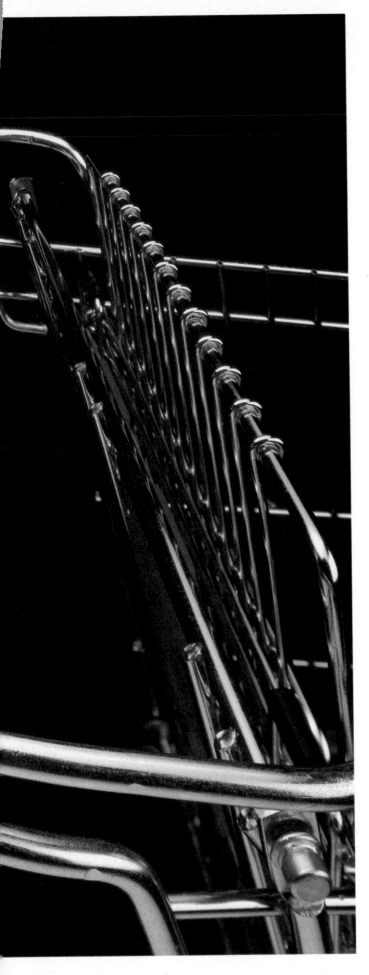

New Ideas in Food Shopping

Coming home with the best
takes some keen strategy
and a love of exploration.

If you took the roof off a supermarket and looked at it from above, the place would seem like a gigantic game board. Well, it is! Only the object of this game isn't to beat your opponent; it's to leave the market with the tastiest, healthiest foods you can find—and with your budget in one piece. To do that, though, you have to know the rules. And the game starts before you walk out your door.

Rule 1: Make a list. Surveys have shown that a woman who goes into a supermarket planning to buy 3 items—but without a list—will usually walk out with some 8 to 10 purchases. A man in the same situation will lug home nearly 20!

On the other hand, don't make your list too rigid. Aside from the ingredients you need to make specific recipes (check the shelves before you go to make sure you really need them), keep the list as flexible as you can within food group categories: green vegetables, meat for Wednesday, fish for Thursday, etc. This will give you the freedom to take advantage of whatever bargains the store may offer.

Rule 2: Leave the children at home if at all possible. Children know exactly what they want (TV commercials have told them), and the junk that food writer Michael S. Lasky has dubbed "kiddie litter" is strategically placed right where they can easily grab it from supermarket shelves. They may sneak candy bars and cheese puffs into the cart without your noticing them. They may scream and turn blue until you give in and agree to buy what they want. And even quiet kids will turn your attention from serious shopping.

Rule 3: Eat before you shop. If you walk into a food store hungry, you're much more likely to be tempted by goodies you don't need.

Rule 4: If you're a coupon clipper, take only those coupons you *know* you're going to need; don't be tempted by junk just because you can get it a few cents cheaper. If possible, shop in the middle of the week, when sales are likely to be on.

That's it for the pregame show. When you arrive at "Go," consider this warm-up advice: Unless your list is a long one, *don't* take a shopping cart. Pick up one of those little wire, plastic or canvas baskets instead, and you'll be less likely to purchase heavy extras.

Rule 5: Hug the walls in circling the "field." Most of the foods you need to create a nutritious diet are placed around the edges of a store rather than in its inner aisles.

Rule 6: Don't be swayed by displays that encourage you to buy more than you need—especially fresh foods. Unless you plan to freeze or preserve things you don't eat right away, you may end up throwing away spoiled vegetables, fruits or meat.

Supermarkets wrap vegetables in clear plastic in an effort to sell more. But if corn is packed in bundles of five ears and there are only four people in your family, you could be gutsy and ask the produce clerk to break open a package for you. He may grumble—but he may do it.

Meat, too, comes sealed in plastic. Looking at the labels, you'll see that the price per pound is much higher for a cut-up chicken than it is for a whole one; you're paying a premium for the convenience of precut chicken. If you can, do the work yourself.

On the other hand, you may want it precut. Ask yourself these questions: Will you eat the skin of that chicken (the part highest in saturated fat)? Will you take the time to make soup or stock from the bones? If not, why pay for them? And, if the white meat is all you're going to eat, you may be getting just

as good a value by buying the skinned and boned breasts.

At the dairy case, how much fat do you want to buy? A quick glance will show you that butter (which is loaded with saturated fat) costs a lot more than margarine (which is made with polyunsaturated fat). Skim milk costs less than whole milk, as it should since it's not mixed with expensive cream. Low-fat plain yogurt will save both money and calories over the fruit-flavored brands that are low in fat but high in sugar. Buying plain yogurt and mixing it with fresh fruit saves money, and is a health plus, too, because you avoid both calories and refined sugar.

But after you've stocked up on the basics, you may still want or need some of the products in those tricky inner aisles. Watch out: This is where the supermarket game really gets tricky.

Rule 7: Look at all the shelves, top and bottom included. The average supermarket shopper is a woman who is 5'4" in height. So where are the most expensive products displayed? *Right at that woman's eye level.* To score points against this positioning ploy, look for the same type of product on higher shelves and then bend down to check the supplies nearer the floor. Chances are, you'll find lower prices in one of these places—and the stretching and bending isn't bad exercise.

Rule 8: Don't be a slave to brand loyalty. That's just what the packager, as well as the supermarket owner, hopes you'll do.

Think of all those TV commercials you've seen that say, "Brand X is the leading brand." Leading in what, nutrition? Fat chance! That phrase means "leading in sales." And why does Brand X lead the sales charts? Because millions of people like us watch TV commercials, that's why. Give the competition a chance!

Rule 9: Read the labels. And that means *read* them, don't just look at them. Rule 9-A is: Look past the package design and find the list of ingredients.

Advertising agencies (which design packaging for supermarket

Beating the Supermarket at Its Own Game

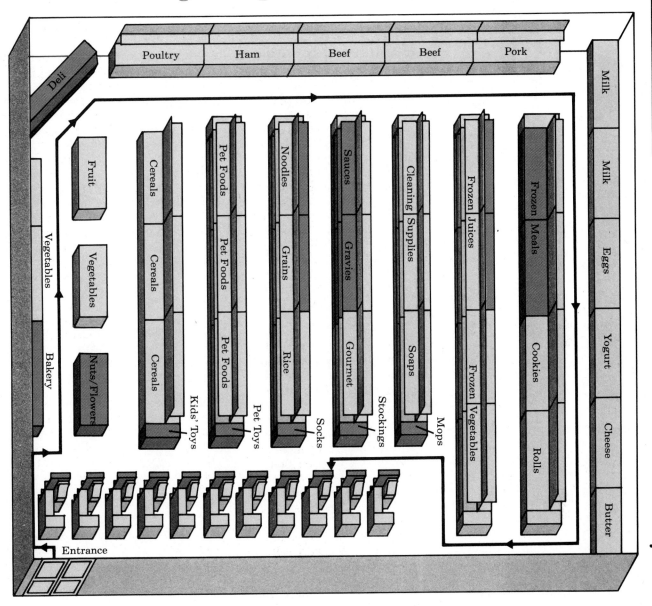

Supermarkets are, in many ways, well-planned money traps. Consider this: You run into the store to pick up a quart of milk. Where is the dairy case? Usually as far from the entrance as you possibly can get. As you hurry down the aisle, you'll probably pass the in-store bakery. (The first shaded area to your left. All the dark areas are traps to snare your money.) "Wouldn't it be nice to have some corn muffins for tomorrow's breakfast?" you're likely to think. And, before you know it, you're paying for the muffins, a package of imported cheese (plucked from the shelf above the milk)

priced for quick sale, a package of crackers to go with the cheese and—oh, yes—a quart of milk.

Consider, too, that if you stop to buy frozen orange juice, chances are you'll soon be face to face with a frozen souffle. (The trap in the aisle nearest the dairy case.) Aisles for low-ticket items like rice are near expensive boxes of pilaf and other gourmet delicacies.

To avoid the traps, follow the arrow —you miss most of the high-cost quicksand, with maximum exposure to the best food in the store.

products) employ people who know as much about our subconscious minds as many psychiatrists do. They know, for example, that red sells. That fancy lettering on a label creates the impression of high quality. That a picture of an appetizing dish can make you crave the contents of a package. If you buy a product simply because of its label, you might as well use it as decoration and forget about opening it.

So "read the labels" means "find out exactly what you're getting for your money."

Rule 10: Watch out for specials. These marketing gimmicks can save you money or waste it, depending on how honest the store management is and how on the ball you are.

Suppose you see a display of Brand X tuna in the front of the store. It's there in front so you'll spot it *before* you see the other brands of tuna. A hand-lettered sign says, "Special!! Brand X Tuna, 99¢ — Today Only!" The sign is hand lettered because that makes it look like a spur-of-the-moment generosity sale rather than a well-planned gimmick.

So, it all *looks* like a good bargain, but before you go for it, take a look at the regular tuna shelf. You may find that Brand Y tuna, or the store's own brand, is selling for 89¢. And if Brand X is going for 99¢ today only, that may mean it's going down to 89¢ tomorrow.

And why do you suppose it's 99¢ instead of an even $1? Because, as simple a gimmick as it is, 99¢ sounds cheap, while $1 sounds expensive. This way, the store can advertise that the brand goes for "less than $1." It's a psychological trick, and it works!

So does the ploy of pricing items at 3 for 99¢ instead of 33¢ each. It makes some people think that they have to buy three packages in order to get the "bargain."

Rule 11: Look straight ahead when going around the corners of aisles. You don't want to bump into another shopper, of course, but neither do you want to get trapped by the "end-of-the-aisle grabbers." Store managers know that people have to slow down when they reach the end of the aisle, so they stock high-profit items there, items that may cost more than other products of the same type. Look out for tempting junk food items here, too.

The Smart Shopper's Tricks of the Trade

Dos

1. Do use a list while shopping; keep a pencil and paper handy in the kitchen, and add to it as you run out of things or make plans.
2. Do plan meals in advance, and do plan for leftovers as you chart your weekly course.
3. Do study the prices of favorite items over a period of time; know when they go up or down.
4. Do comparison shop from store to store and ad to ad.
5. Do try to confine your buying to whole foods and raw materials; beef may be $3 a pound, but the meat in a prepared dinner could be twice or three times that.

Don'ts

1. Don't follow your list blindly; be flexible enough to take advantage of genuine price reductions and in-season surprises.
2. Don't accept a special at its face value; make sure that "special" actually means a drop in price.
3. Don't stop comparing prices once you enter a store; compare national brands with store brands, top-shelf items with bottom-shelf offerings.
4. Don't shop in a hurry, but don't dawdle either; take all the time you need to consider your purchases, but remember that too much time in a store can mean too much exposure to temptation.

These shopper traps are called gondolas, special displays that stand in the middle of your walking space and virtually demand to be noticed. Remember: If it's in a gondola, it's probably going to be overpriced.

Gondola items are hard to resist because they're within easy reach and lurking in a jumble of identical packages. Remember the tidy, sculptural displays that we used to see in stores? We don't see them much any more, do we? The reason is that merchandisers found that customers were reluctant to take packages from such fragile-looking displays. They feared destroying the symmetry or worse—the whole pyramid might come tumbling down! But if the display is a mess in the first place, customers grab with abandon.

As if that weren't enough, there are two more sneaky placement tricks. The first could be called "musical gondolas." How often have you said, "I know the noodle bin was right there last week; where is it now?" You ask, and someone happily points the way. And as you walk to the new location, of course, you have to walk past other displays that are meant to tempt you into picking up a little something extra.

And when you finally find what you're looking for, you also discover an expensive related item right next to it. For example, if you are looking for spaghetti—a fairly low-profit product—there's sure to be some expensive commercial spaghetti sauce placed within easy reach. Ordinarily, you'd probably make your own sauce with fresh, natural ingredients, but there it is, and it's so convenient. . .

Then there's the "last chance" strategy. When you've finally made your way through the maze and arrived at the checkout counter, there are dozens of "goodies" arrayed for you to "check out!" Magazines, batteries, film, chewing gum, candy—stuff that kids can grab at the last minute and toss on the counter before Mom notices—and a jumble of displays of everything from jam to jelly beans. Faced with this gambit, look straight ahead and stick with the things in your basket. You didn't want any of it until the store displays brought it to your attention.

Finding Hidden Health Foods

If you're into healthy eating, you might think of your supermarket as a place to avoid, a tawdry carnival of overprocessed foods. But big stores are also big on healthy foods. Just "check out" the list below.

Fresh, lean meat
Poultry
Water-packed tuna and salmon
Fresh fruits
Apple cider
Dried fruits
Unroasted, unsalted nuts
Fresh vegetables
Dried peas and beans
Natural cheeses
Whole and skim milk
Yogurt
Cottage cheese
Nonfat dry milk
Wild rice
Brown rice
Popping corn
Bulgur
Pearled barley
Dried sweet corn
Unprocessed wheat bran
Rolled oats
Whole grain wheat and rye flour
Whole wheat bread
Shredded wheat
Puffed wheat and rice
Oatmeal
Unsweetened, whole grain granola
Unsweetened jams and jellies
Dried herbs and spices
Honey
Molasses
Tamari soy sauce
Corn, safflower and sunflower oils
Herb teas

Did you make it? Did you get out of the market with the items you wanted and not much more? Are the foods you bought fresh and nutritious and unladen with chemicals? If so, congratulate yourself, you've won the Supermarket Game.

If you do win the Supermarket Game, yours won't be the first name engraved on the gold cup. In fact,
(continued on page 48)

45

Shop the Old-Fashioned Way

Create an old-style Main Street by shopping at specialty stores—where the service is personal and the selection unique.

Butcher. Old-fashioned service is the hallmark of a butcher. He'll trim to order and save the bone for Bowser.

Cheese Shop. A specialty store offers hundreds of delicious alternatives to Swiss and American. It's sure to be love at first bite.

Farm Stand. Produce grown locally is fresh and economical. Take advantage of seasonal bounty like tomatoes, spring peas and pumpkins.

Dairy. The dairy sells milk the same day cows provide it. Refillable bottles—and no middleman—keep the price low.

Orchard. Pick up a basket and head for the trees. Most orchards charge a flat rate per bushel, which is low because *you* do the picking.

Fish Store. The best catch of the day is at the fish store. Small quantities kept fresh on ice—not frozen—insure subtle flavor and flaky texture.

Bakery. More than just birthday cakes come from the bakery. Try hearty sour rye, buttery croissants, round loaves made from whole grains and fresh breakfast muffins.

enough people have mastered the rules (or even become so tired of playing the same game all the time that they're now shopping at some of the alternative markets described later in this chapter) that supermarket managers have introduced some twists.

DOUBLE TROUBLE

One of those new twists is double coupons—that is, the offer to double the value of the manufacturers' cents-off coupons you find in newspapers, magazines and Sunday supplements.

This gimmick can be turned to your advantage if you remember two important points. First, don't try to use every coupon you find. The cardinal rule of couponing still applies: Use coupons only for those items you would buy anyway. Second, don't fall for the market's "we-want-to-save-you-money" ploy and do exactly what the manager wants you

to do—buy a lot of expensive stuff just because you figure you're saving so much on the double coupons that you can afford to splurge. If you do that, you're likely to spend more than if you'd never picked up the scissors in the first place.

Another new angle is generic food items, which offer an additional benefit to people who are interested in saving money without getting second-rate products. You've seen them in most supermarkets: those plain, white boxes and cans that have labels in big, black letters reading "Green Beans," "Spaghetti," or "Laundry Detergent." No fancy lettering, no pretty pictures, just a solid, back-to-basics approach to packaged foods and household items. Or so it *seems*.

The truth is a little more complicated. Supermarkets buy these products from wholesalers and package them themselves, adding either store brand or generic labels. Store brands are usually a little lower in

What's this? Fructose and carob nestled into the supermarket right along with Manhandlers and Snackin' Cake? You bet! The future supermarket will offer health foods along with more standard fare to an ever more health-conscious public. Hopefully, mass marketing also will lower specialty item prices.

price than national brands, and the generics shave a few more cents off the store brand price.

The problem with store brands and generics is that they might be a little lower in *quality,* too. Supermarket managers look for bargains from their wholesalers just as shoppers try to find bargains in the supermarkets. When a big-name food processor has broken or discolored fruits and vegetables that aren't good enough to carry the brand name, they process them and sell the result at a discount to the chain stores, which then sell them as generics. That's great business for the stores and bad luck for you.

Two more points: Generics are not *always* the cheapest brands in the store, especially if there's a sale or you have a coupon for a national brand. And sometimes—with certain products—a generic's strength may be less than a national brand's; that is, you may have to use much more of a generic detergent to get your clothes clean. So, compare prices—and labels—even if it means walking all the way across the store.

"NO-FRILLS" SHOPPING

Supermarkets may be the most convenient, and certainly the most widely advertised, stores, but they are *not* the only sources of food. Recent innovations in this field are warehouse or "box" stores.

These places are operated by professional food merchants but with a difference; to them, "no frills" means "no conveniences" and "no atmosphere." In a box store you'll find both national brands and generics displayed in cartons from which the tops have been ripped off— nothing beckons alluringly from shelves! Prices are announced on big, central signs instead of being stamped on each box or can. And boxes and cans are about all you'll find; no-frills stores don't go to the expense of providing the refrigeration necessary for fresh produce, meat and dairy products.

No-frills also means you'd better bring cash, because most such stores won't take checks or credit cards.

Health food shops offer alternatives to hundreds of usual products, ranging from whole grain cereals and additive-free salad dressings to unsalted potato chips. The growing success of 10,000 or more health food stores has led some giant supermarket chains to open their own health food sections.

And you'll have to do your own bagging in your own bags!

Box stores are big, ugly warehouses full of piles and piles of food products—a sight that some customers find depressing. But the result of this austerity is that most of their prices are 10 to 30 precent lower than those in chain stores.

Another solution to the food price and quality problem is to avoid stores completely and *pick* your own food.

THE PICKY SHOPPER

You can do it just by taking a trip to a nearby farm that allows strangers—even city slickers—to pay for the privilege of doing work the farmer would otherwise have to do himself. For your money, which will usually be about one-third less than you'd have to pay for the same fresh fruits and vegetables in a store, you can get both the produce of your choice and some good, healthy exercise.

A less laborious way to pick your own is to shop at a roadside stand. But make sure you choose one that can deliver the freshness and high nutritional quality you need. Only the roadside stands that are located near the growing fields and have refrigerated storage space are able to deliver truly fresh fruits and vegetables—those that retain the taste and nutrition they were born with. The adorably rustic little stand with no cooling facility and no water supply may be fine for a Norman Rockwell painting, but it is rough on freshness and nutrition. Produce that sits in the sun all day will be wilted and drained of many vitamins and minerals.

IS "HEALTH FOOD" HEALTHIER?

One type of food store that people go to for products that deliver an *extra* dollop of vitamins and minerals (and leave out disease-causing food factors) is the health food store. But anyone who's ever shopped in one knows that health food stores *charge* for that nutrition—at the present markup, the products cost about twice as much as those found in supermarkets. So the important question is, "Is it worth it?"

As far as the organic produce that's often sold in health food stores is concerned, you're pretty much in the dark. That type of produce is *supposed* to be free of pesticide residues and grown in soil enriched by nonchemical fertilizers. But there's no way to tell if that's the case, short of giving the health food store employee or the farmer a lie detector test. And even if the produce has been grown organically, it may have been hit by pesticides blowing in the wind from the nonorganic farm down the road or contaminated by chemical fertilizers used in the soil years before. Equally good produce is probably available from a farmers' market, a greengrocer, or even a supermarket.

The other side of the coin is that organic produce may, in fact, be tastier and loaded with extra nutrients. So the choice is really a personal one—just be sure that the "organic" label is for real.

Another health word that may be more hype than fact is "natural." The government's Federal Trade Commission (FTC) *has* defined the word. They decreed that foods labeled natural must be only "minimally processed" and free of all synthetic and artificial ingredients. But by minimal processing, the FTC meant washing, peeling, homogenizing, canning, bottling and freezing; the baking

---

Healthy Skepticism: Why It's Required in Approaching the Health Food World

Not everything you find in a health food store is a healthy food. Watch out for the following items.

Sugars. Honey and molasses do contain some nutrients, but should be used in moderation. Turbinado sugar and brown sugar are merely cane sugar with some color left.

Sea salt. Salt is salt. Federal regulations stipulate that salt used for food must be 97.5 percent sodium chloride. That doesn't leave much room for the minerals sea salt is supposed to be so rich in.

Granola. Avoid any granola that lists any sweetener as one of the first three ingredients, and watch for hidden ones like corn syrup.

of bread; the aging and roasting of meat; and the grinding of nuts.

What this definition means is that a lot of supermarket products have moved into the natural food category, and food manufacturers, alert to the public's new romance with good nutrition, have rushed to label what seems like every other product on the shelves with the "natural" banner. Once again, you have to be a careful label reader to be sure you're getting what's natural to *you*.

THE COOKIE AND CAROB DROP AISLE

Another way the supermarket executives have tried to corral natural food lovers is with the special health food sections that have begun popping up in chrome-and-plastic chain stores. The trend was started in the late 70s by the Safeway chain in California, which now has added "natural foods centers" to 401 of its stores. At the end of its first year of operation the chain had rung up more than $13 billion in sales of such un-supermarket-like products as fertile eggs, pomegranate juice and seaweed. The Kroger chain then jumped on the bandwagon, opening "healthy" snack departments in 700 stores and selling soybeans, sunflower seeds and carob drops.

This kind of competition can only be good news for consumers because both the supermarkets and the specialty stores will fall all over themselves trying to attract business. Each has its advantages.

The supermarket, in general, has lower prices, and if you can get the same health foods (or all the healthy foods you need) there, why go elsewhere? But the supermarkets still restrict their specialty items to small sections, while health food stores have a much wider range of products, which they often are able to stock and sell in bulk quantities.

On the other hand, most health food stores restrict their stock to packaged goods and do not have much in the line of fresh produce, meat, fish and dairy goods.

Back in the supermarket, where you'll find all the fresh produce you

Say "Good Buy" to Costly Shopping: A Price Guide with Some Surprises

Here are some price comparisons to show you where the bargains *really* are. The point: Shop around!

PRICE COMPARISON CHART

Food	Quantity	Supermarket	Farmers' Market	Food Co-op	Health Food Store	No-Frills Market
Eggs, large	1 doz.	$ .93	$ .95	$ .90	$ .99	—
Chicken, whole	1 lb.	$ .69	$ .69	$ .99	$ .79	—
Beef liver	1 lb.	$ .79	$1.29	$2.49	$1.09	—
Tuna, light, in water	6.5 oz.	$ .89	—	—	$ .93	$ .79
Mushrooms, fresh	1 lb.	$1.39	$1.00	—	$1.09	—
Peanut butter	1 lb.	$1.75	$1.42	$1.93	$1.55	$2.70
Honey	1 lb.	$1.29	$1.55	—	$1.19	$1.19
Safflower oil	1 qt.	$2.39	—	$2.73	$2.33	$1.99
Vinegar	1 qt.	$ .69	—	$1.22	—	$ .59
Navy beans, dried	1 lb.	$ .59	—	$ .61	$ .69	$ .56
Raisins	1 lb.	$1.39	—	$1.43	$1.79	$1.58
Coffee	1 lb.	$2.58	—	—	$2.49	$2.33

want, you won't find anywhere near the supplement selection that's available in the health food store—no alfalfa tablets or brewer's yeast. Wheat germ is about as exotic as most supermarkets get.

Most health food stores also double as book stores, carrying literature you're not likely to find in a supermarket. And since the specialty shops are smaller, often of the mom-and-pop variety, chances are the proprietors and clerks will soon begin greeting you by name, a personal touch only the rarest of supermarkets can muster.

Any way you look at it, getting the most nutrition for the least money is a project, one that requires a lot of label reading, a lot of price comparing, and a lot of selective shopping. But when a goal is as important as this one—your health— it's certainly worth the trouble.

A Farmers' Market Cornucopi

Farmers' markets aren't always run by farmers these days, but they're still worth your shopping consideration. The best ones offer high-quality foods at competitive prices, and even some of the not-so-hot examples can provide a colorful excursion. Ask around to find the market nearest you.

L.A. Farmers' Market

This big market in Los Angeles, California, was founded in 1934 by farmers tired of selling from the backs of their trucks. The 152 merchants now offer produce (purchased from wholesalers), meat, fish, poultry and even a selection of gifts, clothing and cameras that appeal to the flocks of tourists.

Central and Southern Markets

Here's an old-fashioned market building in Lancaster, a city in Pennsylvania's Dutch country. The stalls and stands in this lovely old building are still owned by farmers, and they feature locally grown produce, meats, baked goods and even the traditional handicrafts of the area.

The Haymarket

This *portable* outdoor market in Boston, Massachusetts, was founded over 300 years ago; it still attracts 250 merchants each Friday and Saturday from early morning 'til 8 or 9 at night. The push-carts offer produce and dry staples, while meat is available at a dozen nearby indoor shops.

The Italian Market

The merchants in this Philadelphia market began catering to the food needs of Italian immigrants 100 years ago, and since then they've expanded their offerings to accommodate the tastes of many other ethnic groups. Indoor shops are open all week. Outdoor stands spring to life on Fridays and Saturdays.

Fulton Fish Market

This famous Manhattan landmark is actually a place for wholesalers to sell directly to restaurants and other markets, but there is also a brisk retail trade. Opposite the South Street Seaport Museum, the Fulton opens, Monday through Friday, as soon as the fishermen dock at 5 A.M.

NYC's Chinatown

The merchants of the indoor and streetside shops that link Canal and Mott streets in lower Manhattan are united by their membership in the city's Chinese community. The specialties here, of course, are the herbs, vegetables, meats and fish used in Oriental cooking.

Lexington Farmers' Market

The Lexington Market in Baltimore, Maryland, has recently been spruced up as part of the city's harbor area renewal. The 169 vendors still buy from the growers and producers here, and their emphasis is on high quality and a wide and unusual selection; freshly ground horseradish and muskrat are everyday commodities.

5

How to Pick the Very Best

From apples to zucchini — a bonanza of tips to spot the tastiest, freshest, most nutritious foods.

It's a shopping day. You stroll to the fish section of your supermarket and pick a fillet marked "fresh"—what could be better? Then, in the produce section, you look for the biggest carrots, figuring the small ones can't be as good. Near the carrots are the potatoes, and you buy a 20-pound bargain bag to save money. In the citrus section, you squeeze the limes and buy the hard ones, thinking they won't go bad as fast.

Four purchases. All of them wrong.

It's not that the types of foods you bought were unhealthy. Far from it. But when it comes to freshness, they were second-rate. (We'll tell you why a little later in this chapter.) And that means they were a little less tasty—and probably shortchanged you on nutrients to boot.

But how can you tell which foods are the freshest? There's no one standard, of course. Fish, for example, is only fresh for the day you buy it, while hard, aged cheeses like natural cheddar are fresh for up to two months.

So we're going to show you how to recognize the freshness signs of a wide variety of foods. How to keep an eye out for colors and textures. How to know what the smells mean—and even the sounds! (Thumping a melon is one way to "listen" to freshness.) You'll learn the secrets of buying the best in meat, poultry, fish, vegetables, fruits, eggs, dairy products—dozens of items in all.

And you'll soon find that activities like picking the best of the lot among a bin of oranges, quizzing your local fish dealer, and discovering the subtleties of natural cheese are a lot more fun than mechanically reaching for cello-wrapped or boxed foods. And if you're worried that being choosy will be time-consuming or too difficult—don't. Just consult this guide before your shopping trips, and make a few notes on your list. After a little practice, you'll be perfect. And so will the food!

WILL THE REAL FRESH VEGETABLE PLEASE STAND UP?

Some fruits and vegetables are at their peak during certain months of the year. For instance, April and May are the peak months for *asparagus.* Look for firm, straight stalks with well-formed, tightly closed tips. Thicker stalks are not necessarily better—slender stalks are often the most succulent. Avoid limp, wilted or flat asparagus; it will be tough and stringy. And don't be put off by an extra length of woody stem; it keeps asparagus moist by preventing moisture loss.

Avoid *yellow or green beans* that are broken off below the stem; they'll have lost moisture, too. Look for pliable, velvety, well-colored beans; avoid any that are coarse, limp, spotted, bruised or hard.

Broccoli stalks should be tender and firm, not woody. Look for heads that are compact, with tightly closed flower buds. Pass up broccoli with yellow or flowering buds, wilted or shriveled bunches, or stalks that smell strong and pungent.

Look for small, firm, compact *brussels sprouts.* Like their cousin broccoli, brussels sprouts smell strong when they're too old. Avoid large, puffy sprouts or any with black spots or holes—two signs of insect damage.

Cabbage should be firm, not puffy, and heavy for its size. Avoid heads with a dull color or wilted outer leaves.

With *carrots,* the stems are a good clue to their age; if stems are black or otherwise discolored, they're old. Look for small, crisp, carrots. A bigger carrot has a bigger fibrous core, which is not as sweet as the outer layer.

Cauliflower should have a clean, compact head, free of speckles and smudges. Avoid heads that are loose and spread out—a sure sign of old age in this vegetable.

Avoid limp or woody-looking *celery* stalks, or those with wilted, yellow leaves.

The best *corn* is eaten the day it leaves the field. Look for fresh, green husks, a stem that's not dry or discolored and milky, tender, dent-free kernels.

Bad *cucumbers* are easy to spot: they're dull and yellow, with wrinkled or shriveled skin. Dark, sunken spots are sure signs of decay.

Look for *eggplants* that have smooth, taut skins and feel firm, not spongy. The best months to buy eggplant are July and August.

White-skinned *garlic* has the strongest flavor; pinkish or purplish garlic is milder. Look for large bulbs with good-size cloves.

Lettuce and other salad greens— chicory, endive, escarole, romaine— should be tender and crisp. Reject greens that are yellow, wilted or brown.

Look for *mushrooms* with caps that curl down and cover the fluted gills underneath. If the cap opens like a parasol, the mushroom is past its prime. Avoid spongy-textured mushrooms.

Choose *onions* loose in the bin, and feel for firm, dry ones that crackle or rustle when pressed. Avoid any that are damp, soft or have woody spots on their stem ends.

Parsnips are at their best from October to January. Look for smooth, firm, well-shaped roots; avoid any that are soft or shriveled.

Peas should have small, shiny pods that feel velvety and tender. Reject peas that bulge at the seams— they tend to be old, tough and mealy.

When choosing *green and red bell peppers,* look for firm, brightly colored skins. Check stem ends for early signs of decay. Avoid pale, soft, thin-skinned specimens.

The type of *potatoes* you choose depends on how you plan to cook them. "New" potatoes are best for steaming, boiling and use in potato salads; mature potatoes are excellent for baking and mashing. Look for unsprouted spuds without green spots. Avoid 20-pound "bargain sacks"—many of the potatoes will be split, cracked or decayed, forcing you to throw away a good part of your "bargain."

When buying *radishes,* look for green crisp leaves (if they have any) or smooth, bright, firm roots.

Scallions should have clean, white root ends, with bulbs ½ inch or less in diameter.

Shallots are at their best from July to October; those sold in other months have been in storage. Look

> "Corn kernels should be large enough so there's no space between rows. Avoid ears with immature white kernels or overmature large ones that look tough."
> —from *The Greengrocer,* by Joe Carcione and Bob Lucas.

for large, firm shallots with about ¾-inch bulbs. Like other onions, their outer skins should be smooth and dry, and they should not be sprouted.

Look for large, dark *spinach* leaves that aren't wilted or bruised. U.S. No. 1 Grade spinach is less likely to have a lot of sand and debris clinging to it.

Soft-skinned *squashes* are at their best when small or medium size, with no soft, watery spots. These varieties—like zucchini or yellow crookneck—are at their peak from June to August. When shopping for the hard-skinned variety, pass by those that are bruised or discolored.

The best *sweet potatoes and yams* are small to medium size, tapered at both ends and smooth skinned.

Buy only *tomatoes* that are red, ripe and firm, not split or soggy. If they're underripe, they'll taste flat or sour; if they're overripe, they'll taste bland.

Turnips and rutabagas should be firm, heavy for their size, and not cut or punctured.

FILLING YOUR FRUIT BASKET

Look for firm, well-colored, unbruised *apples.* For best results, pick the type that's most suitable for the intended use: Red or Golden Delicious for eating; Golden Delicious and Rome Beauty for baking; McIntosh and Cortland for eating and cooking.

Apricots are best from mid-May through August; those bought later in the year have probably been shipped from South America—too long a trip for such a delicate, perishable fruit. Ideally, apricots should be velvety golden-yellow, with a blush of red. If they're soft, that's fine.

A ripe, buttery, ready-to-eat *avocado* should feel slightly soft. If you don't plan to eat your avocado for a few days, buy one that's still hard and let it ripen at home. Avoid any that have dark soft spots or that are black.

Most *bananas* arrive at the store with green tips. You can buy them like that, but they're not ready to eat until all the green has disappeared and brown spots appear—at that point, the starch has turned to sugar.

(continued on page 60)

Stalking the Perfect Melon

When pressed, *cantaloupes and honeydews* should have some give. Both should smell sweet and flowery, not fermented. Pass up any melon that sloshes around inside when shaken—it'll be mushy or sour.

For a sweet, orange-fleshed cantaloupe, look for a slightly yellow or tan melon completely covered with a creamy-colored, raised netting. If the rind is green, the melon was picked too soon; too yellow, it's overripe. Fibers hanging from the stem mean that the cantaloupe was picked too early, so look for a smooth stem scar.

Honeydew melons should have smooth skins that feel slightly sticky, perhaps with some scattered patches of netting. The skin should be creamy white or yellowish, not dead-white or green.

A ripe *casaba melon* is deep golden-yellow between the furrows. When you press on the blossom end (opposite the stem end) it should give and spring back.

The flesh of *split watermelons* should be firm and red, not dry and mealy, and it should have no white streaks. The seeds should be full size and black or brown.

The skin of a *whole watermelon* should be dull, not shiny. Turn it over until you find its "ground spot," the place where it rests on the ground while on the vine. The spot should be yellowish, not white or green.

Thumping for the right sound also helps identify a ripe watermelon. Overripe ones sound hollow; underripe, somewhat metallic. A watermelon that produces a deep resonant sound should be just right for eating.

At Its Best

At first glance, it looks like we decided to pose the contents of a savvy shopper's grocery bag for a gorgeous still life. But if you look closely, you'll see that not all the foods here are picture perfect. Can you spot the problems? The stand-outs? Give it a try before you read the captions, and see if you can tell which of this food is "at its best."

1 Celery

For crisp, tender celery, avoid yellow leaves or woody stalks. Green Pascal is less stringy and more flavorful than the paler Golden Self-Blanching.

2 Roast

A well-marbled cut of meat makes a tender, juicy roast, but leaner cuts like top round would be more healthful. Moist cooking methods help retain flavor.

3 Lettuce

Lettuce should smell sweet, not bitter, and be free of brown edges. The greener your lettuce, the tastier your salads.

4 Fish

Whole fish doesn't dry out as quickly as fillets or steaks. Look for bright, bulging eyes, tight, shiny scales and firm, translucent flesh — and no "fishy" smell. Reject fish with dull-looking flesh or a limp, mushy look.

5 Zucchini

A small or medium-size zucchini is the best. The skin should be smooth. Use at once, since it decays quickly.

6 Bananas

The tinge of green at the stem end of these bananas, along with the scattered flecks of brown, shows that they will be perfectly ripe and sweet in a day or so.

7 Onions

The skin of onions should be paper-dry, bright and satiny—so buying them loose from a bin gives you the best selection. Avoid onions that are sprouted or have soggy stem ends.

8 Pineapple

A-O.K.: No soft spots or brown leaves.

9 Chicken

Look for a plump, thick-skinned chicken. Yellow skin is no guarantee of freshness—it only means the bird has been fed on corn.

10 Papaya

A papaya one-third speckled with yellow will ripen in 2 days.

11 Cheese

Natural cheeses like this Edam are much tastier and generally have fewer additives than processed cheeses. However, be sure to trim away dyed wax or other outer coatings.

12 Eggs

Brown eggs are as nutritious as white. Check for cracks.

13 Seeds

The freshest seeds are sold in airtight packages. Keep them tightly sealed to prevent rancidity.

14 Pears

Pears are sold slightly underripe. Buy blemish-free fruit and let it sit on top of the refrigerator for a couple of days.

15 Potatoes

The best-quality potatoes are U.S. No. 1 Grade. Long, oval Idahoes are ideal for baking; red "new" potatoes are great boiled.

16 Avocado

This avocado will be soft and ready to eat in 3 to 5 days. Avoid mushy avocados with black spots.

The perfect banana is solid yellow with brown flecks. Bunches should be displayed on a soft surface to prevent bruising and not piled on top of one another.

Next to apples, citrus fruits are probably our most popular fruit. Good *oranges* are smooth skinned and free of mold or soft spots.

Thin-skinned, heavy-for-size *grapefruit* are the juiciest. Ignore minor blemishes—they don't reflect inner quality. Avoid grapefruit that are puffy or pointed at one end.

The juiciest, tangiest *lemons* have fine-textured skin and feel heavy for their size. Rough, thick skin is a sign of dry fruit. Tinges of green are okay—they only mean the juice will be slightly more acid. Avoid soft, spongy lemons with hints of decay on the stem ends.

Limes should be green, with no yellow. Brown spots are okay. Pass up limes that are hard—the pulp will be mealy and dry. Look for thin-skinned limes that give slightly.

Good *grapes* are bright and plump. A green, firm-looking stem is a sign of ripe grapes; a dry, brown or black stem means the grapes are old—and flavorless.

Kiwi fruit should give slightly when squeezed gently. Or you can buy a firm kiwi and ripen it at home, as you do with avocados.

Nectarines should be firm, plump and slightly soft along the seam. Avoid hard, green or dull-colored fruit—it's not ripe, nor will it ever be. Look for yellow or yellow-orange skin blushed with bright red.

Like avocados, *papayas* are far better bought underripe and allowed to reach their peak at home. A ripe papaya has a slight give and a fruity, pleasant smell.

Peaches are very fragile, so they're sometimes sold slightly hard and underripe. Since they won't ripen at home, look for fruit that's fairly firm yet has some give. And use your nose—if the fruit smells "peachy," it's ripe.

Most varieties of *pears* are at their best from August to October, with Anjou pears filling the demand the rest of the year. Pears are *always* picked before they're ripe, and must be ripened at home. They're ready to eat when they give a little.

Picking a fresh *pineapple* is nearly as tricky as picking a good melon. The most important thing is to choose fruit that's as yellow as possible: Golden-orange or all-yellow "scales" are signs of a sweet-tasting pineapple.

Plums are in season from mid-May to late August; otherwise, they're imported. Plums should be stored chilled at the store, and not piled high, or they'll bruise. Avoid hard and shriveled (underripe) or soft and split (overripe) plums.

BUYING GREAT MEAT

Buying good meat is something of a dilemma for the health-conscious consumer. Marbling—the fine web of fat that runs through roasts and steaks—retains moisture and therefore flavor, making the juiciest, tenderest and most flavorful cuts also the fattiest. Since meat cuts are otherwise equal in terms of nutritional value, you should choose the leanest cuts, trim off all visible fat, and use moist cooking methods like braising and stewing to preserve moisture and texture.

WATER, CORN SYRUP, SALT, DEXTROSE, SUCROSE, MEAT BY-PRODUCTS, HYDROGENATED COCONUT AND PALM KERNEL OILS, TRICALCIUM PHOSPHATE, POLYSORBATE 60, DISODIUM INOSINATE AND DISODIUM GUANYLATE (AS FLAVOR ENHANCERS), RIBOFLAVIN, ASCORBIC ACID, RED #6, BLUE #17, ARTIFICIAL FLAVOR.

Another paradox of meat consumption is that slightly aged beef is considered somewhat better than meat cut fresh from the carcass. The natural enzymes that act on meat in storage break down tough, fibrous muscle protein, tenderizing the meat in the process. For that reason, you may prefer to buy meat from butchers, who usually take time to age their meat, instead of supermarkets, which generally don't. Buying carefully aged meat also enables you to use leaner cuts without sacrificing tenderness.

Ground beef should be as fresh as possible, since bacterial growth speeds up once meat is chopped, ground and exposed to the air. Avoid ground beef with patches of brown among the red; the meat cutter mixed either older beef with fresh or fresh meat with frozen.

The key to buying absolutely fresh, juicy ground beef at the supermarket is to choose a whole cut—or two different cuts—and ask the counterperson to grind it for you. Chuck is the fattiest cut for grinding, and it is also tender, so mixing chuck with a leaner but slightly drier cut like round or sirloin will give you the best features of both.

How to Decipher a Label

The *order* of ingredients on this label is revealing. The substance present in the greatest amount must be listed first, and so on in descending order; here, you pay good money for water. The three forms of sugar show that there's more of that sweet stuff than anything else. The chemicals are added to make the mixture look, feel and taste like real food. Plus two vitamins to return a little bit of the nutrition processing stripped away.

For *roast and steaks,* color is the best guide to quality. Fresh meat is a bright, rosy red. Generally, the brighter the color, the younger—and more tender—the beef. Any fat should be creamy white, not yellow.

When buying *pork,* look for whitish pink flesh and firm, white fat. Avoid meat that's discolored, or wallowing in its own juices. The shoulder chops may be moister and less expensive than the popular center-cut chops.

Lamb bought in spring is the best, since that's when the animals are born, and it is best bought fresh, not frozen. Because lamb comes from very young animals, it's naturally juicy and flavorful—but very bony. So plan on buying twice as much per person as you would if you were serving beef. Generally, a leg of lamb or chops are leaner than shoulder cuts and make the best buy in terms of cost *and* health. And buy small; legs any bigger than 6 to 6½ pounds (trimmed) will taste too strong.

THE PERFECT CHICKEN

For the best-tasting *chicken,* look for birds with plump, rounded breasts and bright skin. Avoid chickens with pointed breasts and thin, dull-looking skin.

Chickens sold in parts may be just as fresh as those sold whole, but tend to be somewhat drier—especially breasts that have been boned and skinned. It's better to buy a whole chicken and cut it up yourself.

For best results, buy chickens suited to your cooking plans. Very young poultry, weighing 1 to 2½ pounds, is best for broiling. Slightly larger birds (2½ to 3½ pounds) may be broiled or fried, since they, too, are moist and tender. Large birds (3½ to 6 pounds) are best roasted, baked or fricasseed. Anything bigger is ideal for the stockpot.

Turkeys, too, vary in taste and texture. Hens, which are broad breasted and relatively small (less than 19 pounds) are juicier than toms, which are pointed breasted and large, and tend to be dry. Regardless of gender, fresh birds are far moister than frozen turkeys, and generally available year-round.

Liten Up!

Many manufacturers now offer "lite" products that contain less salt, sugar or fat—and often fewer calories—than their regular counterparts. A line of low-sodium soups has about 75 milligrams of sodium per serving, compared to 700 to 1,800 for salted soup. A brand of peaches packed in natural fruit juice has 50 calories per serving, compared to 90 for the same peaches in heavy syrup. A line of lite cheeses has just 2 grams of fat per serving, compared to 9 grams for regular cheese.

FISH SHOPPING WITHOUT A CATCH

We urge you to shop at your neighborhood fish market, if at all possible. Since fish is their only commodity, fish dealers are more particular about the quality and age of the fish they sell. Your fish dealer can also tell you where a fish comes from, whether it's been dipped in preservatives (they sometimes are) and when different species are in season.

Whole fish doesn't dry out as quickly as fillets and steaks, so ask for "whole, dressed" fish and cook it whole—keeping the head on holds the juices while the fish cooks. That's a little more of a bother than buying filleted fish, but the organs, scales and fins will have been removed, so the worst part of cleaning is done for you.

When choosing fish, look for clear, bright, bulging eyes; bright, shiny skin with tightly attached scales; and bright red gills and flesh that springs back slightly when pressed. And truly fresh fish smells briny, or salty—*not* "fishy."

Shrimp is packed in ice on the ship and frozen soon after it reaches port, so it's as close to fresh as frozen fish can be. If shrimp in a store is thawed and on ice, it's *not* as fresh as the frozen variety. The shrimp should have a clean, fresh smell; an ammonialike odor means it's begun to decay. And it should look clean and shiny, with translucent shells.

Lobster tastes best when eaten fresh; try to buy it live. The best lobsters come from the cold waters of the Atlantic Ocean, off Maine and Nova Scotia.

A lobster begins to die as soon as it leaves the sea, so a lobster in a tank is no guarantee of freshness. To pick the freshest of the lot, look for one that is active, with lots of leg movement and its tail tucked under its body. A lobster should be alive when it's cooked. The same general advice applies to *crabs*.

Freshness is even more important when buying bivalves—*clams, oysters, mussels and scallops*. A gaping shell means that the animal is dead or dying. Buy only those bivalves whose shells are tightly closed or whose shells close when tapped gently. Shucked oysters (out of their shells) should be plump and creamy colored and sitting in a clear liquid. Scallops are nearly always sold shucked. Tiny bay scallops are more tender and delicately flavored than the larger sea scallops.

Bivalves may harbor bacteria and viruses, so be sure to cook them thoroughly.

DAIRY-FRESH MILK PRODUCTS

Production and distribution of *milk* is closely regulated by the government, since unsanitary conditions can easily make milk a source of serious diseases. So you can buy milk with confidence—just check the expiration date on the carton.

Yogurt is the tangy, custardlike food that results when milk is fermented with special bacterial cultures. Some brands of yogurt are pasteurized after culturing, inactivat-

---

Eight Additives You Should Subtract

Sodium added to food in the form of salt and sodium compounds like monosodium glutamate adds to your chances of getting high blood pressure.

Sugar—in the form of corn syrup and various other sweeteners—adds extra calories, promotes tooth decay and diabetes, and enhances sodium's effect on blood pressure.

Nitrates and nitrites are added in tandem with salt to cured meats like bacon, hot dogs, ham, sausage, corned beef and some cured fish. That lengthens their shelf life but may shorten yours. Nitrates combine with substances in meat and in your body to form nitrosamines—known cancer causers.

Caffeine can be addictive and causes nervousness and loss of sleep; some research links it to breast tumors, peptic ulcers and high blood pressure.

The artificial colorings *FD & C Yellow No. 5 and No. 6* seem to be the most bothersome dyes, causing allergic reactions in many people; and *FD & C Red No. 3* seems to be the most dangerous, as it may cause cancer.

ing the bacteria. Pasteurization also destroys lactase, an enzyme in yogurt that helps lactose-intolerant people digest yogurt easily. So look for brands with active cultures.

Sour cream is a fattier cultured milk product than yogurt, and it should be used sparingly. Be wary of "imitation" sour cream—it's generally made with coconut oil, a saturated vegetable fat that may be no better for you than animal fat.

Buttermilk is a rich, frothy liquid produced by adding a starter of lactic acid bacteria to whole or skim milk. Check the label—some buttermilk is adulterated with artificial coloring.

The best-quality *butter* is U.S. Grade AA, made of top-quality sweet cream. It has a pleasing aroma and creamy texture. U.S. Grade A is close to Grade AA. Lower grades are made from soured cream and may have an acid taste or grainier texture.

For delicate flavor, always buy unsalted butter. Check the sale date on the wrapper, though—since unsalted butter doesn't keep as well as salted, it has to be purchased fresh and used within two weeks or so when refrigerated. Store it in a tightly covered container.

Margarine is a concoction of vegetable oil engineered to taste and perform like butter. The big advantage is that it contains far less saturated fat than butter. The big disadvantage, though, is that margarine usually contains artificial coloring, flavoring, preservatives and other additives in order to change what's basically a white, tasteless mass of vegetable fat into something that looks and cooks like butter. So choose brands that have as few additives as possible—and, as with butter, use as little as possible.

REAL CHEESE, FAKE CHEESE

Cheese is usually made directly from milk curds, or solids, which are formed in a hoop or mold. The curds are created by bacteria found naturally in milk; by the enzyme rennin, which is added; or by other enzymes. These and other factors, like the kind of milk used and the ripening time, give each cheese its distinctive taste,

texture and smell. A few cheeses, primarily soft cheeses like ricotta and cottage cheese, are eaten fresh. Hard or semisoft cheeses like cheddar or Swiss are aged and will keep for a few months.

The cheeses just described are *natural cheeses:* cheddar, colby, Swiss, Edam, Gouda, Parmesan, mozzarella, Romano, blue, Roquefort, brick, Brie and the like. They're living, changing, complex foods, loaded with protein and calcium.

Processed cheeses are a different story altogether. For one thing, they're a lot saltier. For another, they're made by grinding and blending two or more natural cheeses, heating the mixture and adding water, emulsifier, chemicals, additives and artificial coloring. The idea is to create a "homogeneous plastic mass," in the official words of the U.S. Food and Drug Administration (FDA)—a product that tastes and looks uniform and predictable.

How do you avoid processed cheese? A good rule of thumb is not to buy any solid cheese that's presliced, pregrated or prepacked, and instead opt for cheese cut to order off a wheel or a slab. You're more likely to find cut-to-order cheeses at your neighborhood cheese shop, specialty food store or supermarket deli counter than next to the butter and eggs in the supermarket dairy case. When you order the cheese, ask the counterperson to let you read the label. If it's a processed cheese, the label must say so.

Be sure the *eggs* you buy are refrigerated. If cartons are stacked too high, try to take a carton from the back of the refrigerator case. You're probably in the habit of checking the eggs for cracks or dirty spots; it's a habit you should continue. Cracked or soiled eggs may contain bacteria that can produce food poisoning if they're not cooked thoroughly. So don't use them for scrambled, fried, poached or other soft-cooked eggs. If you do get a cracked or soiled egg, use it as soon as possible, hard cooked, or in a thoroughly cooked dish like a quick bread.

Grade A and B eggs are just as good as Grade AA or Fresh Fancy—they simply have thinner whites and less firm yolks.

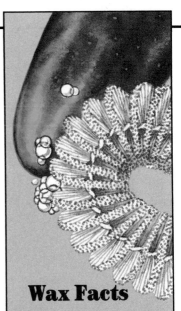

Wax Facts

Why do city apples look so much slicker than their orchard cousins? They've been waxed.

But looks aren't the only reason some fruits and vegetables are waxed. It helps retard water loss, keeping produce fresher, longer.

Is wax safe? The government thinks so. But it's still *wax*—and to our thinking, it belongs on floors and in museum look-alikes, not in our bodies. For maximum safety, buy unwaxed produce when it's available.

6

Keep It Fresh!

You paid for the best. Now, learn how to protect your investment in quality.

We all know what happens when we put the leftovers from Thanksgiving in the refrigerator and forget about them until Christmas—they take on a life of their own, growing to look like something from a horror movie. And much subtler and less noticeable damage can occur in just a few days without the proper precautions. However, you can prevent food from spoiling with a few sensible storage techniques. In fact, by using the same kind of careful planning that helped you win the Supermarket Game, you can safeguard the bounty of nutrition you got there.

TOP-NOTCH FRUITS AND VEGETABLES

If your supermarket is a good one, you probably found fresh produce packed in plastic trays or lying loose in bins that were cool but not cold. These days most stores also provide consumers with plastic bags in which to pack their selections, so you should use a separate bag for each type of fruit or vegetable you buy. Packaging this way not only speeds your way through the checkout line, but it also gives you something in which to store your items at home.

Fresh fruits and vegetables are kept cool for a good reason: Their natural enzymes and certain bacteria—the factors that cause rotting—work faster at warm temperatures.

Green, leafy vegetables also need moisture to hold on to their crispness and nutrients. They dry out very quickly, even when kept cool. This is where those plastic bags (as well as any covered plastic containers you may already have) can come in handy; they seal in moisture.

Those are the general rules. Here are some specific guidelines for particular kinds of fruits and vegetables.

Apples are best kept in the refrigerator. Soft apples should also be kept in the refrigerator, but forget the plastic bags and store them loose; apples need to "breathe" to stay crisp. Use apples within a month.

Citrus fruits—*oranges, lemons, limes, grapefruit, tangerines and tangelos*—should be stored at a room temperature of 60° to 70°F and used within two weeks. If you think they taste better cold, go ahead and refrigerate them, but don't keep them in plastic bags.

Pineapples can be kept at room temperature until they ripen, but then should be used as quickly as possible, or stored in the refrigerator for three to five days.

Fruits that should be kept covered in the refrigerator include all kinds of *berries and cherries.* But don't wash them until you use them, because too much moisture in the package speeds spoilage. Use them within two or three days.

The same rules apply for *cranberries,* but they can be stored for up to a week before use.

Grapes and plums are best refrigerated and kept in plastic bags with holes. They should be used within three to five days.

A number of fruits usually must be ripened before they're refrigerated—unless you're lucky enough to find them beautifully ripened in the market. These include *apricots, peaches, pears, nectarines and melons.* Cut portions should be covered and refrigerated. Use them all within three to five days. (Except a melon, which should be used as soon as possible after ripening.)

Avocados and bananas are usually both stored and eaten at room temperature, but should be refrigerated after they've ripened. Cover any cut portions before refrigerating, and use them within three to five days.

Most fresh vegetables also need to be kept in the refrigerator, but, as usual, there are some exceptions.

Eggplants, mature onions, winter squash, rutabagas and sweet potatoes are best kept at moderately cool (no lower than 50°F) rather than cold temperatures. If you have a cool, dry basement, it can be used for storing these vegetables. *Potatoes* need an even colder area—between 45° and 50°F.

If you don't have access to such a naturally cool storage area, buy these vegetables in small amounts, store them in a pantry or closet, and use them immediately after purchase—within a week at most. Mature onions, however, can last several months at room temperature.

All other fresh vegetables belong in the refrigerator. Keep *tomatoes* uncovered, and *green peas and lima beans* in their pods. If you buy peas or beans without pods, keep them in a plastic bag. They will last three to five days in the refrigerator.

Similarly, keep *corn* in its husk for short-term storage. Use this vegetable as soon as possible after purchase, because its sugar quickly turns to starch, causing it to lose its sweet flavor.

Carrots, radishes, turnips, beets and parsnips should be stored in plastic after you've removed their leafy tops. They'll last about two weeks.

Most other fresh vegetables do well in the bin (sometimes called a crisper) at the bottom of the refrigerator, but even there they usually need plastic coverings to prevent dehydration.

Broccoli, brussels sprouts, scallions and summer squash will last three to five days if stored in plastic bags in the crisper. (However, if the crisper is at least two-thirds full, you

can store the vegetables loose. It's only when it's less than two-thirds full that it becomes important to protect your food with plastic bags or containers.)

Spinach, kale, chard, collards and the greens of turnips, mustard and beets have the same crisper life, but they should be washed in cold water and drained thoroughly before they are packed in bags.

Lettuce, salad greens, peppers and cucumbers should be washed and stored in the crisper or in plastic bags. *Cauliflower, celery and snap beans* don't have to be washed before they're refrigerated. They should be used within a week.

Cabbage is tough and has a long refrigerator life (up to two weeks). *Asparagus* is delicate and should be used within two or three days.

MEATS, POULTRY AND FISH

All meats belong in the coldest part of the refrigerator. *Ground meats* spoil quickly since they've already been exposed to handling, air and the machinery of the grinding process. Supermarket ground meat wrapped in plastic can be kept in the refrigerator for a day or two. But ground meat from a butcher shop, wrapped in paper, must be rewrapped in plastic or waxed paper or cooked right away.

Ground meat can be frozen in plastic wrap for up to two weeks without moisture loss. For longer periods, put it in aluminum foil, freezer paper or a plastic freezer bag. Protected in this way, it will last for up to three months. And remember: Always date anything you place in the freezer.

Other meats—*roasts, steaks and chops*—should be covered loosely and will last in the refrigerator for three to five days at the most. For freezing, use plastic bags or wrap. Steaks and roasts will keep 8 to 12 months, and chops 3 to 4.

Poultry and fish should be used quickly, within a day or two after purchase. If you buy poultry wrapped in plastic, keep it wrapped and refrigerated until cooking. Chicken stored in plastic bags in the freezer will keep for 12 months.

DAIRY PRODUCTS

Milk and cream will last about a week in the refrigerator. Their containers should be kept tightly closed so they don't absorb stray odors and flavors from whatever else is in the refrigerator. Evaporated milk can be kept at room temperature until the can is opened; then it must be refrigerated in a tightly covered container.

If you use dry milk, the powder can be kept for six months at room temperature, but be sure to use a tightly sealed container. Once you've mixed it with water, treat it as if it were whole milk.

When you buy milk, choose a cardboard container instead of a plastic jug. Studies at Clemson University's department of dairy science have shown that milk kept in plastic jugs and thus exposed to a supermarket's fluorescent lighting loses half its vitamin C content after only 24 hours. It also loses some of the B vitamin riboflavin, and takes on a slightly different flavor from milk that's been kept in the dark.

(Sadly, the scientists at Clemson also reported that people have gotten so used to this different flavor

Shelf Life— How Long Is Too Long?

The following list indicates maximum storage time.

Bread: 5-7 days.
Cereals: 2-3 months.
Whole wheat flour: 1 year, refrigerated.
Whole grain rye and barley flour: Same as whole wheat.
Soy flour: 3 months.
White flour: 6-12 months.
Spices: 1 year.
Sugar: Indefinitely.
Nonfat dry milk: At room temperature, 6 months. Reconstituted, 1 week in the refrigerator.

Voilà: A Perfect Jar

It's called a French canning jar, and it can be found in most department stores. Made of glass, it has no metals to possibly rust or contaminate foods.

It has a wide mouth—so there's less chance of spillage as you fill or empty it.

It's airtight, moisture-proof and critter-proof.

One precaution: Some foods are damaged by light, so the glass jar should be amber colored or kept in a closed pantry or refrigerator.

that they now think it's how milk *should* taste.)

Hard cheeses, such as cheddar, Parmesan and Swiss should be wrapped tightly and kept in the refrigerator; they'll last for several months this way. Keep grated cheese refrigerated in a tightly covered jar.

Soft cheeses must be kept tightly covered in the refrigerator. Cottage cheese will last at least three to five days; cream cheese, Camembert and others can be kept up to two weeks.

Cheese spreads that come in jars and crocks can be kept at room temperature until they're opened; then refrigerate and use them within one to two weeks.

Butter and margarine should be kept tightly wrapped in the refrigerator. If you want to soften some in the butter compartment, do it one stick at a time, and use it *quickly.* The rest will keep for about two weeks.

Eggs should be refrigerated in their original carton, large end up, and used within a week after purchase. If you should need to separate the eggs, the yolks should be immersed in cold water and kept in a tightly covered container. The whites must also be stored tightly covered, but need not be submerged. Use both yolks and whites within a day or two.

BREADS, FLOURS AND CEREALS

Whole wheat and other *breads* made without preservatives should be refrigerated and eaten in about a week. Commercial bread will last about a week in a breadbox.

If you want to freeze bread, wrap loaves well in aluminum foil or plastic, or freeze store-bought bread in its original wrapper. It will keep for up to three months.

Flours are tricky—they attract insects and are susceptible to rancidity.

Plenty of insects are so tiny they can sneak right into the paper sack flour comes in. Some have even been known to penetrate the tight metal cover of a canister. Your best bet is to transfer all flours—as soon as you get them home—to clean containers that have tight covers. Then keep the containers on a clean shelf.

Molds need moisture and warmth to grow; therefore, be sure the container is bone-dry before you add flour, and keep it in a cool, dry place, like a pantry or cabinet. You could also store it in the refrigerator.

To prevent rancidity, you have to consider the type of flour you're storing; different types have different fat contents, and it's the fat in flour that goes rancid.

White flour has been "milled," which means the nutritious wheat germ (which is also highest in fat) has been removed. Therefore, white flour will probably last longer than any other kind when stored at room temperature.

Whole wheat flour—the kind that hasn't been stripped of its vitamin- and mineral-packed germ—is a little fussier than its denatured brother. But it will keep for a year in the refrigerator.

Keeping Your Foods Wrapped Right

What's the best kind of wrap for storing food?

Aluminum foil is the strongest and most expensive. It will withstand any temperature, from oven to freezer. It's best used for freezing because it forms a strong barrier against both air and moisture.

Plastic wrap lets you see what's inside; it stretches and clings to form a tight seal; it is relatively inexpensive. It's best used for short-term storage.

Waxed paper won't form a seal, but it is strong, waterproof and fairly inexpensive.

Invest in all three and use each for its best purpose.

Soy flour, high in fat content, will keep for a year in its unopened package if kept in a cool, dry place. Once opened, use it within 90 days.

Cereals, of course, also are made from grains and therefore are subject to similar problems with insects. Even those that are loaded with chemical preservatives are still mighty attractive to bugs. So transfer cereals to clean, dry, airtight containers; leaving them in cardboard store boxes is like giving your front door key to a burglar.

CANNED FOODS

Do canned foods present storage problems? Not many. They're impenetrable to insects, and should last for at least a year if kept in a cool, dry place.

Still, if you come across a can that bulges out at one end, *throw it away!* That bulge means that the container has opened in some way and that mold, bacteria or other organisms have begun to grow inside, and may have made the contents inedible. (A bulging or broken can is *not* a sign of botulism, the potentially deadly food poisoning caused by bacteria. Unfortunately, there's no way to tell if a can harbors the germ.) Also beware of cans that leak or that smell bad when opened.

If you've used only part of a can's contents, the rest should be stored in a covered container in the refrigerator and used within a few days. That's especially true for acidic foods, such as citrus or other juices. Studies have shown that lead levels increased up to sevenfold when juices were stored in opened cans.

CANNED GOODS VS. FRESH

We think there's no contest. In addition to artificial flavors and other chemical additives, canned goods may contain a bunch of flavor "enhancers"—the worst and most plentiful of which is salt. Moreover, the canning process actually robs canned foods of the nutrients in unadulterated foods. For example, take canned peas (please!). Just look at the list of allowed additives: salt,

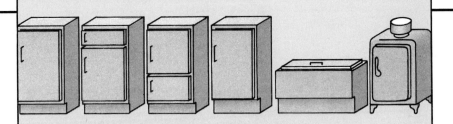

How to Buy a Refrigerator

According to the experts, refrigerators with freezers on top are the only ones to consider. This type is generally cheaper to buy than the others and less expensive to run.

The ability to maintain proper temperatures in both the freezing and chilling compartments of a refrigerator is, of course, also crucial. The thing to look for is a refrigerator's ability to maintain a constant 37°F in the refrigerator and 0°F in the freezer section.

Another thing to look for is one of the U.S. Department of Energy labels that tells you a machine's yearly estimated operating costs and an efficiency rating that implies any energy-saving improvements. According to industry critics, these improvements (better condensors, thicker insulation and better door gaskets) are a good—if initially more costly—investment.

monosodium glutamate, disodium inosinate, disodium guanylate, hydrolyzed vegetable protein, autolyzed yeast extract, sugar (or invert sugar syrup, dextrose, glucose syrup and fructose), spices, "natural flavoring," "color additives," calcium salts, and "seasonings and garnishes" like "pieces of green or red peppers or mixtures of both, either of which may be dried," lemon juice, mint leaves and butter or margarine.

What this long roll of flavor and appearance "enhancers" means is that you're getting a lot of stuff in your canned peas that doesn't exist in fresh peas.

Salt heads that list of foreign substances allowable in canned goods, and so it is the best reason for avoiding them. (Some experts recommend no more than 3 grams of salt a day; most Americans get *12!*) Some of this salt is added for flavor, but more of it is added for no good reason at all. Did you know many manufacturers sort peas using a salt brine? Some bright person, it seems, discovered that old, starchy, and undesirable peas sink in brine, while younger, more tasty ones float, and so a salty selection process was added at many pea factories.

How much salt do we get from the processed foods we eat—exactly? One estimate says we get 3 of our daily 12 grams from natural sources, 3 from the shaker, and up to 6 from processed foods (which include canned goods, of course). Another study, which examined two groups of preschoolers, one eating no processed food and one eating all processed food, concluded that the "processed" kids got six times the salt the "natural" kids did.

We think this information alone should persuade you to swear off canned goods. If it doesn't, consider our container of peas again. According to the U.S. Department of Agriculture (USDA), a cup of raw peas contains just 3 milligrams of sodium. When those peas are canned, the processing brings the sodium level up to 588 milligrams—a nearly 200-fold increase!

Finally, we come to the worst thing about the commercial canning process—the loss of nutrients in the fruits, vegetables and meats that undergo it. Presumably, besides eating to satisfy taste and ease hunger, we eat because we need the calories, vitamins and minerals that food contains. That's why it makes no sense to fill our plates with canned goods that have been robbed of their nutrients.

One systematic study of nutrients lost to canning examined a variety of common vegetables and found they lost an average of 10 percent of their vitamin A, 67 percent of their thiamine, 42 percent of their riboflavin, 49 percent of their niacin and 51 percent of their vitamin C. It seems hardly worthwhile—after seeing figures like these—to open a can.

Finally, let's take one last look at canned peas. The study cited above also made an extended examination of them and produced these alarming numbers: The peas in the particular sample studied lost 78 percent of their biotin to the canning operation,

59 percent of their folate, 69 percent of their B_6, 80 percent of their pantothenate, 30 percent of their vitamin A, 74 percent of their thiamine, 64 percent of their riboflavin, 69 percent of their niacin and 67 percent of their vitamin C. After losses like these, the nuggets left in the can probably should be labeled "pea impersonators," but worse yet is the picture this report paints of a diet that gets most of its fruits and vegetables from cans or jars. Its calories seem almost as hollow as the empty containers.

FROZEN FOODS

If you have a separate freezer or refrigerator-freezer and know that the freezer is capable of maintaining a temperature of 0°F, you can keep frozen foods safely for a fairly long time. Refrigerators that have freez-

Freezing Tips

Among the foods that retain the best flavor and texture after freezing are corn, either on the cob or as niblets; lima beans; brussels sprouts; rhubarb sauce; tomato sauce; whole cranberries, strawberries and raspberries; broccoli; cauliflower; and spinach.

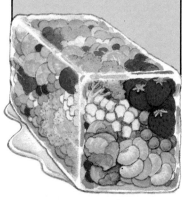

Freezing: Your Costs

Time: Freezing 10 pounds of green beans requires about 1½ hours of your time: 10 minutes to wash the beans, 30 minutes to prepare them, 23 minutes each to blanch and cool them and 8 minutes more to pack and store the containers.
Money: What you save in time you spend in dollars. First of all, you'll need a freezer. Assuming it holds 700 pounds, the amortized cost over 20 years, including repairs, adds 6¢ to the cost of each pound of beans. If you add 4¢ for freezer bags and another 32¢ for a year's electricity, the total cost to freeze 1 pound of beans comes to 42¢.

ing compartments inside them usually are not cold enough to keep frozen foods for more than a few days.

A word of caution: Frozen foods that thaw out completely shouldn't be refrozen, especially if they've thawed over a couple of days. Not only will they refreeze poorly, but the thawing process may have ruined their flavor and safety. If a thawed food still has ice crystals on it or in the package, you can refreeze it. Even so, you should use that food as quickly as possible.

HOME CANNING

If you're fortunate enough to have access to just-picked fruits and vegetables, you may want to do your own canning. If so, you'll need the right equipment.

First, there's the proper canning pot. For certain acidic foods such as tomatoes a simple boiling water bath is sufficient. There are large pots made especially for this task that come with a special rack that keeps the canning jars up off the bottom of the pot and separated from each other. The rack allows the boiling water to get at all surfaces of the jars. You fill the jars with hot food, submerge them in the water, bring the water to a boil, then process for a recommended time that varies with each fruit or vegetable.

For low-acid foods (meats or green beans, for example) you *must* buy a pressure canner, a device that heats food up to 250°F. Finally, there's the proper jar. Those that have a metal cap with a screw-on ring are excellent; the main point is that they have what canning experts call a "self-sealing, vacuum lid." You can recycle old mayonnaise jars, but only for use in a hot water bath, *not* a pressure canner.

One secret of home preservation is to remove as much of the air as possible from the container. Clean both parts of the jar top carefully so that, when the jar cools and the contents contract, the vacuum that results can seal the lid tight. Another secret is to use only fresh, top-notch ingredients. Never try to preserve foods that are battered, bruised or overripe.

Store your canned goods in a space that is dark, dry and fairly cool—between 40° and 50°F. A basement is fine, as is a cool pantry or closet.

If you've followed the rules, your canned foods should last a full year at peak quality. (For more complete details, you should buy a book on canning, with specific recipes. The Ball Company's *Blue Book* is excellent and inexpensive. For $2.50, it can be ordered from the Ball Company, Muncie, IN 47302.)

HOME FREEZING

The amount of freezer space you have will determine how much food you can store. The freezer compartments of most home refrigerators are neither large enough nor cold enough for long-term storage, but home freezers that

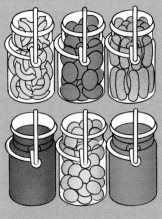

Canning Tips

Peaches, pears, plums, apricots and beets retain their own special qualities even after the rigors of the canning pot. Tomatoes triple as veggie, sauce and juice. Cucumber pickles, applesauce, grape juice and berry jam also are worthy of canning.

Canning: Your Costs

Time: Canning 8 quarts of green beans (10 pounds), requires about 3½ hours: 20 minutes to assemble and wash the jars, about 1 hour to prepare and pack the beans, and about 2 hours to process them. Checking seals and storing jars adds another 15 minutes.

Money: What you spend in time you save in dollars. You'll need a pressure canner, which, amortized over 20 years, adds ½¢ to the cost of each quart of food. Add ¼¢ for repairs, and 8¢ for new lids and jars. With the cost of electricity for processing, canning a quart of green beans costs 12¢, or 9¢ a pound.

Fig Bars

Makes about 4½ doz. bars

Filling
12 ounces dried figs
⅓ cup honey
1 tablespoon lemon juice
2 tablespoons water
2 tablespoons orange
    juice

Dough
½ cup butter or mar-
    garine, softened

½ cup honey
1 egg
½ teaspoon grated lemon
    rind
1 tablespoon lemon juice
3 cups whole wheat flour
1 teaspoon baking
    powder
½ teaspoon baking soda

Filling: Grind figs in a meat grinder or food processor. In a saucepan, combine figs, honey, lemon juice, water and orange juice. Cook over low heat for 10 minutes, stirring occasionally. Remove from heat and set aside to cool.

Dough: Cream butter or margarine and honey together until light and fluffy. Add egg; mix well. Stir in lemon rind and juice. Add dry ingredients to butter mixture, mixing well.

Divide dough in half. Press half of the dough into a 9 × 13 × 2-inch baking pan. Spread fig filling evenly over dough. Roll remaining dough out between 2 sheets of waxed paper into a 9 × 13-inch rectangle. Lay this dough over the top of the filling, pressing down to seal. Bake at 400°F (375°F if using glass pan) for 12 to 15 minutes. Let cool and cut into 1½ × 2-inch bars.

stay at 0°F or colder are available even in small, "apartment" sizes.

Packaging is very important to successful freezing. You need containers that are moisture- and vapor-proof, which means that neither liquids nor vapors can get either in or out. Special freezer foils are available, and so are plastic bags that can be sealed tight enough for freezing. Sealing is important because any air that gets inside a package will diminish the nutrition and flavor of the contents.

Most vegetables and some fruits should be blanched (scalded) before being frozen in order to slow down the enzymes in the food that cause undesirable changes in flavor, color and texture. The blanching time varies from food to food. Most foods are blanched quickly; asparagus, for example, takes two minutes. Scalding is followed by a plunge into ice water to immediately chill the food. Blanching not only slows enzyme action but also helps save vitamins (especially A and C).

Once packaged, food should be frozen as quickly as possible; that means you should introduce only a few packages at a time into the freezer to keep the temperature at 0°F. Spread the containers out in the freezer, so that each one is exposed to as much cold air as possible. Experts say you shouldn't try to freeze more than 2 pounds of food for every cubic foot of your freezer at any one time, because each new warm item that goes in raises the freezer's inside temperature.

In order to keep track of your frozen foods (all those wrapped packages look alike), it often pays to make an inventory of what you have stashed in the freezer. If, for instance, you have 40 packages of peas and only 10 of asparagus, an inventory will remind you to prepare one more frequently than the other. It also will remind you to use foods within their ideal storage time.

Tape the inventory to the door of your freezer. List each food you put in the freezer along with the date and the maximum storage period. Your inventory can be grouped according to food types—meats, vegetables, dairy foods and so forth. Each time you remove a package from the freezer, cross it off the inventory.

With this system, you'll always know exactly what is in the freezer, thus eliminating the problem of packages languishing on bottom shelves until long past their prime.

HOME DRYING

Drying is the oldest method of food preservation, and it is also quite nutritious. What's more, you can do it with ease, indoors or out. An added bonus is that the dried food requires much less storage space than either canned or frozen goods.

Drying also does a fairly good job of preserving the protein, carbohydrate and mineral contents of most foods, as well as safeguarding most vitamins.

As with canning and freezing, you should use the best-quality fruits and vegetables and dry them as soon as possible after they've been picked. They should be washed thoroughly first but *not* soaked; soaking dissolves vitamins and adds water.

Most vegetables should be blanched before drying if they are to be kept for more than six months.

As for the actual drying process, you can buy a commercial dryer (dehydrator) or make one yourself. Some on the market are as small as a hatbox, while others are huge affairs. Your choice can depend on how much you have to spend as well as how much food you have to dry. If you have the time, it's quite easy to build your own. In either case, a dryer simply consists of trays that are exposed to warm, circulating air.

If you have a yard and live in a hot, dry climate, you can let the sun do your drying for you. In that case all you need are some old (but not rusted) window screens to use as trays and another screen and paper towels or a fabric such as cheesecloth with which to protect the drying food from bugs.

If you're drying fruit with pits, begin by removing them. Next, cut the fruit into slices of uniform size for a uniform drying time. The thinner the slices, the faster they'll dry. A food processor does an excellent and fast job of this task.

This is a family of "survivalists"—folks who believe that a modern-day catastrophe could be just around the corner, and who stock food accordingly. These shelves are loaded with grains and other dried foods, along with sufficient fresh water. Here, family members shell nuts for storage in vacuum containers.

It's also possible to dry food in an oven. It's important to keep the temperature at a constant 140°F. (You do not want to *cook* the food, only dehydrate it.) One drawback is that the drying procedure may take a day or more, making the oven unavailable for other uses.

The best storage containers for dried food are clean, dry, insect-proof containers like glass jars or plastic bags put into metal cans with fitted lids.

Some dried foods—such as banana chips or apple slices—are delicious eaten just as they are. Others—such as pepper flakes or celery slices—are best added to soups or stews. All can be brought back to life with a soak in water. Once rehydrated, they should be stored just like fresh foods.

So don't let poorly preserved foods "spoil" your health or eating pleasure. With a little planning, the good food of today will stay nutritious and tasty for many tomorrows to come.

7

Great Kitchen Tools & Techniques

Natural foods need a little help from their friends if they're to deliver their full goodness.

The Saturday morning cartoon show, "The Jetsons," has an A.D. 2100 Mom cooking by computer—she presses a button and in a microsecond the meal pops out of a shiny compartment. No fuss, no muss—just the laugh track turning a reel or two because the kitchen is so ridiculously efficient and work free.

Well, get ready for Future Cook Shock: Ma Jetson probably lives next door. There *are* superfast, oven computers—microwave memory banks that store specific times for specific recipes. You just press No. 1483 and your souffle *can't* be ruined. And it's ready in five minutes, too.

But science has given us more than space age cooking technology. Those folks in white lab coats also have been busy cooking meals of their own and serving them to test tubes. They've evaluated *all* the cooking techniques—old and new—to see what they do to your food. And your health.

Do they preserve nutrients? Do they avoid creating disease-causing chemicals? Do they soak your food in artery-clogging fat? Researchers have the answers—starting right at your kitchen counter.

What do you do to food before you cook it? With vegetables, washing is necessary to remove any traces of dirt. But then what? Do you soak the vegetable or peel it? That may be a mistake.

Soaking leaches out vitamins, especially vitamin C and the B vitamins. (If you're using frozen vegetables, keep them frozen until the very last minute to prevent nutrients from draining away.)

When you peel certain vegetables—potatoes, for instance—you slice off large amounts of vitamins. Other tuberous vegetables, like carrots, also store high concentrations of nutrients in the

Nutrient-Wasting Cooking Methods

Charcoal broiling
Frying
Deep frying
Boiling
Toasting

very part that's commonly pared off and discarded.

What about chopping? Another mistake, if you do it far ahead of eating or preparing the food. This technique exposes more of the surface area of each piece to the air, releasing enzymes that can cause vitamin losses. Carrots are particularly vulnerable. If you slice carrots for a particular recipe, slice them lengthwise. When you cut carrots crosswise, you lose much more vitamin C.

When defrosting frozen meat, do it in the refrigerator, not on the kitchen counter; both nutrition and quality are lost by defrosting at room temperature. When the meat is thawed, use the juices left in the dish to make sauce or gravy. If you don't, up to one-third of the pantothenate and substantial amounts of the niacin and folate you started with end up in the garbage.

THE WORST AND THE BEST OF COOKING METHODS

Now you're ready to cook. But how? No cooking method is *wrong*, of course. But some may do your health a wrong, and you should put them in the "now-and-then" category. Let's look at those methods first.

Charcoal Broiling. That backyard barbecue can be hazardous to your health. No matter how delectable that crusty black steak may taste, the charcoal you burned and its smoke may cause potentially cancer-causing substances to form in and around the meat as it is cooked.

There are, however, three solutions. First, cook only lean meats over charcoal, because it's the fat dripping into the fire that forms the chemical. Second, don't keep the meat right next to the coals. Third, place the meat on foil.

Frying. The saying should be, "out of the fire, into the frying pan." Vitamin A, for instance, is resistant to most forms of mild cooking, but frying does a good job of destroying it. And chemicals that cause cancer have been found in hamburgers fried in a pan or on a grill.

Also, it's well known that frying adds calories to the diet. As much as you may love french fries, you should know that this definitely American kind of frying adds 50 times more fat than baking or boiling.

Boiling. This is one of the best ways to destroy vitamins B and C, as well as potassium and iron. Vitamin C is the most sensitive of these nutrients—boiled asparagus, for instance, retains only 43 percent of its vitamin C.

If you must boil foods, these simple rules will help you hold onto as much nutrition as possible.

First, use very little water and keep the cooking time short. You'll still lose nutrition, but less.

Second, don't put vegetables in a pan until the water is bubbling. If you put them in cold water and then bring it to a boil, many more nutrients will be lost.

Third, use a pan that has a tightly fitting cover. That cuts down the amount of water needed to cook the vegetables.

Fourth, never add baking soda to cooking water to keep vegetables green. In the refrigerator baking soda may absorb odors, but in cooking water, it destroys vitamin C, thiamine and some riboflavin.

Fifth, recycle the water in which foods are boiled. You'll still lose some nutrients into the water, but if you use that water to make soups, sauces or gravies, they won't all be getting away from you.

So much for the worst of the lot. Next are some cooking methods that have to be rated somewhere around B−. They're not bad, but they do have drawbacks.

Microwaving. True, there's the obvious advantage of being lightning fast. And microwave oven cooking also reduces the amount of crude fat, good news for the weight conscious. On the other hand, many more nutrients are lost in the juices that drip from microwaved meats than from oven- or stove-cooked meats.

Slow Cooking. Love that Crock-Pot! You fill it in the morning, disappear, and when you return at night, *voilà*—dinner! But how good a dinner is it?

The long cooking time can destroy thiamine and folate, and riboflavin and niacin escape into the cooking liquid. Those vitamins help protect the nerves, so if you use a Crock-Pot to avoid the frazzle of throwing together after-work meals, you defeat part of your own purpose— less stress. To happily use a Crock-Pot, make sure to use the B vitamin-rich cooking water. You should also know that not all foods are suited to long, slow cooking. If you have a Crock-Pot, use it for meats or beans, but cook your vegetables separately and add them at the last minute.

If you use the less-than-healthy methods sparingly and remember the reservations about the in-between ones, you'll still have plenty of variety in your meal plans. Especially if you also use the following really healthful techniques.

Roasting. If you can't charcoal broil or fry that beef, but you do want to hold onto its flavor and juiciness, pop it in the oven. Slow roasting at a medium temperature (about 300°F) retards shrinkage and keeps meat juicy.

Roasting does cause some loss of the B vitamins, but you'll lose less with roasting than you would with most other cooking methods—about a third of the thiamine, biotin and B_{12}, and less than one-tenth of the riboflavin and niacin. That is, unless you overcook. If someone in your family likes roast beef well done, try to change his mind. The longer it cooks, the more thiamine is lost.

Finally, it's important to ignore the salt shaker when roasting meat. Not only can too much sodium be a factor in high blood pressure, but it will also draw the juices out of meats.

Broiling. This method is as good as roasting when it comes to preserving nutrients. You can usually keep 60 to 80 percent of meat's thiamine and sometimes all of its riboflavin by broiling.

And here's where we save your hamburgers. When you broil burgers, the heat radiates through the air instead of concentrating on the bottom of the patties the way it does

when they're fried. That saves the meat from negative health factors spawned during frying.

Broiling also allows the fat to drain off into the bottom of the broiler, thus reducing calories.

Braising/Stewing. When you cook meat and vegetables in a liquid, then use that liquid to make gravy, you keep almost all the nutrients you start with—as long as you keep the heat low and cook slowly. When you add vegetables, herbs and spices to the pot (but not salt), you come up with a delicious, nutritious one-dish meal. Just don't let a stew sit for hours on the stove.

Baking. The baking of bread, rolls and pastry is easy on nutrients as long as you remember that most items should be taken out of the oven as soon as the crust or top is light brown.

It's also true that the less any dough is exposed to the heat, the better its vitamin retention will be. So baked goods made in pans that have sides are more nutritious than biscuits or cookies baked on a sheet.

Baking is also good for fish; it saves nutrients, calories and flavor.

Stir-Frying. Primarily thought of for cooking Chinese food, this method can be used for just about anything. If you use the Chinese frying pan, the wok, you can cook meat and vegetables more quickly and safeguard their nutrients. Stir-frying also saves on calories, because it uses much less oil than skillet frying.

Steaming. When you steam a vegetable, no part of it touches the water. It also cooks quickly, and you use no fat at all.

Boiling, remember, destroys 57 percent of the vitamin C in asparagus and 67 percent in broccoli; with steaming, only 22 and 21 percent are lost. Protein, mineral and other vitamin losses are also considerably less with steaming than with boiling.

Pressure Cooking. You need a special piece of equipment for this method, and it's not cheap—but it is worth the investment.

Pressure cooking requires very little water and very little time, and,

Nutrient-Saving Cooking Methods

Roasting
Broiling
Braising/Stewing
Baking
Stir-frying
Steaming
Pressure cooking

therefore, it is considered better than any other method for preserving nutrients.

THE TOOLS OF THE TRADE

Pots and pans are the backbone of any kitchen, and they range from primitive clay pots to state-of-the-art nonstick cookware. Which are best, both nutritionally and economically?

No matter what a cooking utensil is made of, its size and shape are important. It should, as closely as possible, fit the heating units of your stove. If it's too small, heat will escape around its edges, wasting energy. If it's too big, the heat distribution won't be uniform and some heat will be reflected back onto the stove top, possibly damaging it.

Another feature to look for is a heavily clad bottom. It will distribute heat evenly so that you're less likely to burn food.

One utensil that usually doesn't have a heavily clad or flat bottom is the wok made for stir-frying. It has a rounded bottom like a bowl, which prevents the concentration of heat on the bottom, and it comes with a ring stand to hold it level over the heat source.

Clay and pottery cookware can be dangerous if it is glazed with a lead-containing substance and fired at too low a temperature. The lead in such a glaze can be drawn out by acidic foods (anything containing tomatoes, for instance). Low levels of lead in your body can chip away at the immune system; high levels can poison you.

You can't tell by looking at a glazed pot whether it's safe or not. So it's best not to use one unless it came with a manufacturer's certificate of safety.

Unglazed pottery, however, is both safe *and* healthful because the clay is porous and absorbs water. That means you need very little liquid and oil or fat to keep food from sticking—water that could leach nutrients; fat that could add calories.

There are some drawbacks, however. Clay pots are easily broken; handle them with care and never put hot food into a cold pot. Place the filled pot in a cold oven; set the temperature, adding 100 degrees to the temperature recommended in your recipe directions; and cook slowly.

After use, clay pots require very careful cleaning. Fat from the food can get into the pores and turn rancid. Also, never use soaps or

One of the simplest ways to improve your diet is to steam, not drown, your vegetables—it keeps vitamins and minerals from going down the drain. For instance, raw vegetables emerge from a steamer with a full two-thirds of their vitamin C intact. Boiled vegetables, however, *lose* up to two-thirds of this nutrient. And as vitamin C goes, so go several other water-soluble vitamins—like B complex—and all minerals.

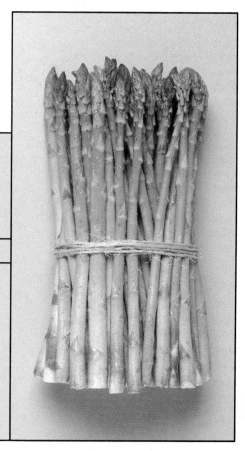

Cooking with the Percentages: Why Steaming's a Winner

VITAMIN C CONTENT (mg.) OF RAW, STEAMED AND BOILED VEGETABLES

Vegetable	Portion	Raw	Steamed	Boiled
Asparagus	4 medium spears	17.5	13.6	7.5
Beans, wax	½ cup	27.3	20.4	12.3
Broccoli	1 medium stalk	171.0	147.0	61.4
Brussels sprouts	4 sprouts	66.9	57.5	23.4
Onions, chopped	¼ cup	6.9	4.6	2.5
Peas	½ cup	19.7	13.2	8.7
Rutabagas, cubed	½ cup	25.3	16.4	9.1
Spinach, chopped	1 cup	49.6	31.8	22.3
Squash, cubed	½ cup	10.5	8.0	6.3
Turnips, cubed	½ cup	16.1	9.8	7.2

detergents for cleaning; they can get into pores and spoil taste. Instead, fill the pot with a strong solution of baking soda and water and bake it for an hour at 400°F.

Copper conducts heat rapidly, is lightweight, and is beautiful to boot. But the metal can release toxic minerals, which is why copper utensils must be lined with stainless steel or tin. As long as a pan's lining remains intact, it is safe, but as soon as the lining wears thin or is chipped, the utensil *must* be relined.

Cast iron pots and skillets can still be found secondhand at antique shops and flea markets and even new at some hardware stores. They're heavy and take a long time to heat, but they can actually add some beneficial iron to your diet.

Stainless steel does not conduct heat well, but some cookware comes with copper- or aluminum-clad bottoms that heat foods evenly and do not allow the contents to touch the copper.

Metal pots and pans that are enameled with a porcelain glaze will conduct heat as well as whatever metal was used in their manufacture. This cookware is likely to be heavy, and very high temperatures can damage its glaze. However, foods don't stick as readily to porcelain as to metal, and these utensils are easy to clean, although you must be careful not to scratch them with scouring pads or cleansers.

The glass that is used for top-of-the-stove saucepans and ovenware will not transmit anything into food, but it breaks easily and heats unevenly.

Some glass utensils will shatter from sudden changes in temperature; others, such as those sold under the names Pyrex or Corning Ware, are designed to go from hot to cold to hot without sustaining damage. Check labels carefully to make sure you know a utensil's capabilities. Also check to see whether the manufacturer recommends using it both on top of the stove and in the oven—if there's no label saying you can, don't try it.

Nonstick finishes are very convenient because they keep foods from sticking and they are easy to clean. They can also contribute to

Do You Need a Food Processor?

It mixes, blends, chops, slices, grates, grinds, minces and makes dough. Julia Child calls it "the most useful machine a cook can have," and James Beard says it *might* be possible to live without one, but he'd rather not try.

It's not a French maid or a *sous chef*, it's a food processor, and it's turned out to be much more than just a fad.

Do you need one? That depends on how much cooking you do, how much time you have to do it, how much you enjoy chopping and kneading by hand and how varied your menus are.

You *probably* need (and could make good use of) a food processor if you cook mostly from scratch and don't have all day to do it; if you have a large family or entertain lots of guests; if you like elaborate recipes that contain many steps and require last-minute steps like the grinding of meat or nuts; or if you can or preserve large quantities of homegrown food.

healthful cooking because they require very little fat or oil.

Pressure cookers work by compressing steam at very high temperatures, but not everything cooks well in a pressure cooker. It's good for beans, potatoes and beets, and not so good for the leafy green vegetables like spinach and broccoli.

When you're shopping for pots and pans, be sure to include a couple that will fit together as a double boiler. This makes smooth, creamy sauces possible, sauces that won't scorch or curdle because the bottom of the sauce-containing pan is not in direct contact with a flame or electric coil.

Choose pots and pans that are heat efficient, easy to handle and clean, have heat-resistant handles and tight-fitting lids and do not contribute undesirable substances to foods. That way, you'll have a well-equipped and healthy kitchen.

The 10 Best Cooking Utensils

Your cooking is only as good as your tools—so here are 10 great kitchen helpers to make sure that even the most challenging recipes turn out right.

1 **A Good Set of Knives.** The best are high-carbon stainless steel with hard wood or hard plastic handles. The blade should extend through the length of the handle for good balance.

4 **Spatulas and Scrapers.** They should be made of stain-resistant material, such as metal, plastic or rubber, and they should have flexible ends and be rigid toward the handles.

2 **Sharpening Steel.** A knife is only as good as its edge and knives dull quickly with frequent use. To keep them sharp, straighten the edges with 4 or 5 swipes along a sharpening steel each time they're used.

5 **Wok or Vegetable Steamer.** An alternative is to buy a collapsible basket steamer to set inside a tightly covered pot.

3 **Plastic Cutting Boards.** Wooden boards can harbor bacteria; plastic boards don't allow these germs to breed, nor do they hold onto grease or odors—and they're lightweight.

6 **Colander.** This gadget is great for rinsing and then draining produce. Be sure yours has a firm base so you can set it in the sink.

7
Wire Whisks.
These are the most
efficient tools for thor-
oughly mixing and
beating. Buy them in
sizes ranging from
tiny for sauces and
dressings to large,
heavy-handled models
for big jobs.

8
Stainless Steel Bowls.
Steel is lightweight, unbreak-
able and easy to clean, and can
be heated or chilled according
to a recipe's needs. Good
bowls are shallow and have
flat bottoms.

9
Wooden Spoons.
Wood won't scratch
your pots and pans
like metal or melt like
plastic, and it won't
burn your hand during
long stirring jobs.
Hardwood spoons don't
absorb odors.

10
**Measuring
Cups and Spoons.**
You'll need a heat-
resistant glass cup for
liquids, a set of cups
for flour and other dry
ingredients, and a set
of metal spoons for
spices and small
amounts of liquids.

8

The Healing Garden

Start a partnership with Mother Nature, and open a health pharmacy in your own backyard.

The quality of vegetable gardening is thrice blessed, to paraphrase a speech from Shakespeare's *Merchant of Venice*. It blesses the gardener with a crop of wholesome, nutritious food. It provides healthy, vigorous exercise. And homegrown vegetables offer a refuge from the chemical fertilizers and pesticides of commercially grown vegetables. Let's count those blessings one by one.

Backyard gardens offer tastier food because their bounty reaches the dinner table within minutes of picking. Freshness and vitamin content are subtracted from most vegetables the moment they're plucked from the plant. Add shipping to that equation—the thousands of miles and minutes vegetables travel before they reach your supermarket—and you've got one worn-out head of lettuce. Garden-ripe tomatoes, for instance, may have up to 30 percent more vitamin C than those you buy in the store. Growing your own vegetables allows you to eat them while they are still rich in nutrients and full of flavor.

Gardening's second blessing, healthful exercise, is as inexpensive as it is good for you. The exercise you get from gardening—the bending, stooping, lifting, digging—could hardly be improved upon at a costly spa. It's also *outdoor* exercise, vigorous, satisfying activity in sunshine and fresh air.

Third, by using mulches, compost and natural pest control methods you also bring to your table vegetables that are free of chemicals. A backyard gardener can avoid all chemical sprays, and even use plant-derived insect poisons only as a last resort. Chemical sprays, and even many of the organically approved botanical sprays, may be toxic to people. In a garden it is next to impossible to spray an insect without getting poison all over vegetables.

All gardening is blessed with these qualities—nutrition-packed and chemical-free food, and exercise. But the health benefits of your backyard garden increase even more when you plant a "healing garden."

By that we mean a plot against disease—a few feet of turf to produce the vegetables that scientists have discovered may protect against major problems like heart disease and cancer. Sound incredible? It won't after you meet our lineup, the nine stars that can help you beat illness: broccoli, brussels sprouts, cauliflower, carrots, spinach, garlic, cabbage, onions and potatoes.

MOTHER NATURE'S HELPING HAND

To a nongardener, growing vegetables might seem like a lot of work. All that digging. And bending. And weeding. But when you plant a garden, you automatically have an assistant: Mother Nature. In fact, you're really the helping hand, since it's nature that does all the hard work of gardening; it's the combination of sunshine, rain, fresh breezes and rich soil that makes little seeds grow into hardy, productive plants. To be a successful gardener, all you have to do is help nature along. And if you want to pitch in and grow great vegetables, the first step is: Feed them. Plants need nourishment,

just as humans do, and they "eat" the minerals that are in the soil (along with generous helpings of sun and rain). You might want to check your soil to see if it lacks the nutrients plants relish. Your local Cooperative Extension Service will help you get your soil tested and tell you if you have to add such elements as nitrogen, phosphorus or potassium.

You can also improve your soil by mixing compost with it. Compost is a blend of decayed organic matter and soil. You can make your own compost pile in a corner of your yard by layering your kitchen garbage (except meat, bones and fat) with lime, grass clippings or shredded leaves and layers of loose soil. When you add this compost to your garden soil, you give plants the rich, organic matter on which they thrive.

But gardening really starts in winter when seed companies send out their catalogs. Looking through the catalogs, you can anticipate the different kinds of vegetables you will plant and where you will plant them. You might want to sketch out a simple map of your garden at that time, similar to the one shown here. Order your seeds as early in the year as possible. Pick the most disease-resistant strains and the ones best suited to the general weather conditions in your area.

The right tools can keep drudgery at arm's length. All you really need to garden are a few well-made

Nutritional Potencies in a Healing Garden

Vegetable	Portion	Calories	Calcium (mg.)	Iron (mg.)	Vitamin A (I.U.)	Vitamin C (mg.)	Fiber (g.)
Broccoli	1 stalk	48	156	1.7	3,780	171	5.4
Brussels sprouts	½ cup	28	25	0.9	405	68	2.2
Cauliflower	½ cup	16	15	0.7	35	45	1.2
Carrots	1 carrot	30	27	0.5	7,930	6	2.3
Spinach	½ cup	20	84	2.0	7,290	25	5.7
Garlic	1 clove	4	1	trace	trace	trace	NA
Cabbage	½ cup	11	22	0.2	60	21	1.2
Onions	¼ cup	16	12	0.2	18	4	0.6
Potatoes	1 potato	145	14	1.1	trace	31	4.0

NA—information not available.

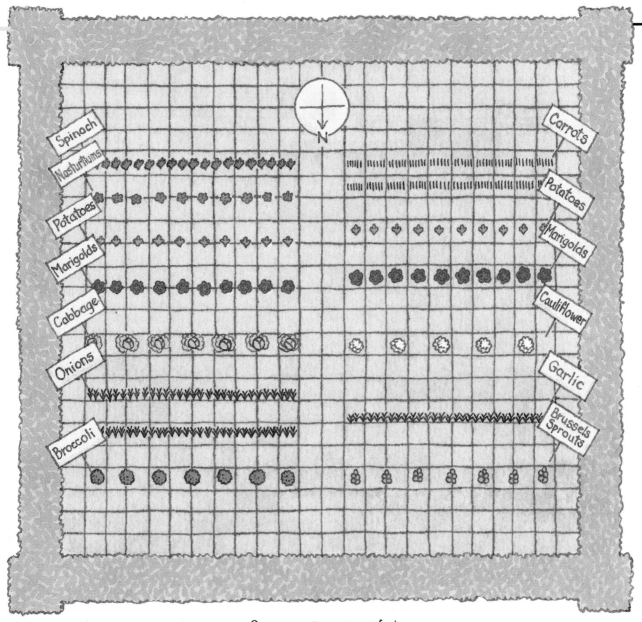

Spinach

Nasturtiums

Potatoes

Marigolds

Cabbage

Onions

Broccoli

Carrots

Potatoes

Marigolds

Cauliflower

Garlic

Brussels Sprouts

One square = one square foot

tools with firmly attached handles. You need a shovel to dig and something to break up the soil—either a spading fork or a heavy metal rake—and a trowel for planting.

For the very best results, another tool you might consider is a hoe. A lightweight hoe with a rectangular blade is good for weeding. For a second hoe, choose one with a V-shaped blade that will let you work close to plants.

You also might want to have on hand a sharp knife for harvesting broccoli and cauliflower, a watering can or galvanized bucket for watering, and bushel baskets, pails and large cans for carrying weeds and harvests.

If you're planting your very first vegetable garden, you may want to buy prestarted plants from a garden center and save yourself the work of growing vegetables from seeds. You can buy prestarted broccoli, brussels sprouts, cauliflower and cabbage. These prestarted plants may be purchased either in individual containers or in shallow, soil-filled boxes, commonly called flats. If you buy such plants, check with your local nurseryman for advice on how to plant them best.

If you decide to grow your garden from seeds, read the planting instructions on the seed packets carefully. Stagger the planting dates of the crops to give yourself staggered harvests.

You can help keep your garden pest free by interspersing certain plants with those you want to protect. Garlic, onions, marigolds and nasturtiums may help repel the bugs. As an added bonus, all but the marigolds are delicious foods, too.

Healing Herbs

Camomile
The flowers of this perennial are used to make a tea with a soothing, sedative effect.

Catnip
Catnip tea is often used as a sleep aid. A poultice made from the leaves may also relieve swelling of bruises and bumps.

Plantain
Plantain leaves can be applied whole or in a poultice to treat insect bites and stings and to relieve the itching of poison ivy.

Rosemary
As a tea, rosemary has long been prescribed for bad breath, hair loss and headaches, and as an appetite stimulant and cough quieter.

Sage
The gray-green sage leaves are used as a spice to counteract rich, greasy foods like duck. They also make a strong tea that can be used as a digestive aid.

Now to work. Never plant when the ground is wet. The soil is packed down firmly then, and this limits the movement of air through it. You should transplant seedlings you have grown or have bought from a nursery on cool, cloudy days or during the evening when bright sun will not wilt the young plants. Water the garden thoroughly after placing the seeds or transplants. Once your plants take hold, remove weeds that develop as soon as possible—before they grow large and sprout deep roots. The longer you allow weeds to stay in the ground, the more nutrients and water they can steal from your vegetable plants. Mulching can check the growth of weeds while it keeps the soil warm and moist. Spread your choice of mulch throughout the garden, but only after the season has advanced and the soil is thoroughly warmed.

Finally, after the first autumn frost stops your garden's growth and production, turn small plants like spinach into the soil to decompose. The larger plants that remain should be pulled and added to your compost pile (except for those that are still producing, like broccoli). Most important, keep a record of each year's garden layout to help you to recall the location of your crops. By rotating each crop to a new position each spring, you can go a long way toward preventing nutrient deficiencies in the soil and the spread of pests and plant diseases.

Along with our nine health-insuring vegetables, you might want to spice up your healing garden with medicinal herbs. Herbs have been staple natural healers in folk medicine for generations, and they work just as well today as they did in Great-Grandmother's day. The five herbs we recommend for your healing garden are camomile, catnip, plantain, rosemary and sage.

SPECIFIC PLANTING TIPS

Here are some specific tips on how to grow the nine disease-fighting vegetables and the five healing herbs.

Broccoli is a hardy, fairly quick-maturing plant that likes it cool and moist. It grows best in the spring or fall. For spring planting, start in late winter by sowing the seeds ½ inch deep in flats placed in a sunny window or greenhouse. You can move the seedlings to your garden in early spring, or as soon as the soil can be worked. Later, when the danger of severe frost has passed, sow more seeds directly in the garden. When their stalks are 3 or 4 inches tall, thin the plants or transplant them so that they are 18 to 24 inches apart.

Broccoli that is direct-seeded in late May will mature during the cool, early autumn months. Be sure to harvest the greenish heads well before their flower buds expand and dry out. After the main heads have been cut, the side-shoots will continue to produce smaller heads, so be careful to leave a long stub when you harvest broccoli.

Brussels sprouts are actually walnut-sized buds that grow on the stem of the plant. It is a long-season crop that likes to mature in cold weather. By starting your seeds in flats inside in April or May and then moving them outside in July or August, brussels sprouts may be harvested until December. In the South, they can be picked from November to March.

To prepare for planting brussels sprouts, till an ample amount of compost into the soil about two weeks before you move the plants to the garden. As you set them out, pinch off a few leaves and place the plants 16 to 20 inches apart in evenly spaced rows, 16 to 20 inches wide. In late summer, remove most of the lower leaves to concentrate the plant's growing power on the immature buds. Your sprouts will be ready to pick when heads are 1 to 1½ inches wide; be sure to pick the lower buds first. While it's a good idea to keep the soil around your sprouts free of weeds, be careful of their shallow roots as you cultivate.

Cauliflower does well in cool weather and poorly in hot, dry weather. It grows best when the daytime temperatures average between 60° and 65°F. It needs rich, moist, well-drained soil with lots of humus, so add large amounts of compost or rotted manure to the bed before planting, and nourish it with phosphorus and potassium in the form of phosphate rock or wood ash.

Spring crops are best when started from transplants. Fall and winter crops can be either seeded directly or transplanted. Start seedlings indoors in spring 10 to 12 weeks before the last frost. Do your transplanting only after the plants have developed three true leaves in addition to the first two seed-leaves. Direct-seed your fall crop about 12 weeks before the first expected frost; drop two or three seeds every 24 inches along rows that are spaced 36 inches apart.

You should thin clusters of direct-sown seedlings when they reach 1 inch in height, leaving only the sturdiest plants to grow. Keep the soil moist at all times, and mulch thickly with straw or compost. To insure that you have good-looking white heads to harvest, protect them from the sun by gathering up the longest leaves around the head and tying them in place with a strip of cloth or twine. To harvest, cut the heads well below the innermost leaves with a large knife.

Carrots should be planted successively from early spring through midsummer to insure a constant supply. Because the edible portion of the carrot is actually the root of the plant, success in growing carrots depends on good soil. Carrots require a deep layer of topsoil that is loose and well drained. Sandy loam that is free of stones and lumps is best. The tiny seeds are hard to handle, and thinning is usually necessary after the seedlings have grown to 2 or 3 inches.

Mulching helps to retain soil moisture and keep weeds down. Carrots should be harvested as needed after their roots reach a diameter of ½ inch.

Spinach is easy to grow in any decent garden soil that is well drained. Spinach grows rapidly as long as temperatures remain relatively cool. Planting can be done in April in most regions, and again in August for a second harvest in the fall.

Spinach can be harvested by cutting the whole plant, but for a prolonged harvest, cut the outside leaves from the plant as needed and allow the small inner leaves to continue growing.

Calming Camomile

The benefits of camomile have long been appreciated by the Europeans, especially the Germans, who praise one type as "capable of anything."

Herbalists use the plant to treat skin disorders, sore gums, menstrual cramps, indigestion and occasional fevers. Many people drink the tea at bedtime for a restful sleep.

You can make camomile tea with flowers picked from your herb garden. Dry the flowers, then brew 1 ounce of them in a pint of boiling water.

Scientific research and European folklore agree that the tea's benefits come from long-time use. The reason is that brewing brings out only a small amount of the plant's volatile oil, the source of its soothing qualities. By drinking it often, the beneficial effects of the tea will accumulate.

Not all of us, however, can become camomile fans. People with severe allergies should beware due to pollen in the plant's flowers.

Garlic should be planted just as you plant onions—with one notable exception. Garlic plants are almost always started from sets or cloves. As with onions, you can interplant garlic among your other vegetable plants to help keep creepy-crawly pests in check. Garlic thrives in well-drained, moist soil that is loose and moderately acid. Garlic cloves can be started indoors very early in the spring or planted directly in the garden four to six weeks before the last frost. Garlic is ready to harvest when the tops start to turn yellow and droop. At that time, knock down all the tops. Harvest the bulbs three to five days later and cure until dry before storing.

Cabbage, like broccoli, brussels sprouts and cauliflower, prefers cooler temperatures, plenty of moisture and heavy mulching. Early varieties will get off to a quicker start if you plant seeds inside and then transplant to the garden. So place the seeds in fine soil in flats or pots about four to six weeks before transplanting. In northern states, this can be done in February or March.

When the seedlings reach a height of 3 or 4 inches, they should be thinned to insure the growth of strong, stocky plants. When you're ready to transplant, choose a well-drained spot and add a good amount of compost or manure to the soil about two weeks before planting. Early varieties of cabbage are best set 14 inches apart in rows that are 28 inches apart. Midseason varieties should be 16 inches apart in 28-inch rows and late varieties should be 24 inches apart in 36-inch rows.

Onions that are grown in home gardens are of two types: bunching onions, which are grown more for their stems, and storage onions, which are grown mainly for their large, pungent bulbs. All kinds of onions are the answer to a garden planner's prayer. They can be used as companion plantings to fill in the spaces between well-separated vegetables like broccoli, cauliflower and cabbage, where their pungent nature will drive away pests from the neighborhood.

Onions can be started from seeds or sets (small, dormant bulbs). Sow onion seeds indoors very early in the spring or outdoors four to six weeks before the last frost. Sow the seeds ½ to 1 inch deep. Keep indoor seedling tops trimmed to a height of 1 inch until a week before setting out; this can be done up to six weeks before the last frost. Plant onion sets in the garden after the last frost; they should be 1 to 2 inches deep with their pointed ends up. Space seeds, sets or seedlings 3 to 4 inches apart in rich, loose, well-drained soil.

The rest is simple. Thin large onion plants to prevent crowding, don't allow the soil to become completely dry and keep down weeds. If the bulbs break the soil surface, surround them with a light mulch. You may pull bunching onions as you need them. As storage bulbs mature, their tops wither and fall over. When most plants have fallen, you can help the others along by knocking them over with a broom handle or rake. A week or so later, when the leaves are brown, the onions will be ready to pull or dig up. Onions should be cured before storing—either in the sun or indoors, if the weather is wet.

Potatoes develop best in cool areas where they are planted in early spring. They thrive in well-drained and loose soil that is high in organic matter like compost or well-rotted manure. Catalogs usually offer seed "eyes" or potato pieces, while garden centers usually sell whole seed potatoes, but either can be used successfully for starting your crop. Do *not* use potatoes bought in a grocery store in your garden, because they often are treated with chemicals to inhibit sprouting. Before planting, cut each whole seed potato into individual pieces so that each one contains one or two eyes and a good deal of flesh. Let the pieces dry

An Invigorating Tonic for Your Soil

The best way to improve your soil is to make and use compost—a mixture of organic matter like grass clippings, a nitrogen-rich substance like manure or bone meal, and soil. That mixture, broken down by microorganisms, turns into humus, a critical ingredient for healthy plants.

Compost provides a number of benefits. It feeds the microorganisms that aid plants.

It adds nutrients to the soil.

It breaks down nutrients already in the soil into forms that plants can use.

It improves soil structure, making it easier to cultivate, easier to aerate and kinder to roots.

It helps retain moisture.

It makes for soil that warms up faster in spring.

And it leads to soil that resists packing down.

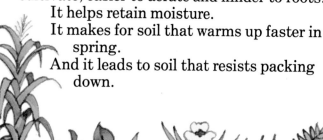

overnight before planting, and then sow them two to four weeks before the last frost.

Rows of potatoes should be 20 inches apart for smaller, early varieties, and 30 inches apart for mid and late-season varieties. To prepare rows, dig furrows that are 4 inches deep in heavy soil and 6 inches deep in light soil. Set the potato pieces, cut side down, 12 inches apart for the smaller varieties and 15 inches apart for the larger varieties; when the pieces are in place, cover them with soil. Then, when the plants grow to 6 or 8 inches in height, pack soil around the stems, leaving the tops uncovered. As the stems grow taller, keep them covered with hills of earth. This loose soil covering the growing potatoes also provides good drainage and discourages weeds. If your potatoes outgrow their hills, recover them immediately to avoid discoloring their skins. If these hills are properly constructed with loose soil, your potato harvesting will be greatly simplified. You can merely break into a hill, find a good-size tuber, and gently separate it from the mother plant.

HEALTH FROM THE GROUND UP

Herbs practically raise themselves. Most like a sunny, well-drained spot that is sheltered from the wind, but their soil need not be rich. In fact, some herbs actually grow better in poor soil. And, best of all, herbs are seldom bothered by bugs. The five herbs we are recommending for your healing garden are also perennials, which means that they'll come up year after year with no replanting. While the plants themselves may be killed by frost, their roots will hibernate during the winter and send up new shoots at the first sign of spring. Since some herbs are more sensitive than others, it's better to plant them outdoors for the first time after all danger of frost has passed. As for harvesting, the leaves of most herb plants can be picked at almost any time, but peak flavor is usually reached just before flowering. And because picking stimulates growth, don't hold back. You can harvest up

to one-third of a plant at any one time without harming it.

Camomile can be started from seeds in well-drained, rather dry and sandy soil. Thin the seedlings until they are about 18 inches apart, and keep them free of weeds. Once established, camomile plants produce runners, which can be divided the following spring for further plantings.

Catnip will grow into a large, leafy bush when planted in well-drained soil. It can be started from seeds, seedlings or stem cuttings. In the spring, it's easy to use cuttings; stem ends about 4 inches long will usually root right in the garden within a week. Harvest catnip when half the blossoms are open and as soon after the dew has evaporated as you can manage.

Plantain grows so profusely—especially in the wrong places like lawns and meadows—that you should think twice when placing it. It can easily take over the entire garden and choke out other plants if not kept in check. Watch the plant closely—and thin ruthlessly—to prevent such a spread.

Rosemary is a sun-loving evergreen that grows best in poor, sandy and well-drained soil that has been limed.

Sage plants start easily from seeds after the last frost. The plants grow in any kind of soil if they have full sun, but take care not to wet the leaves in the evening; sage leaves are prone to mildew.

PEST ADVICE

Here is a seven-pronged natural pest control strategy whose steps should be used in the order in which they are listed here.

1. Encourage soil health. Use plenty of rich compost and a mulch that will decay over the growing season. Use only natural fertilizers, animal manures and natural rock powders as fertilizers.

2. Interplant. When you interplant garlic and onions with your other vegetables, you disrupt a pest's ability to find its favorite vegetable. Many insects

Garden Guard

Practically any organic material can be used as mulch—a blanket-like layer that helps protect your garden—and each has its own benefits. Hay is high in nitrogen. Try rain-spoiled hay to cut costs. Buckwheat hulls are clean and attractive but can be expensive and hard to obtain. Cocoa bean hulls are excellent and very absorbent; they soak up 2½ times their weight in water. Ground corncobs are high in sugar and can boost the number of microorganisms in your soil. Lay down at least 6 inches of cobs after applying a nitrogenous material like blood meal, cotton-seed meal, bone meal or compost to the soil. Shredded cornstalks are another excellent mulch. Grass clippings are also very good, and they are cheap and readily available. Shredded leaves are worth consideration, too. They enrich the soil more quickly than unshredded leaves and do not mat down.

These guidelines will help you grow vegetables *and* pick them — seeds that are planted in the wrong place or improperly tended may not reach the table as hearty, healing food. Those with little room to garden should try compact varieties, which take up less space. (And those with little patience should try fast-maturing varieties, for an earlier harvest.)

even have an active dislike for onions and garlic and avoid gardens filled with them.

3. Plant pest-resistant varieties. One of the best ways to thwart an insect invasion is to plant vegetables that thrive despite the pests. You can find out about these varieties from your local Cooperative Extension Service.

4. Practice garden hygiene. Till the soil between plants as often as necessary. A good tilling kills many pests.

5. Add some beneficial bugs to your garden to control pests. One California businessman ships more than a half billion ladybugs all over the country each year, and other commercial insect breeders provide gardeners with helpful predators like praying mantises, tiny wasps of several species and even predatory mites. If you populate your garden with these beneficial insects, you'll surely keep pests on the run.

A Harvest of Smart Tips

Vegetable	Time to Plant	Location
Broccoli	For a spring crop, sow seeds indoors 8 to 10 weeks before the last frost. Transplant seedlings from 4 weeks before to 3 weeks after the last frost. For a fall crop, sow seeds outdoors 14 to 18 weeks before the first expected frost.	Well-drained, nitrogen-rich soil with plenty of moisture
Brussels sprouts	Seeds can be started indoors or outdoors 15 to 18 weeks before the first killing frost. If you plant indoors, transplant the seedlings 10 to 12 weeks before the frost.	Rich, heavy, well-drained soil with plenty of moisture, phosphorus and potassium
Cauliflower	For a spring crop, sow seeds indoors 10 to 12 weeks before the last frost. Transplant seedlings from 4 weeks before to 2 weeks after the last frost. For a fall crop, seeds can be sown outdoors 12 weeks before the first expected frost.	Rich, moist, well-drained soil with plenty of phosphorus and potassium
Carrots	Sow seeds for first crop outdoors 4 to 6 weeks before the last frost.	Light, well-drained, deeply tilled sandy loam with plenty of moisture
Spinach	For a spring crop, sow seeds 4 to 6 weeks before the last frost. For a fall crop, sow seeds 8 to 10 weeks before the first frost.	Rich, well-drained sandy loam
Garlic	Cloves can be planted outdoors 4 to 6 weeks before the last frost. In northern areas, cloves may be planted in fall and mulched over winter for early spring growing.	Fertile, well-drained, finely tilled sandy loam with plenty of moisture
Cabbage	For early varieties, start seeds indoors 11 to 13 weeks before the last frost. Transplant seedlings from 5 weeks before to 3 weeks after the last frost. Sow midseason varieties outdoors about the time of the last frost, and late-season varieties 4 weeks later.	Rich, well-drained loam with plenty of moisture, phosphorus and potassium
Onions	Seeds can be sown indoors 10 to 12 weeks before the last frost. Transplant seedlings from 6 weeks before to 2 weeks after the last frost. Onion sets can be planted outdoors soon after the last frost.	Rich, well-drained, finely tilled soil
Potatoes	Sow seed "eyes" 2 to 4 weeks before the last frost.	Rich, well-tilled, well-drained, acidic sandy loam with ample phosphorus and potassium

6. Set physical traps. Several excellent kinds of beetle traps are available at most garden centers. These traps lure the beetle away from your vegetables and to imprisonment. You can also hand-pick pesky worms, bugs and beetles off your plants and flick them into a small container of kerosene or soapy water. Jar lids filled with beer and buried to the rim in the garden will attract slugs and kill them.

7. Use botanical poisons. After you have tried these first six methods, *if* you still have trouble with pests, *then* you can think about plant-derived (botanical) poisons. These include pyrethrum, rotenone and ryania. They're effective, but they *are* poisons, and can be toxic to humans and animals in heavy doses. Still, they can be used safely, and because they are made from plants, they degrade quickly— unlike the chemical poisons.

Compact Variety	Fast-Maturing Variety	Major Pests	Best Natural Controls
Green Dwarf	Green Comet Hybrid	Imported cabbage worm Cabbage looper	*Bacillus thuringiensis*
Long Island Improved	Jade Cross Hybrid	Imported cabbage worm Cabbage looper	*Bacillus thuringiensis*
Early Snowball	Snow Crown Hybrid	Imported cabbage worm Cabbage looper	*Bacillus thuringiensis*
...	Kundulus	Carrot rust fly	Sprinkle wood ashes in furrow when sowing seed. Cover plants with cheesecloth or fine screening to prevent flies from laying eggs nearby. Sprinkle phosphate rock around plants.
...	Melody Hybrid	Leaf miner	Remove and destroy infested leaves. Cover plants with cheesecloth or fine screening.
...	White or Mexican cultivars	...	Garlic is rarely bothered by pests.
Morden Dwarf	Earliana	Imported cabbage worm Cabbage looper	*Bacillus thuringiensis*
...	Ebenezer	Onion maggot	Cover plants with cheesecloth or fine screening. Sprinkle diatomaceous earth around plants.
...	Red Pontiac	Colorado potato beetle	Hand-pick and destroy eggs, larvae and adults. Dust with rotenone.

The Healing Garden

Mother Earth was the first woman doctor. But her black bag is dark, rich soil. Dig into it and plant a healing garden, and you'll pull out natural medicines more powerful than any drug—because they help *prevent* disease. So enroll in Mother Earth's Medical School. It takes only one summer to grow a degree.

1 Broccoli

Researchers conducted interviews with hundreds of men and women with colon or rectal cancer to compare their diets with those of people who didn't have the diseases. People free of these cancers, the researchers found, tended to eat more broccoli, more brussels sprouts and more cabbage than those who had cancer. Although the scientists couldn't pinpoint the anticancer factor, they *knew* it was there.

2 Brussels Sprouts

Other studies confirm that brussels sprouts, broccoli and cabbage contain a defender against cancer. In one study, rats were fed these vegetables in powder form, and the feedings increased a chemical reaction in the rats' intestines that can prevent tumors. Scientists also fed rats indoles, substances found in these three vegetables, and again, the cancer-fighting chemical reaction increased. In a third study, two groups of animals were exposed to cancer-causing substances. One group was then fed indoles and developed less cancer.

4 Carrots

Doctors reported in a 1981 issue of the *Lancet*, a world-renowned medical journal, that a substance found in carrots may reduce the risk of lung cancer—even among cigarette smokers. The protective substance is called beta-carotene, a chemical that's also plentiful in leafy greens and red fruits and vegetables.

3 Cauliflower

This vegetable is a dieter's friend. A ½-cup serving has only 16 calories and lots of fiber—the roughage that fills you up so you don't overeat. Fiber can also erase up to 100 calories a day by helping to escort dietary fats out of our intestines before they're absorbed. Cauliflower is a healing vegetable because overweight is underhealthy; obesity is a major factor in a number of diseases.

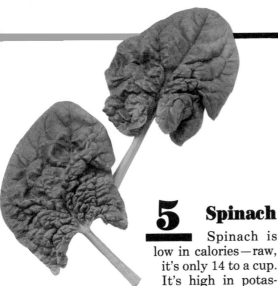

6 Garlic

This powerful bulb has proved to be quite potent in combating heart disease. A doctor in India found that garlic increases fibrinolytic activity—the body's ability to dissolve heart-threatening clots. A high level of fibrinolytic activity is especially important for people who have had heart attacks, to prevent recurrences. When the doctor gave people garlic oil in the crucial recovery period after a heart attack, fibrinolysis increased by 63 percent.

5 Spinach

Spinach is low in calories—raw, it's only 14 to a cup. It's high in potassium, iron and vitamin A. And it's *very* high in chlorophyll, another substance that may protect against cancer. Chiu-Nan Lai, Ph.D., of the M.D. Anderson Hospital and Tumor Institute in Houston, Texas, believes that the key anticancer agent in spinach is chlorophyll. "My laboratory research has demonstrated that extracts of chlorophyll [from spinach] definitely lower the mutagenic [cell-warping] activity of cancer-causing agents," she says.

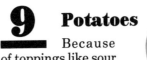

7 Cabbage

Cabbage is more than a cancer fighter. The juice of this vegetable may heal ulcers. Garnett Cheney, M.D., treated 13 ulcer patients with a mixture of fresh cabbage juice and celery juice 5 times daily. In 11 of these cases the ulcers disappeared in 6 to 9 days. Seven years later, Dr. Cheney and his associates healed over 90 percent of 45 ulcer patients with a cabbage juice concentrate derived from fresh pressed raw cabbage.

8 Onions

These pungent vegetables are good sources of folate, iron, and potassium—three nutrients that can do wonders for your energy levels. And during the last several years, studies have noted onions' ability to lower cholesterol. One study also showed that people who ate onions along with a fatty meal had far less "platelet aggregation," a chemical change in the blood that can lead to an artery-clogging clot. All of which means that onions are a great food for your heart.

9 Potatoes

Because of toppings like sour cream, potatoes have a reputation as a no-no for calorie counters. But the truth is, a good-size baked potato has only 145 calories, the same as a cup of low-fat milk. The potato also resembles fruit. A medium-size spud has almost as much C as half a grapefruit. And more vitamin C may mean fewer colds and gum problems, not to mention less risk of heart disease and cancer.

The World of Edible Sins

Like a rainbow it beckons; the colors artificial but the calories all too real.

Fast food is big business with a capital "B"— over $20 billion earned in a typical year. Consider these facts:

- 90 percent of Americans eat at a take-out establishment at least once within any six-month period.
- The average American spends more than $400 a year to buy fast food.
- Customers under 35 years of age will choose a fast food restaurant 60 percent of the time when dining out.

McDonald's, Burger King, Kentucky Fried Chicken, Dairy Queen, Jack-in-the-Box, Gino's and countless other fast food franchises are good at getting us to eat at their restaurants. What they're not so good at is telling us that their foods are loaded with fat, salt and sugar. That the nutrients in most of their foods are dwarfed by a devastating number of calories. That the types of food they offer, the way the food is prepared and the amount eaten are practically an exact profile of the very diet that contributes to overweight, high blood pressure, hardening of the arteries, diabetes and even cancer. In short, that there's an undeniable link between the all-American fast food habit and the all-American health hazards.

THE TROUBLE WITH FAST FOODS

Fat. The deep fryer ranks as the biggest offender of all. And we're not looking just at french fries. A piece of fish—low in fat and only 100 calories to begin with—can emerge from a bath of hot oil toting twice the calories. Once it's been slapped into a bun and smeared with tartar sauce, more than 60 percent of that fish sandwich's calories may come from fat. Condiments like mayonnaise

What's Cooking at Hamburger U.

A dean, an assistant dean and 8 professors— all to teach aspiring students how to make *hamburgers?* Yes, that's Hamburger U., McDonald's very own institute of higher learning (and *earning*) in Elk Grove Village, Illinois. The students not only learn how to use a grill, but also learn management techniques (including psychology) and the fine art of refrigeration and equipment repair. Is the reward for diligent study a McD? Or a Phi Beta Ketchup? That's close: The diplomaed manager is a "certified hamburgerologist."

sauces and creamy salad dressings at franchises featuring coleslaw and salad bars tend to put fat on the hips even while you're congratulating yourself for eating your vegetables. "Fast" scrambled eggs give you 230 calories, 75 percent of which come from fat. At home, a scrambled egg has about 142 calories, with only 67 percent derived from fat.

Salt. Potato chips are salty. Milk shakes are sweet. So how is it that a typical chocolate shake has almost 300 milligrams of sodium—at least 100 milligrams *more* than ten tangy potato chips?

The sodium content in nearly all categories of fast food is outrageously high. Meanwhile, the potassium needed to balance or flush out all that sodium is dangerously low. If the sodium onslaught keeps up day after day, the kidneys are forced to work overtime and high blood pressure may be the result.

The next time you order fast food, keep in mind these sample sodium shockers: At Dairy Queen, a plain hot dog has 830 milligrams of sodium; a super hot dog with cheese has 1,605 milligrams. A fish sandwich has 875, and a chicken sandwich, 870 (at home, a roasted drumstick has just 47 milligrams of sodium). McDonald's breakfasts are a morning salutation to sodium: an Egg McMuffin has 885 milligrams and Hot Cakes have 1,070. At lunch, a Quarter Pounder with Cheese hits hard at 1,236 milligrams of sodium. That means a breakfast of pancakes and pork sausage, and a lunch of a burger, shake, fries and pie can come to approximately 2,913 milligrams of sodium.

Sugar. Ample amounts of sugar are found in shakes, sodas, condiments and desserts. But the *combination* of sugar plus salt means double trouble in terms of high blood pressure, for reasons that are not yet clearly understood. A research study published in the *American Journal of Clinical Nutrition* indicates that sugar increases salt's ability to bring on hypertension.

And if you eat lots of fast food, you probably get more salt and

sugar in your *non*-fast foods. A study sponsored by the USDA showed that fast food fans have bigger appetites for salt and sugar. The average American already consumes at least twice as much salt and sugar as the government considers healthy, but fast-fooders get up to 60 percent more than that. They sprinkle extra salt over their food, saturate their coffee with sugar and end up eating 5 teaspoons of straight sugar daily, while the average person eats one-fourth of that. The typical fast food addict gives his meals over six shakes of salt daily, compared to half that for a nonaddict.

Caffeine. Soft drinks are so integral a part of the fast food scene that a word about caffeine cannot be avoided. We know that coffee contains caffeine and that too much can cause irritability, insomnia, the "jitters," upset stomach and the like. Plus caffeine robs the body of thiamine and other B vitamins essential to steady nerves.

Most of us wouldn't offer a cup of coffee to our toddlers and teenagers—but we do offer the equivalent in caffeine by buying them colas, Mountain Dew, Dr. Pepper, Mello Yello, Sunkist Orange and various other sodas, all of which contain caffeine. Though a can of soda has about one-third the caffeine in a cup of coffee, its impact on a child is similar to that of coffee on an adult because of the child's smaller body weight. A child who drinks several cans of soda a day may become overactive, may have trouble sleeping and can suffer withdrawal symptoms when he or she misses out on a soda "fix."

Lack of Fiber. In many fast food meals, there is precious little fiber to clear our digestive tracts and keep our intestines in good working order. Salad bars, available in some restaurants, provide an exception to the rule.

Lack of Nutrients. In a report in the *Journal of the American Dietetic Association,* two researchers from Pennsylvania State University presented a comprehensive analysis of the nutritional pluses and minuses in sample fast food menus. They found that values for protein rated high at 30 to 50 percent of the Recommended Dietary Allowance, and "almost all of the menus also contained items which, if selected, . . . would provide 20 to 30 percent of the recommendations for thiamine, riboflavin, ascorbic acid [vitamin C] and calcium." However, they say, people do *not* always select foods that give them these four nutrients. Furthermore, nearly all of the menus "lacked a rich source of vitamin A" and "other nutrients commonly in short supply in sample meals were biotin, folacin [folate], pantothenic acid [pantothenate], iron and copper." These inadequacies are due to the "limited nature of fast food menus which . . . offered little in the way of fruits and vegetables, particularly those rich in vitamin A." Other nutrients making a less than decent appearance in a fast food meal include magnesium, vitamin B_6 and

vitamin E. In one study mentioned by the researchers, the calcium intakes of 280 fast food patrons were "quite low," not only because the meals they selected were low in calcium but also because the overwhelming majority of interviewees chose soft drinks and coffee instead of milk (less than 5 percent bought milk).

Over the long run, a steady diet of fast foods and junky snack foods can, in fact, create nutritional deficiencies. What father and mother would believe, for instance, that their child could develop symptoms that suggest beriberi, the thiamine deficiency disease? Yet 20 youngsters under the care of an observant pediatrician, Derrick Lonsdale, M.D., of Cleveland, Ohio, did develop thiamine deficiency, or "overconsumption malnutrition," many from their junk food habits. Symptoms included recurrent abdominal or chest pain, sleeplessness, depression, recurrent fever and chronic fatigue. After

Nutrition in the Fast Lane Is Slippery Going

Percentage of Recommended Dietary Allowances in Fast Food Meals

McDonald's Breakfast
Egg McMuffin
Sausage
Hash browns
Orange juice

Pizza Hut Lunch
Thin 'n' Crispy
Pepperoni Pizza
(3 slices of a
10-in. pie)

Kentucky Fried Chicken Dinner
Original Recipe
chicken (drumstick
and thigh)
Mashed potatoes
with gravy
Coleslaw
Roll

Nutrients				Total %
Protein	50.7	35	54.0	139.7
Vitamin A	19.8	20	5.1	44.9
Vitamin C	146.9	—	61.0	207.9
Thiamine	63.3	20	16.7	100.0
Riboflavin	32.2	30	18.8	81.0
Calcium	24.7	30	11.6	66.3
Iron	23.1	25	21.7	69.1

Salt in Snack Foods: A Better Shake

Snack	Portion	Sodium (mg.)	
Pretzels, thin twisted	10	1,008	
Cheese crackers	10	325	
Corn chips	1 oz.	231	
Potato chips	10	200	
Doughnut, cake type	1	160	
Peanuts, roasted, salted	¼ cup	151	
Peanut brittle	1 oz.	145	
Almonds, roasted, salted	¼ cup	78	
Ice cream	½ cup	42	
Pumpkin seeds, unsalted	¼ cup	17	
Sunflower seeds, unsalted	¼ cup	11	
Cashews, unsalted	¼ cup	5	
Peanuts, roasted, unsalted	¼ cup	2	
Popcorn, unsalted	1 cup	1	

When it comes to snacking, snack the natural, nearly salt-free way. A handful of unsalted popcorn has 1/1000 the sodium (salt) content of just 10 pretzels.

taking thiamine supplements, all 20 youngsters improved or lost their symptoms completely.

DINING WELL ON FAST FOOD

But with all those drawbacks, can you still have it your way—healthfully? Here are five tips to help you make your next fast food meal better for you.

First of all, patronize restaurants that feature a salad bar. Choose romaine lettuce over iceberg when you have the choice, and take generous helpings of sprouts and fresh-cut vegetables such as tomatoes, broccoli, carrots and cauliflower for vitamins A and C. Go easy on dressings that look like glue (they're probably full of fats) and shun salty, pickled condiments. Hard-cooked eggs are full of protein and vitamin A; cottage cheese supplies protein and calcium.

Second, remember to order less than you think you want. This technique is surprisingly effective; you may well find yourself feeling full on less food. And if you're really hungry, you can always order more.

Third, try to cut the fat. When ordering pizza, for example, choose the green pepper and onion combo instead of the sausage. Ask if you can get dishes like meat and fish without the sauce. Foods that are baked, broiled or boiled obviously contain less fat than those that are deep-fried.

Fourth, request that the chef "hold the salt." Do your part, too, by avoiding condiments and pickles (for example, just telling the person who takes your order "no pickle, please" on a Whopper Junior at Burger King cuts out 93 milligrams of sodium). Counter a salty meal by eating high-potassium foods some other time during the day—potatoes (baked or boiled), raisins, dried apricots, skim milk, tomatoes, orange juice and bananas are all good sources.

Fifth, do whatever you have to do to avoid wolfing down the meal. If your food comes to you in boxes and bags, pull it out and arrange it on a tray. Take your meal outside (weather permitting), away from the zippy music.

SNACK ATTACKS

On the first day of the big experiment, the 30 willing participants were divided into three groups. One group received wholesome meals. Another group dined exclusively on potato chips, cookies, sugary cereals, gelatin desserts and peanut butter, washed down with milk and fruit-flavored drinks. The third group had a choice of wholesome meals or snack foods.

For 11 weeks, scientists at the Beltsville Human Nutrition Research Center in Maryland kept a close eye on things, recording blood sugar levels and cholesterol. At the end of the trial, the effects that junk food had on the participants (for that, of course, was the study's focal point) were clearly negative: The snack-fooders had "significantly higher" levels of blood sugar and "significantly greater" levels of cholesterol in the blood than the other two groups. When the participants took a glucose tolerance test—a standard medical test for diabetes—the snack-fooders and the group that ate both snacks and wholesome food came out with heavy-duty insulin responses (a sign of disordered blood sugar metabolism), compared to the normal insulin in the group that ate a good diet. The junk-fooders had put on the most fat.

Sound like anyone you know? Well, responsible researchers can't have people participate in experiments they *know* might ruin their health, so they use rats. Judith Hallfrisch, Ph.D., and her colleagues employed male albino rats in the above study. But scientists think there's a definite similarity in behavior and body responses in rats and people when it comes to junky snack foods.

There's really nothing at all wrong with snacking per se. Lots of

Americans—an estimated 60 percent—have something to eat or drink between meals every day. At the University of Illinois, over 90 percent of the students reported snacking during just one 24-hour period, according to nutrition professor Mahmood A. Khan, Ph.D. Snacking, he says, can be important in helping students meet daily nutritional requirements—if properly planned.

Unfortunately, most Americans do *not* plan their snacks well. It's all too easy and convenient to reach for a bag of pretzels, snap off the flip-top lid of a soda can, or unwrap two or three cream-filled chocolate cupcakes. Before you have time to sit down, you've polished off more salt, sugar and fat than your body needs or wants and at a very high calorie cost (not to mention dollar cost).

But convenience can't explain why our hearts leap at the sight of Boston cream pie. We do not lust after celery sticks in the same manner. And hunger has little to do with pumping handful after handful of buttery, salty popcorn into our mouths at the movies. Hunger doesn't drive us into a bakery to buy a dozen eclairs and other gooey goodies—just after we've had a full lunch. It doesn't explain how jelly doughnuts can turn an intelligent adult into an impulsive child—or why a simple lollipop can turn a child into a tantrum-throwing maniac.

Somewhere along the line, nature gave us an enormous appreciation for foods that taste sweet or salty. Our taste buds are especially sensitive to these flavors. Food processors know this. And junk food represents the calculated exploitation of these instincts.

In a very real sense, junk food is to natural food what pornography is to real sexuality. In the latter instance, images of nudity push the automatic response button, but the contact, the companionship and a whole lot more are missing. With junk food, the sugar or salt is there as a lure, but the *purpose* of food—nourishment—is missing. What we do get with "porno food" is sugar to rot our teeth and disrupt our blood sugar levels, calories to make us overweight, salt to play havoc with our blood pressure, and hundreds of food additives that could be giving us

Potassium Scores

Beverage	Portion (oz.)	Potassium (mg.)
Tomato juice	8	552
Orange juice	8	496
Grape juice	8	293
Apple juice	8	250
Coffee	6	117
Tea	6	44
Orange soda	12	37
Cola	12	7

Soda, coffee and tea may beat any juice in popularity, but not in potassium content.

The Greasing of the Spud

What's brown, has more than 2 eyes, and lives in Idaho?

Right: the potato.

It's also the most commonly eaten vegetable in America, a nutritional masterpiece low in fat and calories, high in fiber, and packed with vitamins, minerals and protein. One problem, though. The potato has been perverted.

Almost everything good about a potato —not many more calories than an apple, only 0.1 percent fat, plenty of vitamin C, all of the B complex vitamins, minerals, protein—has been made bad. Made into greasy french fries. Salty potato chips. Frozen potatoes. Canned potatoes. Made into foods high in fat, salt and calories and low in nutrition and fiber. Made into junk food.

You know the potato has really gone downhill when a brand of potato chips comes stacked in a can that looks like it ought to hold tennis balls. And in order to fit so neatly into that can the potato was practically beaten up. It was peeled, cooked, mashed and dehydrated. Then some water was put back in to make a smooth dough, and sugar (dextrose) was added for uniform browning. The dough was cut into uniform chips, which then were quick-fried for 15 seconds. Next the chips were salted and sealed in airtight, crush-proof cans.

One nutrient that really loses out in processing like that is vitamin C: Potato chips have 75 percent less C than a plain potato. Canned potatoes have lost about 50 percent, and mashed potatoes in frozen dinners have lost over 70 percent.

anything from hyperactivity to cancer.

Once you can see that junk foods are *designed* to exploit, you will find it much easier to resist them. The most important time to gear up resistance is just prior to going food shopping. Remember, if junk foods are not on hand, they can't be eaten. Studies on vending machine buying tell us that people will buy healthful snacks if that's what the vending machine offers. Availability counts. And because we don't want to have to clean and chop a carrot, for example, each and every time we feel like snacking, it's a good idea to prepare wholesome snack foods upon returning from the supermarket.

SNACKING HEALTHFULLY

Making the transition from chocolate bars to wholesome, satisfying and delicious snacks is a lot easier than it sounds. It requires some experimentation and creativity, to be sure, but no more time than a snack should take. The best part is, once your palate becomes accustomed to a true taste experience—instead of salt and sugar—you won't be able to tolerate the chips and gumdrops; they'll taste too salty or too sweet.

Unsalted, dry-roasted mixed nuts and peanuts, or peanuts in the shells, are good snacks for weaning away from salted cocktail nuts. So are roasted sunflower seeds and pumpkin seeds. Raw, unsalted seeds and nuts are also delicious, as are whole wheat pretzels covered with sesame seeds instead of salt. Many health food stores carry such items.

Popcorn is an excellent food, high in fiber and low in fat and calories—only 6 calories in a handful compared to 114 calories in ten potato chips or 104 in ten jelly beans. That's *without* butter and salt. Air popper appliances, which are enjoying tremendous popularity, make it easy to have popcorn ready within the space of a TV commercial. Try sprinkling on a favorite seasoning for zesty flavor; garlic powder, grated cheese, chili and curry powders are all delicious.

Muffins and breads made with whole grains are complex-carbohydrate foods that are digested more slowly than snacks made with refined flour. Sweetened with fruit rather than table sugar, they're more filling and just as delicious.

Buy natural peanut butter (without salt and sugar), or make it at home, to spread on whole grain breads and crackers. Cashew butter and sesame butter are available also, for high-protein, zinc-rich snacks.

Cut up cauliflower, broccoli, carrots, sweet red peppers and other raw vegetables for eating as is or dunking in dips of cottage cheese and yogurt. Let bowls of fresh cherries, strawberries, grapes, plums and other fruits in season take their place near the TV. Cut up cantaloupe, honeydew melon and peaches and top with a dollop of plain yogurt. Add chopped Brazil nuts, wheat germ or raisins. Make a big bowl of tabbouleh salad, which combines fresh parsley, bulgur, tomatoes, onions, lemon juice and vegetable oil.

Dried apricots, pears and raisins are nutritious, but they're sticky and can lead to tooth decay unless you brush and floss soon after eating them. Some cheeses, on the other hand, seem to help prevent tooth decay, especially aged cheddar, Monterey Jack and Swiss.

For a cold snack from the freezer, have "juice cubes" all ready to pop out of the ice cube trays. They're easy to make: Pour orange juice or any juice into the tray and let it freeze.

Weaning yourself and the children off soda may take some doing. Milk, fruit juices, spring water and herbal teas are alternatives, but for a soda substitute, try mixing various fruit juices with such effervescent bubbles as Perrier water, which is high in calcium and low in sodium. White grape juice and Perrier make a great-tasting, refreshing "grape soda."

Finally, if you're still lusting madly after french fries, shakes and a hot dog with everything on it, we know of at least one video game on the market that lets you gobble up pizzas and root beer with a vengeance— and without a trace of guilt. Just watch out for the purple pickle.

10

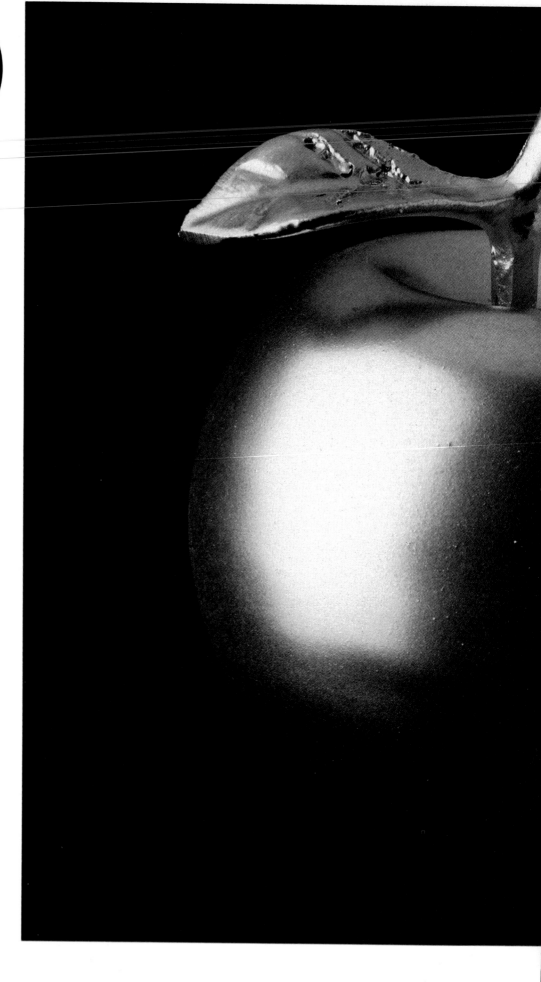

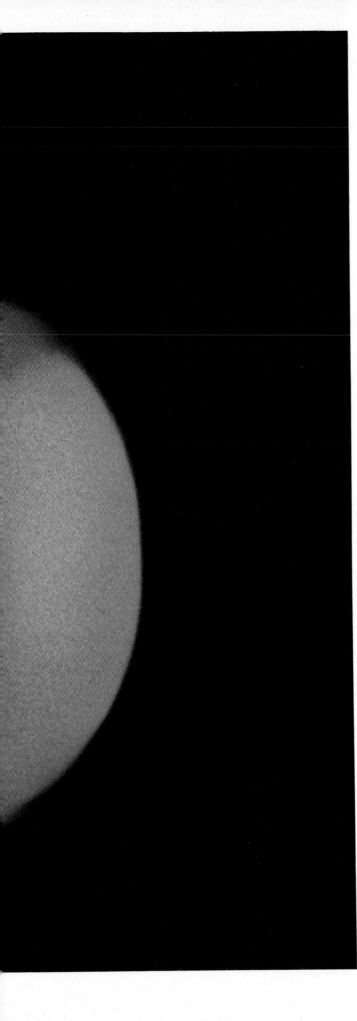

The Encyclopedia of Food & Health

In a world of confusing choices, here's your guide to the wisest nutritional investments.

■

By now, we trust you've gotten a clear idea of what we mean by the "revolution." You've seen how modern food processing methods and our own ill-informed eating habits have been shadowed by the steady rise in degenerative diseases—the cancers, the heart disease. How a new consciousness of the *nutritional value* of food can help reduce your chances of becoming one of those statistics—and help you roll out of bed each morning to a brighter day.

We've shown you some ways you can take life into your own hands—how to plan a "supermarket strategy" for healthy shopping, how to grow and store your own food, how to plan a lifetime of good nutrition, how to recognize a junk food when you see one.

But so far, we haven't really gotten down to specifics. Which is leaner, white meat or dark? How much fat is in an avocado? What's the best vegetable source of fiber? Of vitamin C? Of vitamin A? That's what we'll tell you in this final chapter.

To do this, we've divided all the foods on the world's table into eight basic groups: meat, poultry, fish, vegetables, fruits, grains, nuts and seeds and dairy products. We've analyzed the nutritional value of a representative sampling of foods chosen from each of these groups, and you'll find the result in the form of a "food target" at the opening of each section that follows. Our targets are meant to serve as a quick, simple way of comparing the nutritional merits of foods in each of these eight groups—and to accurately set your sights on health.

Meat

An archer drawing a bead on a target has a vivid image of his arrow's goal—the bull's-eye. Surrounding that sweet, far-off disk are a series of rings he'd be less happy to hit—increasingly less happy the farther they are from the center. But when you're combing the supermarket aisles in search of next week's meals—and doing your best to find the most nutritious food for your money—how do you know exactly what to shoot for?

To answer that question, we've put together the food targets you'll find here and at the beginning of each of the seven sections that follow. To do that, we enlisted the help of a computer and the latest scientific information on the nutritional value of 243 different foods and used them to rank the foods for you; foods from each of eight different food groups are arranged on the targets from best to worst order.

In each bull's-eye you'll find our "nutritional superstars," the foods in that category richest in vitamins, minerals, fiber, protein and other health-building necessities, and lowest in fat, sodium, sugar and other health "baddies." In the surrounding rings, we've arranged the other members of the food group in descending order of nutritional glory; that is, the farther out a food is, the less healthy it's apt to be. Finally, we've exiled the lowest-ranking foods in each group to the outermost ring—though, as we'll explain later, these last-ringers range from just plain awful to not so very bad depending on the food group they're in.

We started by evaluating the nutritional makeup of each item in the eight food groups. The nutrients we used for our evaluations were slightly different for each food group; generally, they were the ones which that particular group was richest in. For example, when we decided to take a look at meat—the target you see on this page—we looked at each kind of meat's protein content, its fat and sodium levels, its total calories, and its complement of iron, potassium, and the B vitamins thiamine and niacin. But when we looked at fish, we considered the protein, fat, sodium, vitamin B_6, potassium, iron and niacin content of each variety for the same reason.

You'll notice that some of these component parts, like fat, can be a genuine threat to well-being when they're consumed in large quantities. To balance a food's potential dangers with its benefits, we gave fat a negative value and nutrients like iron or thiamine a positive value.

As you can see from the meat target, liver is one of the superstars in a butcher's lineup. For one thing, it's a rich source of high-quality protein, essential for the growth and maintenance of a healthy body; one 5-ounce serving of liver provides more than one-third the Recommended Dietary Allowance of protein for adults and two-thirds for children. It's also one of nature's own multivitamins. Liver is loaded with vitamin A, vitamin C, all the B vitamins and trace minerals like iron, chromium and zinc. Plus—compared to other meats—it's also low in fat.

Fat, of course, is meat's main drawback, but, as the target illustrates, you can keep fat to a minimum by aiming for leaner cuts like round or flank steak. The target also shows that highly processed and additive-laden meats like bacon and knockwurst have nothing much to recommend them; they are best eaten in moderation or not at all.

Anybody who's ever bitten down into the juicy red heart of a charcoal-broiled steak fresh from the grill has

Polish sausage

Salami

Cured ham

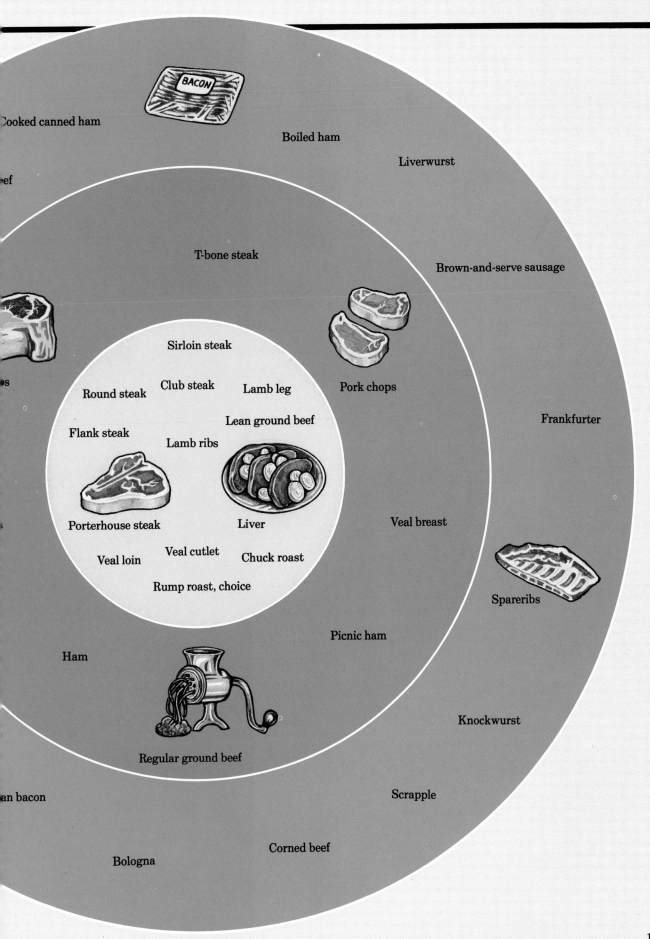

Cooked canned ham

BACON

Boiled ham

Liverwurst

...ef

T-bone steak

Brown-and-serve sausage

Sirloin steak

...os

Round steak   Club steak   Lamb leg

Pork chops

Flank steak   Lean ground beef

Frankfurter

Lamb ribs

Porterhouse steak   Liver

Veal breast

Veal loin   Veal cutlet   Chuck roast

Rump roast, choice

Spareribs

Picnic ham

Ham

Knockwurst

Regular ground beef

Scrapple

...an bacon

Corned beef

Bologna

one idea why meat has long been part of man's diet, but our relationship to animals as food providers goes far beyond good taste; it is a very old and natural thing. Even when health enters the picture, there's a lot to be said for meat eating.

For one thing, red meat is full of the high-quality, complete protein that your body needs in large amounts for the building of everything from fingernails and hair to nerves and blood cells. Getting adequate protein from a plant-based diet is certainly possible, but it is a bit trickier. That's because the body produces the raw materials for growth from 20 simple molecules called amino acids, which it shapes into protein substances to fill its current needs. Eleven of these amino acids are manufactured in the body; nine of them are found in food. Meats, because they supply high levels of all nine, are easily transformed into the growth proteins the body needs. Plants, on the other hand, have low levels of some of these nine essential acids; it's necessary to combine vegetable and grain foods to supply our bodies with the best array. Animal protein, in short, is much closer in composition to the protein substance in the human body, and so it is more readily usable.

Meats are also abundant sources of minerals that are often tough to find in other foods. Zinc, for example, is necessary for everything from healthy skin to normal growth, and many meats are loaded with it. Meat is also one of the best sources of iron, which is necessary for the prevention of anemia, and a good source of selenium, which is thought by many to protect against cancer.

Many meats are also packed with the B vitamins—thiamine, riboflavin, niacin, folate, pantothenate, biotin and vitamin B_6. And at least one B vitamin, B_{12}, is almost impossible to get anywhere else except in meat.

And yet, there's just no way around it: When it comes to your health, meat is a mixed blessing. There are serious problems with a diet too rich in meat, especially the fatty red meats and highly processed meat products like hot dogs and sausage. In fact, many studies suggest that too much meat in your diet can lead to elevated blood pressure, osteoporosis (demineralization of the bones), and an increased risk of heart disease and cancer (particularly colon cancer).

What's worse is that many of these health risks seem to be directly linked to the fats that "marble" most of the meats on your butcher's counter—the very marbling that marks them as gustatory treats.

FATS AND HEART DISEASE

Much of the evidence linking animal fats to the increased risk of heart disease comes from the branch of science known as epidemiology, the comparative study of disease in the world's populations. Sometimes an isolated population group, because of its unusual dietary habits or an extraordinarily high (or low) incidence of disease, can provide scientists with what amounts to a real-life laboratory experiment. By examining the group's eating habits and its incidence of disease, they can draw reasonable—though not 100 percent

It looks like Americans have a beef with their own health—rising beef intake has paralleled a rise in colon cancer, for example.

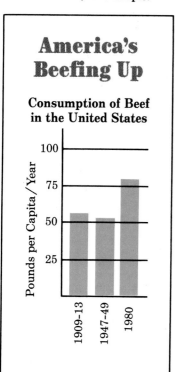

America's Beefing Up

Consumption of Beef in the United States

Take a Vacation from Meat

Scientific studies show that vegetarians have a 30 percent lower risk of dying of a heart attack, and that vegetarian women have a lower risk of breast cancer.

In short, a vegetarian diet is healthier. But where do you start?

You might follow the advice of those vegetarians who recommend a

certain—conclusions about the effect of diet on health.

Seventh-Day Adventists, for example, eat much less meat than most other Americans. One study showed that, while Adventist men have heart attacks, they tend to have them about ten years later in life than the rest of us.

A closer look at this fortunate group turned up some even more incriminating evidence against animal fats. When deaths among Adventist men were compared to the expected number of deaths in men the same age in the general population, the figure for the Adventists was about one-half of the other. Adventist men who ate no meat but did eat eggs and dairy products (which are also high in animal fats) had only 39 percent of the expected mortality rate. And the total vegetarians, those who ate *no* food of animal origin, had only 14 percent of the expected rate. In short, the study seemed to support the link between meat and heart disease.

But epidemiological studies aren't the only evidence strengthening this link. It's known that elevated levels of cholesterol and triglycerides tend to increase a person's risk of heart

gradual change of diet. "After all," says one vegetarian, "you've been eating meat for a long time. You shouldn't go overboard and cut it out all at once."

For a start, cut meat down, not out. Try dishes where meat is just one of several ingredients, like casseroles or stir-fried Chinese food. Or have one vegetarian meal each day. After several weeks of this, cut out meat entirely.

disease. Though the details of this connection are complex and controversial, it appears that circulating blood fats contribute to atherosclerosis, the gradual buildup of fatty plaques on artery walls that impede the passage of blood and can lead to the sudden and dramatic blockage of blood flow we call a heart attack or stroke. Studies of individuals, rather than populations, have shown that animal fats in the diet can raise the level of cholesterol and triglycerides in the blood.

In one such study, the blood fat levels of 21 vegetarians living on a "macrobiotic" diet consisting mostly of whole grains, vegetables, legumes and fruits were measured. Then, for a month, the subjects added 250 grams of beef to their diet each day, and their blood fat levels were tested again. This time, their total cholesterol levels had risen an average of 19 percent, and their blood pressures had gone up, too. "The study suggests an adverse effect of consumption of beef on plasma lipid [fat] and blood pressure levels," the scientists concluded.

Another researcher, after reviewing similar evidence, concluded that "it [has been] established beyond reasonable doubt that saturated fat, and specifically meat, is a factor in heart disease mortality."

Elevated blood pressure, a condition that is often a silent prelude to heart disease, has also been linked to meat-laden diets. In one study, 210 vegetarians living in the Boston area were found to have blood pressure readings significantly lower than their meat-eating peers. An average blood pressure of 106/60 was found among the 16- to 29-year-old vegetarians and that is much better than a typical "healthy" American male's 120/75. Moreover, those who reported that more than 5 percent of their diet consisted of foods of animal origin had higher blood pressures than those who said their diet contained less animal foods.

INCREASED CANCER RISK

Increased risk of heart disease isn't the only potential problem with a

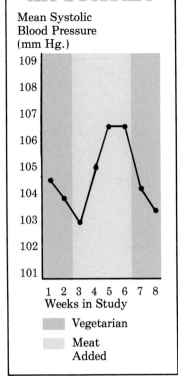

Meat Puts On the Pressure

Mean Systolic Blood Pressure (mm Hg.)

Weeks in Study

- Vegetarian
- Meat Added

What happened when researchers added beef to the diet of vegetarians? Their blood pressures went up (a major risk factor in heart disease and stroke)—but came right back down when they stopped eating beef.

meat-centered diet. Other medical studies suggest that too much red meat, particularly too much beef, can increase your chances of developing cancer of the colon (large intestine) and rectum. And it may be true that our taste for meat has made colorectal cancer the most common form of cancer in the United States and the second leading cause of death from cancer.

Again, some of this evidence comes from epidemiological studies. Americans consume over 40 percent of their total calories as fat, much of it animal fat. And, although colon cancer has reached epidemic proportions here and in many other industrialized Western nations where meat is a substantial part of the national diet, the incidence of colon cancer is far less common in other parts of the world, like Japan and

Africa, where most people eat much less meat than we do. When people move from these "low-risk" countries to "high-risk" countries—like the Japanese immigrants to the United States—and begin to adopt Westernized eating habits, their colon cancer rates rise to the level of those of the host country.

In fact, a National Cancer Institute review of many studies on this subject concluded that all the research, taken together, "points to meat as a food item associated with the development of malignancies of the large bowel, and suggests that fish is not an associated item. Beef or cattle meat is probably the most suspect of the meats."

Yet, despite this long list of minuses, you still may not want to give up meat. So here are nine ways to have your steak and eat it, too.

Hop To Good Nutrition

Along with their celebrated ability to multiply, rabbits have another quality going for them that may someday add to their fame: Their meat is nutritious and delicious to eat. In fact, rabbit meat is higher in protein and lower in saturated fat, cholesterol and calories than either beef, pork, chicken *or* fish. What's more, their tender, all-white meat tastes remarkably like chicken.

In recognition of rabbit's low cholesterol content, the American Heart Association recommends it for heart patients. Because it also goes easy on the calories, rabbit has been endorsed by Weight Watchers. And, due to rabbit's low sodium content, it's a boon to meat eaters on a low-salt diet for high blood pressure.

With all these health benefits, you'd think that rabbit meat would be available on every supermarket meat counter, but it isn't. The fact that Americans ate about 25 million pounds of rabbit in 1980 only means that we consumed less than ½ ounce per person. In Italy, where rabbit has long been popular, the average person consumes over 5 pounds a year.

Another great thing about rabbits is that they produce more meat per pound of feed consumed than any other domestic animal. They produce twice as much meat from the same amount of alfalfa as sheep do, for example—and 4 times as much as cattle.

Tip 1: The most obvious tip, of course, is to eat less. Try one vegetarian meal a day and/or explore recipes that use just a bit of meat for flavoring. We know one that deluges whole wheat noodles with a flood of vegetables that have been stir-fried in chicken broth, with just a hint of salami.

Tip 2: When making meat the main event in a meal, use the leaner cuts like flank or round steak.

Tip 3: Trim all the visible fat from even these skinny examples.

Tip 4: Serve your soups and stews the *second* day. Rather than carry them directly from stove to table, let them sit overnight in the refrigerator, and, next day, peel off the hard layer of fat that forms in the cold. Not only will your meals be less greasy, but they may well taste better, too. The added time in the fridge allows their flavors to mix and mingle to perfection.

Tip 5: Avoid those chemically cured meats that employ the mixed blessings of nitrates and nitrites, preservatives that have been linked to cancer. If you can't give up hot dogs or ham, try to find uncured varieties that are free of these evildoers.

But if you lust for regular bacon or sausage at breakfast, accompany them with a *big* glass of orange juice or a whole orange. The vitamin C in the juice or fruit will help keep the nitrites in the meat from forming the cancer-causing substances.

Tip 6: Balance a meal whose star attraction is a rich cut of meat with carrots and onions, two vegetables with proven cholesterol- and fat-fighting records. In fact, add a salad filled with vitamin C-freighted ingredients and a low-calorie dressing with garlic as well. All that C will help stand off what's wrong with the meat, and recent studies have shown that garlic will enlist in the battle, too.

Oxtail, Barley and Braised Cabbage Stew

Makes 6 servings

2½ pounds oxtails, cut into 1-inch pieces (or use beef shank with bone in)
3 tablespoons whole wheat flour
3 tablespoons oil
2 cloves garlic, minced
4 thin leeks, white and green parts both thinly sliced
2 stalks celery with leaves, thinly sliced
3 or 4 tomatoes, chopped
2 bay leaves
1 cup barley
¾ teaspoon marjoram
2 cups water or beef stock
1½ pounds cabbage, coarsely chopped
8 cups boiling water
3 tablespoons butter or margarine
1 medium onion, coarsely chopped
2 tablespoons minced fresh dill
sour cream or yogurt

Dredge meat in 2 tablespoons flour. Heat oil in skillet and brown meat on all sides. Transfer to 3- to 4-quart stew pot. Add garlic, leeks, celery, tomatoes, bay leaves, barley, marjoram and water or stock. Cover pot and bring to a boil. Then lower heat and simmer for 1 hour. Meanwhile, place cabbage in deep bowl and cover with boiling water. Drain after 5 minutes, reserving liquid.

Heat butter in a heavy saucepan until browned. Add onion and 1 tablespoon flour. Cook, stirring constantly, until browned. Add cabbage and stir. Cover pan and simmer for 15 minutes, or until cabbage turns pinkish. Add a few tablespoons of reserved liquid, if needed, to prevent scorching.

Add cabbage to stew. Cook for 20 minutes or until meat is tender. Remove bay leaves. Sprinkle with dill and serve hot, topping each serving with a dollop of sour cream or yogurt.

A Smart Shopper's Guide to the Lean and Fat Cuts of a Steer

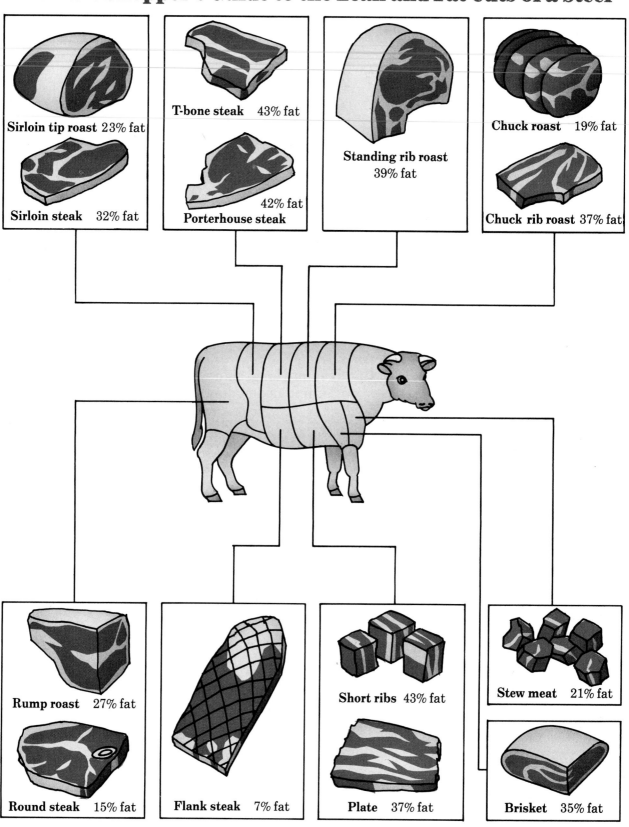

Sirloin tip roast 23% fat

Sirloin steak 32% fat

T-bone steak 43% fat

42% fat
Porterhouse steak

Standing rib roast 39% fat

Chuck roast 19% fat

Chuck rib roast 37% fat

Rump roast 27% fat

Round steak 15% fat

Flank steak 7% fat

Short ribs 43% fat

Plate 37% fat

Stew meat 21% fat

Brisket 35% fat

Tip 7: In fact, while you're at it, add a few new wrinkles to your vitamin and mineral supplementation program, wrinkles directed right at what ails meat. Try zinc and selenium as cancer fighters, and build up your C ration for both cancer and cholesterol blocking.

Tip 8: Specifically to fight cholesterol and to move wastes—which can contain cancer-causing agents—add bran to your daily health routine. Try it mixed with juice or sprinkled on cereal, but do try *two* kinds and alternate them. That is, have wheat bran for intestinal health one day, and then switch to the cholesterol-lowering properties of oat bran the next.

Tip 9: Finally, while we're on the subject of fat and changes in daily patterns, add exercise—fairly vigorous and regular exercise—to yours. A good aerobic workout, one that gets the heart and lungs pumping, has been shown to be a great boost to the body's ability to process and dispose of fat.

WILD FLESH AND STUFFED STEERS

"You talk about *natural* food," my friend exclaimed out of the blue. "Now, what could be more natural than this," he went on, jiggling his knife at the few remaining mouthfuls of his porterhouse steak. "So what's all this I've been reading lately about *meat*? You say, don't eat so much meat, don't eat so much beef. It's going to do this to you, it's going to do that to you. But what could be more natural than a piece of meat? And aren't natural foods good? I mean, take that wine. That's been processed ten times more than this steak. Or that cheese. I mean, cows don't *give* cheese. You have to *make* it. Now *this*," he declared, spearing the last piece of his pink, plump steak, "this is what I call *natural* food!"

Probably many people wonder about that same question. But we aren't the only ones suggesting that a diet in which red meat plays a prominent role is, to put it politely, less than optimally healthful. Lately, the scientific literature has been full

Liver with Mixed Vegetables

Makes 2 servings

¾ pound calves' liver	2 scallions
3 tablespoons whole wheat flour	1 small zucchini
2 teaspoons dried basil	10 cherry tomatoes
1 tablespoon corn oil	2 teaspoons tamari soy sauce

Cut liver into long, thin strips. Combine flour and basil on waxed paper, and dredge the liver slices in the mixture.

Heat oil in a medium skillet or wok, and cook or stir-fry the liver over low to moderate heat. The inside of each strip should remain pink. Do not overcook.

Now chop the scallions. Cut the zucchini in half crosswise, then lengthwise. Cut each section into long, thin strips. Halve the cherry tomatoes.

When liver is cooked, remove to a serving plate and keep warm. Add the scallions to the pan or wok, add a few spoonfuls of water to prevent sticking, and stir. When the scallions wilt, add the zucchini.

When scallions and zucchini are softened, add cherry tomatoes and tamari, and stir to combine. Place a lid on the skillet or wok and allow vegetables to steam until tender, about 10 minutes, stirring occasionally.

To serve, arrange vegetables around the liver. Serve hot.

of evidence, direct and indirect, that a meat-centered diet may well tend to invite a number a fairly common modern diseases, including heart disease, cancer, osteoporosis, kidney stones and possibly others. But—as our friend asked—what could possibly be wrong with a food that's so natural and so minimally processed? Has nature somehow gone wrong? Were we not meant to eat flesh?

Those are perfectly legitimate questions, and even some scientists have asked them—often with an edge of protest.

The answer to this confusion is that beef may not, in a manner of speaking, be natural at all.

And what manner of speaking might that be? Well, here is the gist of the answer given by scientist Michael Crawford of the Zoological Society of London in the pages of the *British Medical Journal.*

Crawford acknowledges that the hunter/gatherers and nomadic tribes of yesteryear raised and ate meat on the hoof, and this might be taken to suggest that meat, and meat eating, are natural in the historical sense. But, Crawford says, the meat we eat today bears little resemblance to the meat eaten by generations past, because of radical changes in farming practices.

Body tissues, Crawford explains, contain two distinct types of lipid (fatty) substances. One kind is structural lipids that form cell membranes, and are rich in polyunsaturated fatty acids (PUFA) that are necessary for health and even survival. The other type is storage fats that are a potential energy source. Storage fat is largely saturated and is not necessary to survival, as it can be produced by the body from other fats.

In free-living animals that forage over pastureland, and in the herds of nomads who may travel many miles, Crawford points out, considerable muscle tissue develops, which is a rich source of structural, or polyunsaturated fats. Only small amounts of saturated, "carcass storage fats," are accumulated. And such meat, he says, "is what Moses ate, what the hunters and gatherers ate and still eat." In contrast, "modern intensive farming methods in which the animals are fed on high-energy foods and deprived of exercise produce pathological tissues loaded with saturated fat and deficient in the muscle cells that carry PUFA in their membranes. The ratio of nonessential fatty acids to PUFA in free-

living animals is about 2:1 and in the modern domestic animal about 50:1."

Just what are these intensive farming methods that produce "pathological tissues loaded with saturated fat"? For the first part of its life, nine months to a year, a steer spends most of its time on the range or in a pasture, eating grass; nothing particularly unnatural about that. But things change fast when the steer is sent to a feedlot for fattening. For about four months, the animal has nothing to do all day but consume huge amounts of corn, sorghum, wheat, barley or other grains, supplemented with an average of 270 pounds of protein concentrates. The protein may or may not come from natural food sources: Chemical urea may supply significant amounts of nitrogen to the animal, from which it manufactures protein. During this time, a minimum of roughage is fed to the steer, and since it is living in a feedlot devoid of all vegetation, the little roughage it does get may come from supplements of ground-up corncobs, sand, or even rough plastic pellets. The general idea is to get the animal as big and beefy as possible in the least amount of time. And not just with lean meat, but with plenty of marbling, or fat, which adds tenderness and flavor to the meat.

Recently, there has been a tendency to cut back a little on this fattening process, to save money and to turn out a somewhat leaner animal. But the net result is still meat that's far fattier than that from animals foraging for their food in the wild state.

That porterhouse steak our friend was eating, for instance, is 36 percent fat. Detailed information about the fat content of undomesticated grazing animals is not plentiful, but data supplied to us by government nutrition experts indicates that the meat of such animals as deer, moose, caribou and reindeer has an average fat content averaging from 2 to 4 percent—an incredible 90 percent less than the porterhouse steak.

As for those saturated fats—the kind believed to be particularly harmful to human arteries—wild animals generally weigh in at less than 1 percent saturated fat. Choice

porterhouse checks out at a booming 17 percent, chuck comes in at a more modest 9 percent, while regular hamburger is 10 percent saturated fat. Even lean hamburger has more than five times as much saturated fat as the meat of wild ruminants.

Besides the composition of the meat from modern steers, there's also the question of how much it is eaten. No one can say for sure how much meat our early ancestors who hunted consumed, but most scholars in the field think that the basis of most primitive diets was not meat. Meat may have been eaten on occasion, but wild and cultivated grains, roots, seeds, vegetables and fruits were the staples. Certainly, people today in Third World countries that raise

livestock get most of their nourishment not from meat, but from rice, millet, corn, potatoes and other vegetable products. Meat is usually reserved for special occasions, or is eaten in small portions along with lots of rice or wheat. So when we in North America or Europe eat meat or meat products two or three times a day, we are not only eating meat which is unnaturally fat, but eating what may be said to be an unnatural amount as well.

That's why we suggest that red meat not be a dietary staple, but perhaps an occasional dish. When you do eat it, choose a lean cut and eat relatively small portions, rounding out your meal with plenty of grains and vegetables.

Meat is natural—so why isn't it healthy? Well, the feedlot-grown, fatty beef that modern man eats every day is a far cry from the lean, wild meat that our prehistoric ancestors ate—if and when they could catch it. The antelope in this cave painting, for instance, were certainly not a risk factor for heart disease.

113

Poultry

In 1932, when the Republican party vowed to put "a chicken in every pot," it was a promise that seemed about as keepable as "a Cadillac in every garage!" Times were tough then, money was scarce, and chickens—at least partly because they were disease prone and tough to raise—were expensive.

Today, of course, that old campaign slogan seems absurdly modest. Chicken is the most inexpensive meat, and we Americans consume it at an annual rate of about 50 pounds apiece. Over four *billion* chickens are produced in the United States each year, and the "poultry industry," what economists call the raising of chickens, turkeys, geese and ducks, is the fourth largest agricultural enterprise in the nation.

You probably have your own favorite chicken dish—and so, it seems, does everybody else. Practically every country has its own version of a "national" chicken recipe, from Italy's chicken cacciatore and France's *coq au vin* to Japan's chicken teriyaki and a covered dish dinner's chicken a la king.

But how does poultry stack up when it comes to your health? Again, very well. All meat is loaded with protein (since that's mainly what meat *is*), but, as we've seen, red meat delivers a tremendous load of fat with its protein. A 3-ounce serving of hamburger, pork or chicken, to take just three examples, will deliver between 22 and 25 grams of protein. The pork comes packed with up to 331 calories, and hamburger has about 186. But the chicken—when the fattier parts of the birds are avoided—delivers around 163 calories.

And *that* is just the beginning of the advantage story. An added bonus is that most of the fat in beef or pork is spread throughout the muscle mass, where it's hard to avoid, while in poultry much of the fat is concentrated in or just beneath the skin. That means that simply by avoiding the skin, we can halve the amount of fat. A 3-ounce serving (equivalent to half a breast) of white chicken meat, including the skin, is about 10.8 percent fat; skinless, there's only about 4.5 percent fat in the same piece. On top of all that, the fats in chicken are not as harmful as those in red meat because they're higher in polyunsaturates.

If you take a look at the poultry target shown here, you'll notice that the *parts* of the birds don't run neck and neck. A chicken breast, for example, is much higher in fat than a turkey breast. A chicken leg, however, is about 25 percent lower in fat than the same part of a turkey. But, as with all the targets, both the first and second rings are good choices. The meats in the first ring, though, are jampacked with iron, zinc, niacin and B6, the nutrients we picked to rate poultry. On the average, the second ring offers slightly lower levels of those goodies.

You'll also notice we've exiled processed poultry meats like turkey loaf and chicken franks to the outer ring of the target. That's because they contain additives like phosphates and nitrites, which scientists believe may be transformed into cancer-causing nitrosamines in your stomach. Turkey and chicken franks *are* considerably less fatty than hot dogs made from beef or pork, however.

The wild game birds are all in the second ring—mainly because you don't eat this kind of food too often unless a butler serves it. But pheasant and quail are *very* lean. Duck and goose, on the other hand, are somewhat fatty.

But talking about poultry and health doesn't mean just considering whether it has less fat and more of

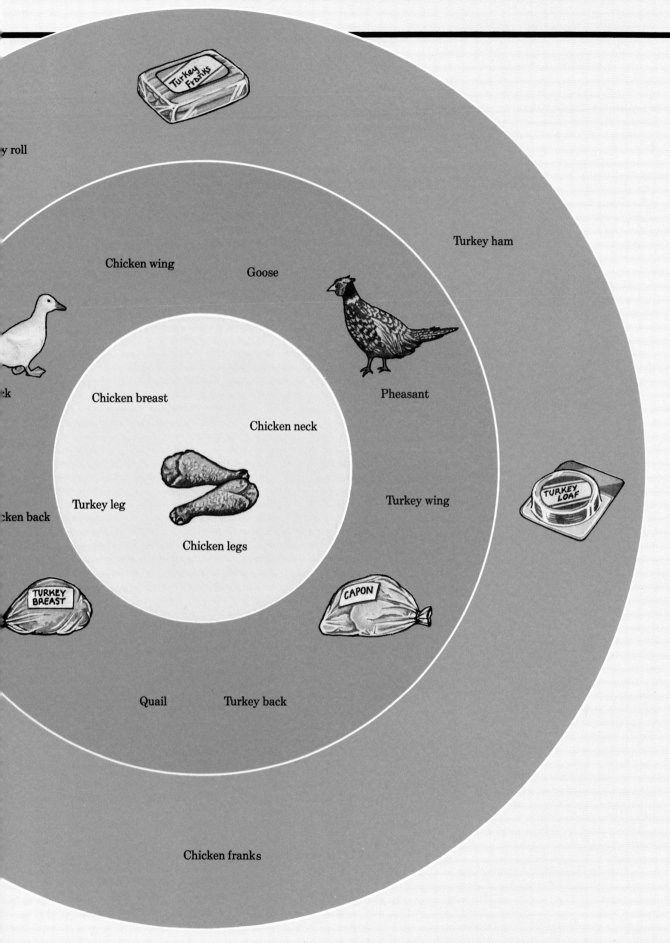

Turkey Franks

y roll

Turkey ham

Chicken wing

Goose

Pheasant

k

Chicken breast

Chicken neck

TURKEY
LOAF

cken back

Turkey leg

Turkey wing

Chicken legs

TURKEY
BREAST

CAPON

Quail

Turkey back

Chicken franks

Spicy Chicken Soup

Makes 6 servings

2½ to 3 pounds chicken
12 cups chicken stock
2 pounds veal bones,
    cut into small
    pieces
2 stalks celery, with
    leaves
6 to 8 thin leeks, split
    and washed
    well under cold
    running water

2 small carrots
1 bunch parsley
3 whole cloves
2 bay leaves
½ cup barley
1 teaspoon curry powder
1 teaspoon ground
    allspice

Place chicken, stock and veal bones in a heavy 8-quart pot. Bring to a boil, then lower heat and skim the accumulated foam. Simmer for 5 minutes. Tie celery, carrots, 1 of the leeks and the bunch of parsley together with string and add to pot along with the cloves and bay leaves. Cover and simmer for 45 minutes.

Remove chicken. Cook stock for 30 minutes more, then remove and discard the vegetable bouquet, veal bones, cloves and bay leaves. Bring soup to a boil, slowly add barley and then lower heat. Cut the tough green parts off the remaining leeks, leaving 1 inch of green. Cut leeks into 1-inch lengths and add to the pot with curry powder and allspice. Simmer, covered, for 40 to 45 minutes, or until barley is tender.

Meanwhile, remove skin and bones from the cooled chicken and tear the meat into chunks. Add to the soup and heat together for 5 minutes.

certain vitamins and minerals. It means chicken soup, that proverbial nostrum for colds and flu. But does chicken soup *really* battle the common cold?

We were pleased to learn that at least one medical researcher wondered, too, and had done a little investigating on the subject. That researcher, Marvin A. Sackner, M.D., of the division of pulmonary disease at the Mount Sinai Medical Center in Miami Beach, Florida, reasoned that since the nose is our first line of defense against upper respiratory infections, perhaps hot soups (and maybe all hot liquids) might help the nose do its job: to stop germ-carrying particles before they cause damage by trapping them in a flow of nasal mucus bound for the stomach. Anything that triggers and increases that flow, Dr. Sackner proposed, would help the body rid itself of cold-causing agents.

To test this hypothesis, he asked 15 healthy young people to drink (and then to sip through straws) three liquids: hot chicken soup, hot water and, finally, cold water. After each trial sipping, Dr. Sackner and his nasal sleuths measured the speed of the mucus flow. The liquid and method of ingestion that moved the fluid most efficiently would obviously be the most effective in freeing the nose of germs.

When the results were tabulated, these answers emerged: *drinking* chicken soup produced the largest increase in mucus flow; drinking hot water came in second; and sipping soup through a straw was a respectable third. Because cold water taken by *any* method slowed the flow significantly, some skeptics on the research team suggested that it was simply the steam from the hot liquid (and the resulting rise in nasal temperature) that generated the speed-up. But Dr. Sackner countered their charges by pointing out the success of the soup-through-a-straw method. Because *it* worked well, too, he "speculated that the rise in nasal mucus velocity . . . could be related to an aromatic compound . . . or a mechanism related to taste." In other words, hot chicken soup—spicy and delicious—is good for a stuffy nose.

THE INDUSTRIAL CHICKEN

After reading the health information in this section, many people may decide to stock up on chicken. Which is a fine idea with one potential problem. *Lots* of people have made that decision over the years. As a result, chicken has gone from a backyard by-product to an industrial commodity. To keep up with the increasing demand, chicken farmers have turned their coops into factories, their pecking orders into assembly lines. These days, the modern poultry industry can transform an egg into a market-weight broiler in about 60 days, and it does so literally billions of times each year.

To meet our demand for chickens, poultry magnates have done three things: They've begun to feed their birds "enriched" (and hormone-packed) feeds to speed their growth; they've confined their chickens to prevent weight loss; and they've pumped the animals full of antibiotics to defeat the disease that comes with the close quarters.

What does this do to your health? No one really knows. But if you want to be cautious and avoid these chemicals, there's still an easy way to keep chicken on your table: find barnyard or so-called free-range chickens that have been raised without the industrial improvements.

For advice on buying down-home birds, we talked to Bob Hofstetter, an agronomist and poul-tryman at the Rodale Research Center in Maxatawny, Pennsylvania. He claimed that it was tough to find old-fashioned birds these days, but that it was worth the effort. Their meat is firmer, tastier and more natural—even though it may cost considerably more because barnyard birds grow more slowly and thus require more feed.

A chicken grown locally and allowed to range freely is more apt to be one of the tall, rangy birds of the Plymouth Rock family, he told us. That's because these are "dual purpose" breeds—good for both meat and eggs—and thus more practical for a small farmer to keep. To find these good values, look for chickens that are taller, heavier (up to 8 pounds) and leaner than the birds that are raised strictly for meat, which tend to be squat and compact, and look like little turkeys.

You can also get to know your butcher and ask him to order you such birds. Or, perhaps best, you can seek out a small chicken farmer and buy directly from him.

The Great Chicken Face-Off: Which Meat to Eat, White or Dark?

It's a question asked in millions of homes every year: "White meat or dark?" Most people decide with their taste buds. But if you're trying to lose weight or eat less fat, white is "lite."

For instance, a 3-ounce serving of skinless, white turkey meat checks in at around 3 percent fat. In the other corner, skinless dark turkey meat contains 7.2 percent—or more than twice the amount for white. And the same is true with chicken. Skinless white meat—4.5 percent fat; skinless dark—9.7 percent.

When it comes to vitamins and minerals the tables are turned. Dark chicken meat, for example, has about twice as much zinc, folate and vitamin A as white. So if you're on a low-fat diet, choose white. If you want more nutrition, choose dark. And if you're opting for taste—well, the choice is all up to you.

Fish

From haddock to halibut, this animal's variety runs as deep as the waters it swims. And no matter how you catch it—whether with hook, line and sinker or a trip to the market—the net effect of fish is great nutrition.

Almost all fish delivers high-quality, easily digestible protein along with a minimum of saturated fat, cholesterol and calories. For good measure, the sea god, Neptune, has thrown in generous amounts of many vitamins and some hard-to-get trace minerals like iodine, zinc and selenium. But what may prove the most important bonus in fish is its oil. Fish fats and oils have recently been shown to contain an ingredient that may have the power to control heart disease—but more about that later.

When it comes to fat, the great thing about fish is that most of it comes to us in polyunsaturated form rather than the saturated fats associated with red meats—and with a higher risk of heart disease. Also, fish are *low* in fat—most contain less than 5 percent, while most meats have higher levels; a prime porterhouse steak, for instance, is 36 percent fat.

There's a tremendous range in fat content among the various species of fish and shellfish, however. As we said, most members of the underwater tribe contain less than 5 percent fat. This group includes tuna, halibut, cod, flounder, haddock, pollock, mullet, ocean perch, carp, whiting, crabs, scallops, shrimp and lobster. In fact, some of these fish contain almost no fat at all. (And that's why many of them made it into the center ring.)

A second, smaller group offers 5 to 15 percent fat. Anchovies, herring, mackerel, salmon and sardines belong to this group. Only a few fish species deliver more than 15 percent fat. These are certain kinds of lake trout and (during particular seasons) herring, mackerel and sardines.

But low fat content isn't the only criterion a food must meet to be considered healthful. Cholesterol—a component of fat—is another factor that's become a concern to many people, particularly those prone to (or recovering from) heart disease. And people on low-cholesterol diets have traditionally been told to avoid shellfish.

But that may have been bad—or at least unnecessary—advice. New laboratory methods of measuring cholesterol in foods have produced some surprises, particularly in studies of oysters, clams and scallops. The old method, it now appears, measured *all* members of the biochemical family called sterols, of which cholesterol is just one. With a new, more precise method, scientists have found that only 30 percent of the sterols in scallops, for example, are actually cholesterol and that in clams and oysters, they represent only 40 percent. So the actual cholesterol content of these mollusks is less than half the amount it was once believed to be. Shrimp is the *only* shellfish that contains too much cholesterol to be considered for a cholesterol-lowering diet.

Finally, fish contains substantial amounts of many vitamins and minerals. Growing up earlier in this century, many a youngster knew this all too well: Cod-liver oil, a rich source of vitamins A and D, was dutifully administered to them by determined mothers as a daily tonic. Though commercially produced vitamins have largely replaced that vile-tasting preventive, A and D can still be found in the meat of most of the fattier fish. Fish and shellfish are also good sources of the B vitamins niacin, biotin, B_6 and B_{12}.

The dietary minerals potassium

Anchovies

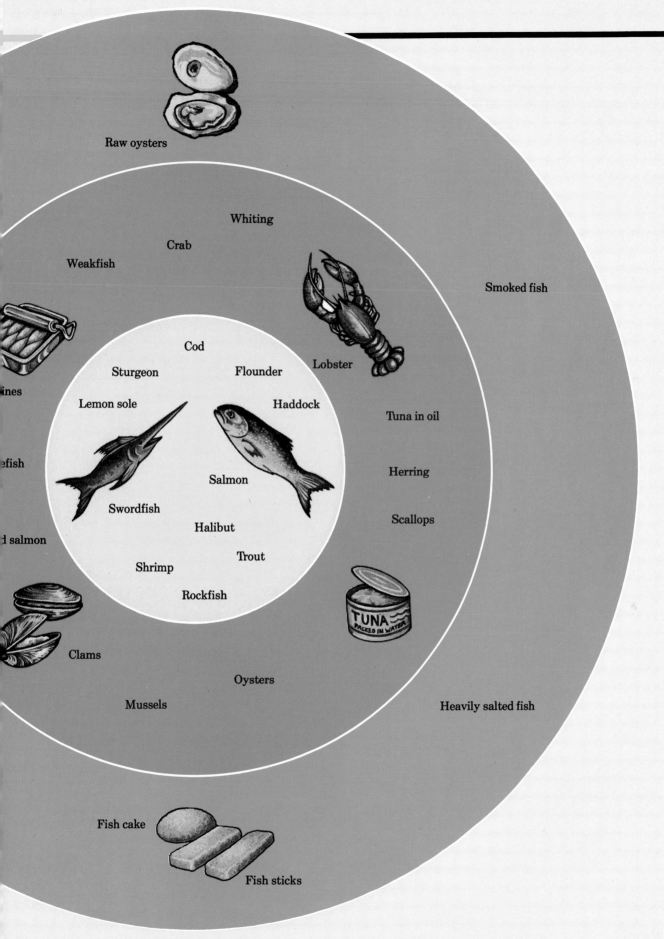

Raw oysters

Whiting

Crab

Weakfish

Smoked fish

Cod

Sturgeon

Flounder

Lobster

...ines

Lemon sole

Haddock

Tuna in oil

...efish

Salmon

Herring

Swordfish

Scallops

...d salmon

Halibut

Trout

Shrimp

Rockfish

TUNA
PACKED IN WATER

Clams

Oysters

Mussels

Heavily salted fish

Fish cake

Fish sticks

and iron, which the body needs in fairly large amounts, are also generously supplied by seafood. Marine foods are the best source of iodine in most of our diets. They're also an excellent source of the trace minerals zinc and selenium.

A closer look at salmon—one of the fish in our bull's-eye—will give a good idea of what fish can do for your health. A 3-ounce serving of canned pink salmon, including the bones, delivers better than 17 grams of protein. The Recommended Dietary Allowance for an adult man is only 56 grams, so salmon is a very high-powered protein source. There are only 5.1 grams of fat in this serving—compared with nearly 35 grams in a cooked rib steak of the same weight. It also offers goodly amounts of calcium (168 milligrams) and potassium (309 milligrams), plus 60 I.U. of vitamin A and traces of the B vitamins thiamine, riboflavin and niacin. All very impressive numbers. But there's something *else* in salmon (and many other fish) that's an exciting and unexpected bonus.

THE HEART LOVES FISH OIL

The first clue that there might be something very special about fish turned up wrapped in a puzzle. Scientists studying the health of various people in the world noticed that two isolated population groups— certain Eskimos and the Japanese living in coastal fishing villages— were remarkably free of the heart disease that was nearly epidemic in more developed areas. Further study revealed that both protected groups ate tremendous amounts of fatty fish, fish oils and other marine life that fed on fish. The confusing thing was that these findings appeared to contradict decades of research: Diets high in fat, particularly animal fat, have long been suspected as a *cause* of heart disease!

Digging deeper, researchers found that these fish-loving people had high blood levels of a certain group of fatty acids called eicosapentaenoic acid (EPA) and docosahexaenoic acid (DHA). And where do EPA and DHA come from? From fish, fish oil and the fat of marine animals that feed on fish. It seemed fairly obvious that these substances were the key to the fish lovers' healthy hearts.

Recent work in the United States and abroad tends to confirm the early conclusions. At the Oregon Health Sciences University in Portland, researchers asked people to eat lots of fish oil and salmon meat, which are rich in both EPA and

Young Calamari Salad

Makes 12 servings

4 pounds cleaned, young calamari (squid), sliced
½ cup olive oil
    juice of 3 lemons
10 slivers pimiento
10 black olives, pitted
1 cup croutons
2 teaspoons chopped parsley
1 teaspoon finely chopped garlic

Place calamari in a large pot, cover with water, add 1 tablespoon olive oil and cook for 10 minutes. When done, mix together with remaining olive oil, lemon juice and other ingredients.

Arrange the calamari on serving dish and let cool for at least 1 hour. Refrigerate and serve chilled.

DHA. After 28 days on the salmon diet, cholesterol levels in healthy volunteers dropped 17 percent and triglycerides 40 percent. Among subjects whose blood fats were already high, even more dramatic changes occurred: Their cholesterol levels dropped 20 percent or more, and their triglycerides went down by as much as 67 percent.

"Subjects with elevated cholesterol and triglycerides seemed to show the most marked response to fish oil," wrote William S. Harris, Ph.D., one of the Oregon researchers, in the *Journal of the American Medical Association*. "As a rule, the higher these levels at the outset, the further they dropped when the fish oil program was started."

These high cholesterol and triglyceride levels, of course, are considered warning signs of heart trouble. But there's another measurement scientists use to assess cardiovascular health: a patient's clotting time, the time it takes a cut to stop bleeding. This is important because tiny blood cells, called platelets, which help the blood to clot, may also clump up along blood vessel walls and form clots that can lead to heart attack or stroke. Apparently, because their platelets are less "sticky," and less apt to clump, fish-eating Eskimos and Japanese have long clotting times. So do experiment subjects who add fish oil to their diets.

In one British study, 76 subjects were given either 1.8 or 3.6 grams of EPA daily. Although the volunteers taking 1.8 grams showed no change in clotting time, those taking 3.6 grams "showed a highly significant increase in [clotting] time," the researchers observed. And their triglycerides dropped as well.

"These changes," the scientists noted, "are consistent with a reduction in the incidence of thrombosis [clotting] and a slowing down of the atherosclerotic [heart disease] process. An increased dietary intake of marine oils, particularly those rich in EPA, may reduce the risk of coronary artery disease."

Which fish are richest in EPA? Almost all fish contain some EPA, Dr. Harris says, but among the richest sources are salmon, trout, haddock, mackerel and sardines.

THE SHELL GAME

The term "shellfish" actually refers to two quite different kind of animals: bivalve mollusks (like oysters, mussels, clams, scallops) and crustaceans (like shrimp, crab, lobster). The bivalves are called filter feeders because they "eat" by pumping water through their bodies, a feat that oysters manage at the rate of 20 quarts per hour. But these bottom-dwelling creatures, which thrive in shallow coastal waters, also imbibe toxic chemicals, heavy metals, sewage and some poisonous organisms along with their meals. These nasty substances become concentrated in the mollusks' bodies and, as a result, the FDA still considers oysters, clams, mussels and scallops high-risk foods. The crustaceans, on the other hand, since they are not filter feeders and live in deeper, cleaner water, do not become as frequently contaminated.

Outbreaks of hepatitis, paralytic shellfish poisoning (PSP) and other diseases have been traced to contaminated mollusks and crustaceans. In 1981, for example, seven outbreaks were reported to the Center for Disease Control in Atlanta.

The government, fortunately, is looking after us to the extent it can; it's illegal to harvest shellfish from waters that have been designated as polluted. The interstate shipment and retail marketing of mollusks is also monitored under the National Shellfish Sanitation Program, administered by the FDA.

Still, this safety net is not without its holes, and contaminated shellfish do get through and into our kitchens. We can protect ourselves against this possibility by taking the simple precautions of buying from reputable dealers and avoiding containers unmarked with state identification numbers. Clams and oysters in their shells should be tightly closed. If their shells are open and do not close when you tap them, the animals are dead and should not be eaten. Shellfish also should be bought in small numbers, kept only a few days, and thoroughly cooked before serving.

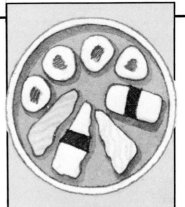

Sushi: A Raw Deal

The preparation of raw fish in ways that please the eye as well as the palate is a venerable tradition in Japan. Fresh, raw fish served with vinegared rice, and sometimes seaweed, is called *sushi; sashimi* is the fish that goes into *sushi,* a special raw material that is ritually selected and cut according to density and texture.

Unfortunately, these rituals aren't enough, and thousands of cases of food poisoning from raw fish occur every year in Japan. Cooking usually protects us against this unpleasant side effect of fish, and so—unless you're absolutely certain the raw fish in *sushi* is clean, fresh and germ free—say *sayonara* to this Japanese eccentricity.

Vegetables

It was on every channel's nightly news. To economize, the government had proposed changing the rules of the national school lunch program, allowing a hamburger's condiments—ketchup or a pickle—to be the meal's vegetable.

The other political party quickly called a press conference and showed the TV cameras a plate with a red dab instead of spinach or potatoes or tossed salad. The proposal was quickly dropped.

It's not surprising that people feel strongly about vegetables. They seem so powerfully alive with nourishment, so basic to health. The word "vegetable," in fact, derives from a Latin word meaning "to enliven, or animate." The description fits: Eat more vegetables and you'll probably feel livelier. And live longer, too.

Vegetables are health champs. That's why the vegetable target is a little different from the meat, poultry and fish targets. *All* the foods on the target are A-O.K. It's just that the inmost ring is A+, the middle ring A and the outer ring A−. In short, there's no such thing as a vegetable that's bad for you. Those in the bull's-eye, however, are especially rich in the health factors that make vegetables winners—the infection fighters, vitamins A and C; the energy minerals, potassium and iron; the bone and muscle mineral, calcium; and the all-around body cleanser, fiber. Let's look more closely at how vegetables can keep you healthy— free of lung cancer, for instance.

Since 1957, a team of researchers had been keeping tabs on the eating habits of almost 2,000 middle-aged men employed at a Western Electric plant in suburban Chicago. At the end of the 19-year observation period, each of the surviving men was examined by a doctor, and the medical and hospital records of those who had died were studied with care.

After tabulating all this information, the researchers announced their conclusions: The men who remained free of lung cancer during the 19 years had been eating a significantly greater amount of one dietary substance than those who had succumbed to the disease. That sub-

stance was beta-carotene, which the body transforms into vitamin A. How were they getting this wonderful stuff? "The principal sources of carotene are dark green, leafy vegetables, carrots, and certain yellow and red fruits and vegetables," the scientists wrote in the *Lancet*, a leading medical journal. "These results support the hypothesis that dietary carotene decreases the risk of lung cancer."

Actually, this finding didn't come as a complete surprise. Earlier studies in Norway, Japan, Britain, Singapore and the United States had all shown a strong association between diets rich in vitamin A and a reduced risk of lung cancer. But the Western Electric study was an advance because it pinpointed the precise *form* of vitamin A that was working these protective wonders. (Ready-made vitamin A, or retinol, can be found in animal foods like milk, cheese, butter, egg yolks and liver. But carotene—the anticancer factor—occurs in great abundance only in vegetables.)

The threat of prostate cancer may also be lessened by the powers latent in many vegetables. A 10-year study of 122,261 Japanese men, age 40 and over, revealed a substantially lower death rate from prostate cancer among men who ate green and yellow vegetables each day.

This study also showed that American men consume fewer vegetables than Japanese men, and their incidence of prostate cancer is higher.

Eggplant

Turnip

Asparagus

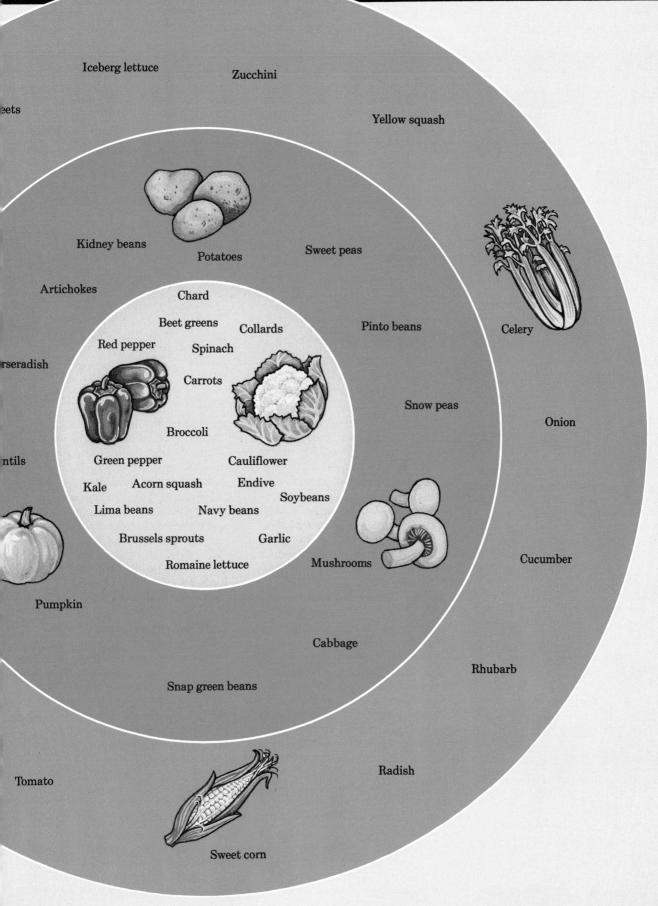

Iceberg lettuce

Zucchini

eets

Yellow squash

Kidney beans

Potatoes

Sweet peas

Artichokes

Celery

Chard

Beet greens

Collards

Pinto beans

Red pepper

Spinach

rseradish

Carrots

Broccoli

Snow peas

Onion

ntils

Green pepper

Cauliflower

Kale

Acorn squash

Endive

Soybeans

Lima beans

Navy beans

Mushrooms

Cucumber

Brussels sprouts

Garlic

Romaine lettuce

Pumpkin

Cabbage

Rhubarb

Snap green beans

Tomato

Radish

Sweet corn

Leafy Vegetables

There's more to greens than the anemic iceberg lettuce that's the mainstay of most salad bars. Pictured here are leafy vegetables that, nutritionally, would make iceberg green with envy. In the top row, from left to right, are spinach, brussels sprouts, leaf lettuce and kale; in the bottom row are cabbage, endive, chard and collards.

We've talked about the health-building power of vegetables in general; now let's look at them one by one. To do this in a practical way, we've broken down the whole vegetable kingdom into five smaller realms, fiefdoms named for the part of the plant that's most commonly eaten. What follows, then, are good words on the nutritional and healing properties of those vegetables we eat as leaves, roots and bulbs, stems and flowers, pods and fruits.

Our categories are more practical than scientific. Brussels sprouts, for example, are a stumper: They're called *sprouts,* yet look like tiny cabbage heads whose *leaves* we eat. Fortunately, things like brussels sprouts are in the minority. Most people know that potatoes and carrots are roots, that spinach and lettuce are leaves, and that peas and beans are pods. So, we decided to deal with exceptions as they came up and talk about vegetables in ways that people in supermarkets do.

First, the leafy vegetables: Swiss chard, spinach, cabbage, kale, brussels sprouts, collards, endive and the various kinds of lettuce. They're *all* nutritional gold mines (especially if they're fresh and properly prepared), but significant differences do exist among them.

All dark green, leafy vegetables contain quite a bit of calcium, for example. But they also contain varying amounts of oxalic acid, a substance that clings to calcium in the stomach to form an indigestible compound, calcium oxalate. In effect, this reaction makes the calcium useless to the body. Some greens have far more oxalic acid than others, and so some are good sources of calcium and others are not. Beet greens, spinach and chard have as much as eight times more oxalic acid than calcium, and so they're considered poor calcium sources. Other greens—especially kale, collards, mustard and turnip greens and broccoli—contain up to 42 times as much calcium as oxalic acid—making them superb sources of calcium.

In general, leafy greens are good sources of vitamins A and C, fair sources of the B vitamins, and contributors of minerals like potassium, magnesium and iron. One of those greens—kale—is a perfect example. A half cup of cooked kale packs 4,565 I.U. of vitamin A, a figure that almost matches the RDA. That amount of kale also delivers 51 milligrams of vitamin C—again, almost equal to the RDA.

In that same ½ cup there's 121 milligrams of potassium and

103 milligrams of calcium. And on top of all that, this amount of kale checks in at only 22 calories and has less than 1 percent fat.

Leafy greens also contain something else important to health: chlorophyll.

GREEN MEDICINE

Chlorophyll is the green substance that helps plants perform a most useful little miracle: changing sunlight into food. Earlier in this century, scientists discovered that there's a remarkable similarity between chlorophyll, the pigment in plants, and hemoglobin, the pigment in human blood. Both consist of a ring of molecules around a central dot of an essential mineral. In the case of hemoglobin, it's iron; with chlorophyll, it's magnesium. To say that chlorophyll is the "green blood" of plants isn't really stretching the point.

Excited by this startling parallel, researchers began exploring the medical possibilities of this "green blood" during the 1920s. After two decades of work, they concluded that a purified, water-soluble derivative of chlorophyll, called chlorophyllin, could be used to help heal skin ulcers, infected wounds and rashes. Though medical interest in this natural healer waned when antibiotics came into widespread use during the 1940s and 1950s, other researchers have more recently "rediscovered" the various green wonders of chlorophyll. In unrelated studies, it's been shown to help prevent tooth decay, to decrease inflammation of the pancreas and to possess certain cancer-fighting properties.

Chiu-Nan Lai, Ph.D., a researcher with the M.D. Anderson Hospital Tumor Clinic in Houston, has observed that spinach and leafy lettuce are rich in chlorophyll. "My laboratory research," she says, "has demonstrated that extracts of chlorophyll from those vegetables definitely lower the mutagenic activity [the tendency to cause harmful cellular changes] of known cancer-causing agents."

Ever Greens

You can keep fresh greens on the table all through the winter by growing your own in a small solar greenhouse called a "growing frame."

Basically a well-insulated, draft-free, south-facing lean-to, a growing frame collects solar heat through its "French doors" during the day, stores it in rock, masonry or earth, and releases that bottled-up heat back to the plants overnight. In effect, plants think it's May no matter what the outside temperature.

A growing frame can supply enough greens to make 200 salads between January and April—a wintertime miracle in anyone's book.

For more specific—and practically foolproof—plans for making a growing frame, we recommend *Solar Growing Frame* by Ray Wolf (Rodale Press, 1980).

Roots and Bulbs

From left to right, the roots and bulbs shown above are beets, rutabagas, parsnips, carrots and turnips. If you're wondering how to use rutabagas — which are high in potassium — simply think of them as turnips. Like turnips, they're best steamed, mashed or added to soups or stews.

The Dani people of New Guinea are probably the world's greatest lovers of the sweet potato. Something like 90 percent of the Dani's diet is composed of these nutritious roots, and the rest is a smattering of greens, fruits and an occasional wild pig. Sound a little dull? Not according to the Dani; they cultivate some *70 different varieties* of sweet potatoes and claim that each has its own distinctive appearance and flavor.

Though their menu isn't exactly a smorgasbord, the mere fact that it sustains life and health says a lot about the nutritional virtues of the root vegetables in general and potatoes in particular. Take the common Idaho or "white" potato. It's a good source of fiber, vitamin C, several of the B vitamins and essential minerals like potassium and magnesium. But it also contains calories, right? That potatoes are fattening, says one researcher, is no more than a "well-established fallacy." A baked potato delivers all its nutrition at a cost of only about 145 calories. When it comes to potatoes, what gets them into trouble is what we pile on top.

Garlic and onions, two vegetables in this category, contain substances that may offer protection against that demon of modern, fast-paced life, the heart attack.

In one study, researchers compared the blood levels of cholesterol and triglycerides in three groups of people: one that ate garlic and onions in liberal amounts, one that ate small amounts and one that didn't eat any. The group that ate the most garlic and onions had the lowest levels of blood fats; they were 23 percent lower in cholesterol and 52 percent lower in triglycerides than the folks who ate none — and high blood fats are often warning signs of heart trouble.

To understand the rest of this pungent story, we need to say more about heart attack. One cause of a heart attack is when blood flow to the heart is cut off by a dam of tiny blood clots (thrombi). The central disaster in the process of thrombi formation is a microscopic dance of cells called "platelet aggregation," so reducing platelet aggregation may well reduce the risk of a heart attack. The latest news about garlic and onions, reported in the journal *Atherosclerosis,* is that a substance common to both of them has the ability to do just that.

Researchers hot on the trail of this story took blood samples from six healthy people and added chemicals to speed platelet aggregation — that is, speed blood clotting. Then they added garlic to this experimental brew — and the platelet aggregation dropped dramatically, in one case by 98 percent. The volunteers then added garlic to their diets for five days, after which blood samples were taken a second time. Compared to the pregarlic samples, the platelet aggregation in the second tests had decreased substantially.

Clots are held together by a sort of "paste" called fibrin. Blood that has a tendency to dissolve these fibrin-bound clots is said to have "fibrinolytic activity" (FA). Both garlic and onions, it seems, increase the protective FA of blood. One research team gave garlic oil to three groups: healthy people, people who had just had a heart attack, and people who'd had a heart attack at least one year earlier. Then they measured the FA of everyone's blood. Garlic oil increased the fibrinolytic activity of the healthy subjects' blood by 130 percent; those with recent heart attacks had an increase of 96 percent; and those with less recent heart attacks saw an 84 percent rise. "Garlic," the researchers observed, "may prove to be an important dietary measure" for persons likely to have a heart attack.

Some of the other root vegetables have highly nutritious parts that most people neglect—their greens. Turnip greens, for example, are among the richest of all vegetables in vitamins A, C and E and riboflavin, plus some minerals. Beet greens, too, are rich in vitamins A and C.

Sprouting: Now You Can Tend Your Garden in a Jar

Whatever vegetables can do, sprouts can do better! Most sprouts have 12 percent more protein than their resident seeds. What's more, the B vitamins jump threefold to tenfold, as vitamins A, E and K also increase. And, perhaps best of all, the sprouting process actually creates vitamin C where there was none in the dry seeds.

The best seeds for sprouting are those of the legume family (like beans, peas or alfalfa) or the grasses (wheat, rye, oats and barley). All you'll need to sprout is a glass quart jar and a piece of cheesecloth to cover its top. (You can also buy special sprouting lids.) Start by soaking the seeds overnight to soften.

The next day, pour off the water and use it for cooking; it's loaded with minerals, vitamins, enzymes and amino acids. Rinse the seeds and drain them again. Now cover the sprout jar and put it in a warm, dark place. It should be tilted slightly to let moisture out and oxygen in.

Over the next 2 to 6 days, you should rinse and drain the sprouts several times a day. Mung beans (the easiest to sprout) should be rinsed 3 or 4 times a day; alfalfa, radish and sunflower seeds, twice; lentils 2 to 4 times; soybeans, 4 to 6; and wheat, 2 to 3 times each day.

When the sprouts have reached a desired length, bring the jar out of hiding and set it in a sunny spot. The tiny leaves will turn bright green with chlorophyll. Finally, give them a final rinse, drain and store in the fridge. They'll stay fresh and healthful up to 2 weeks when tightly sealed in a plastic bag or glass jar.

Stems and Flowers _____

From left to right, the vegetables above are broccoli, leeks, artichokes, celery and cauliflower. For a dip for artichokes that's lower in fat than butter, whir up 2 tablespoons mild vinegar, 1 tablespoon buttermilk and ½ teaspoon Dijon-style mustard in a blender, then gradually add ¼ cup soy or sunflower oil until the mixture thickens.

In the mid-70s a large batch of wholesale chemical feed in Michigan was accidentally mixed with the fire-retardant PBB (polybrominated biphenyl). Before the error was discovered, cows all over the state had been contaminated—and farm families who regularly consumed PBB-tainted milk and meat had symptoms like weight loss, fatigue, loss of hair and aching joints. And one study showed that many Michigan women—not just farmers' wives—had PBB in their breast milk.

There's no way you can protect yourself against exposure to this type of pollution—it's a hazard of modern life. But if those farmers had been eating more cauliflower, they might not have had as many symptoms. A study published in *Environmental Health Perspectives* shows that when rats fed PBB were also fed cauliflower, they had less PBB accumulated in their bodies than did PBB-fed rats that didn't get cauliflower. The researchers who ran the study say that cauliflower increases the activity of the enzyme system that helps clear the body of pollutants.

A scientific study of a stem vegetable—celery—shows that it, too, protects health; in this case, against stomach cancer. Researchers compared the diets of 783 people with stomach cancer to those of over 1,500 people who didn't have the disease and found that those free of cancer ate more celery and lettuce.

Here's a rundown of the health values of the other vegetables in this category.

Broccoli. A cooked stalk of broccoli delivers over twice the RDA of vitamin C, all the RDA of vitamin A and respectable amounts of riboflavin, iron, calcium and potassium. Both the flowering, tightly clustered tops and the stalks can be eaten raw, steamed or stir-fried until tender-crisp.

Leeks. These onion relatives have been a staple in European gardens since ancient times and are quickly catching on here. They're low in calories (about 34 in each 1-ounce serving), and they supply good amounts of vitamins A, C and E. Eaten raw in salads, added to soups or stews, or sautéed as a vegetable side dish, the leeks' most famous role is as costars with potatoes in a soup that is known as vichyssoise when it's served chilled.

Kohlrabi. Described by some as a "turnip growing on a cabbage root," this strange mixed vegetable is a member of the cabbage family that has a turnip-size swelling on its stem. Odd as it may appear, the kohlrabi is a good source of vitamin C, some of the B vitamins, calcium and iron.

Celery. A celery stalk has 7 calories—so it makes a perfect snack for dieters in desperate need of something crunchy.

Asparagus. Years ago, white asparagus (which is denied sunlight to inhibit photosynthesis) was very popular. But today's nutrition-conscious shoppers have turned to the green variety because it is considerably more nutritious. The green spears are rich in vitamins A and C and offer small amounts of thiamine and riboflavin, plus some calcium.

Rhubarb. The pink, red or reddish-green stem is the only part of the rhubarb that's edible. Both the roots and leaves are toxic to humans and should never be eaten. The stems, however, are commonly used in sauces, pies and jams, and are a good source of potassium. They also provide some vitamin C.

Cauliflower. The hard, greatly enlarged flower head of the cauliflower plant (sometimes called the curd) is usually white, but there are purple- and green-headed varieties, too. One-half cup of white cauliflower has 150 percent of the Recommended Dietary Allowance of vitamin C.

Artichokes. The globe artichoke is a rosette of tender, fleshy leaves that is actually an immature flower head. The only part of the flower that's not edible is its thick center; if allowed to grow, this bud forms a violet-colored, thistlelike flower. Artichokes contain relatively small amounts of the vitamins A and C and some trace minerals.

MEATY VEGETABLES

Peas and beans are reliable providers of good nutrition. Beans, for example, are good sources of thiamine, magnesium and vitamin B_6. They contain more potassium than steak and two to six times as much calcium, and many varieties are an especially good source of iron.

But the legumes are perhaps best known as "poor man's meat," a rather unflattering (but accurate) reference to their extraordinary protein quality.

Though they're not the equal of eggs, soybeans deliver protein that's as high in quality as that in beef or chicken. Certain legumes *are* light on a protein component (amino acid) called methionine and a bit high on one called lysine. Fortunately, many cereal grains are slightly imperfect in just the opposite way: They're high in methionine and low in lysine. So, by serving these two food groups at the same meal, a cook can fill in the gaps in each and create a single high-quality protein. That may explain why so many traditional dishes all over the world match up legumes and grains, like the red beans and rice that are popular all over the American South.

Stuff Your Stalks with High Protein

Peanut butter isn't the only high-protein spread that tastes great with celery. Try out some of the other combos described below.

Chicken Pâté
This spread is made by blending a mixture of ground almonds, vegetable oil, sautéed chicken, tamari, vinegar and a touch of garlic powder.

Salmon Special
Salmon, cream cheese, lemon juice, grated onion, horseradish, paprika and ground pecans are the ingredients of this spicy spread.

Herbed Liver Spread
This mix contains onion, garlic, savory and thyme—along with a tablespoon of oil, a hard-cooked egg and, of course, chicken livers.

Beans and Peas

The lowly bean (from left to right, the beans are mung, navy, pinto, red kidney, yellow lentils, green lima and Great Northern) has gotten some bad press. Truth is, they're disease fighters; research has shown them to be particularly effective at lowering cholesterol. Of the pod vegetables (left to right, sugar peas, peas and snap beans), peas are loaded with fiber—cup for cup, they have more than brown rice.

Proteins from legumes have some real advantages over proteins from meat, milk or eggs. For one thing, they're much cheaper. The proteins in beans cost about $3 per pound—roughly half the cost of egg protein, and less than one-fourth the cost of round steak protein. Vegetable proteins are also much lower in fat than animal varieties: Beans have one-tenth to *one-hundredth* the fat of club steak.

And if you're worried about cholesterol, don't be! Beans and peas have none. What's more, they've got something that can help lower the cholesterol already in your system and thus protect your heart and digestive system: fiber. A cup of uncooked navy beans contains about 9.6 grams of fiber, as much as four slices of whole wheat bread.

But the legumes' story isn't all positive: Beans, especially, are notorious for their ability to produce intestinal gas. The substances in beans that produce flatulence are called oligosaccharides; they're broken down by fermentation in the lower intestine and gas ensues. Fortunately though, you can leach much of this material out of beans before you eat them. Before cooking, soak dried beans in water for at least three hours. Then throw away the soaking water and cook the beans in fresh water for at least 30 minutes. Finally, discard the cooking water, add fresh water, and continue cooking.

Dried Beans. Among the most

popular dried beans are mung, pinto, kidney, Great Northern and navy beans. They're good sources of the B vitamins thiamine and B_6, and they also contain significant amounts of niacin, folate, calcium, iron, magnesium and potassium. A half cup of kidney beans provides about 4 grams of fiber—a very respectable amount; the same amount of pinto beans delivers even more.

Fresh Beans. Green, yellow and lima beans are much richer in vitamins A and C than dried beans. And they share most of the other advantages of beans, too. They're low in calories and fat, contain no cholesterol, pack a protein punch, and—all the while—deliver vitamins B_6, niacin and riboflavin along with calcium, iron and potassium. Being low in sodium as well as high in potassium, they're good for people on salt-restricted diets.

Dried Peas. Versatile foods, dried peas deliver thiamine, riboflavin, iron, calcium and potassium.

Fresh Peas. Sweet peas, snow peas and the recently introduced sugar snap peas are rich in vitamins A and C and several of the B vitamins, plus calcium, iron and fiber. Snap peas can be eaten unshelled, pod and all—and their natural sweetness makes them delicious raw. They also contribute more vitamin C, niacin and potassium and fewer calories than the other pod peas.

Beans Packed with Power

Considered "beans of good fortune" by the Japanese, soybeans contain no cholesterol and almost none of the saturated fats associated with animal proteins. The advantage of that was shown in a study published in *Nutrition Reports International* in which 7 men with elevated cholesterol levels were switched to a new diet, one that substituted soy protein for meat and dairy proteins. The result? Over a period of about 7 weeks, the subjects' average cholesterol level dropped 13 percent and their triglycerides 23 percent.

That study proves soybeans are good for you.

But to hear William Shurtleff tell it, soybeans may be the world's most important protein source, as well. "The protein in soybeans is equal in quality to that of beef or chicken—and everyone agrees that soybeans are the least expensive source of protein in the world, far lower than meat," says Shurtleff, who, with his wife, Akiko Aoyagi, directs The Soyfoods Center in Lafayette, California, and has written numerous books on the virtues and uses of soybeans.

Soybeans are also amazingly versatile, he goes on. "You can make almost anything you can think of out of soybeans—including *all* the dairy products like milk, yogurt or cottage cheese, plus tofu, tempeh or soyburgers—all in your own kitchen." For the millions of people who can't drink milk because of a lactose intolerance, soy milk is a delicious alternative, he says.

From a planetary perspective, soybeans offer exciting possibilities in a world troubled by hunger and declining resources: 20 times as much protein can be produced from each acre of land planted in soybeans rather than given over to beef cattle. What's best is that this message is catching on: Over the past 70 years, Shurtleff says, soybeans are the only crop in the world that has steadily increased in total acreage under production.

It's not that all this is terribly new, he adds. "Soy foods have been used by roughly a quarter of the world's population for the past 2,000 years. So they're time tested by millions of people."

Still, all those arguments would be unconvincing if foods made from soybeans just didn't appeal to modern tastes. Yet soy foods, especially tofu and tempeh, *are* rapidly gaining in popularity in the United States, Shurtleff says.

Resembling a soft cheese, tofu is a custardlike food made from soybeans in much the same way cottage cheese is made from milk. It's quite mild tasting, and has been called the "food of 10,000 flavors" because it tends to borrow the flavor of the foods, sauces and marinades it's prepared with.

A simple, quick and delicious way of using tofu (now widely available in supermarkets) is as a salad dressing or dip. Simply spin a bit of tofu, some salad oil, lemon juice and your favorite spices in a blender, and you've got a creamy dressing that's cheaper than commercial dressings made from dairy products—and has only *one-third* their calories. Tempeh is a fermented soy food made into compact cakes or patties that has been a popular food in Indonesia for centuries. "People like it because it reminds them of southern fried chicken . . . it's something you can really sink your teeth into," says Shurtleff. It can be used as a meat substitute in tempeh burgers, tempeh Sloppy Joes, or mock tuna salad.

Flowering Vegetables

From left to right, the vegetables in the top row are mushrooms, pepper, corn and eggplant; in the bottom row are tomato, cucumber, squash and pumpkin. The pepper here is green; a red pepper is simply a green one that has grown older. It's almost doubled in vitamin C content, and has 10 times more vitamin A.

Back in 1581, the herbalist Matthias de L'Obel made this less than brilliant observation about the tomato: "These apples were eaten by some Italians like melons, but the strong stinking smell gives one sufficient notice how unhealthful and evil they are to eat." The tomato's early reputation as a foul, probably poisonous plant—and it *is* related to poisonous members of the nightshade family, like belladonna and mandrake—proved amazingly difficult to shake. In fact, for centuries after their introduction in Europe, tomatoes were cultivated mainly as curiosities or ornamentals.

It was up to Robert Gibbon Johnson, a man otherwise forgotten by history, to set the world straight. In 1820, he stood on the steps of the courthouse in Salem, New Jersey, and—before an incredulous world—ate a tomato. *And did not die!*

Today, of course, the tomato has outgrown its bizarre history and, in fact, has achieved a certain preeminence among vegetables; it now provides the average American with a greater percentage of his total nutrition than any other vegetable. Still, the tide of popular opinion turned in the tomato's favor only during this century: In 1920, the per capita consumption of tomatoes in the United States was about 18 pounds a year. By 1978, it had topped 56 pounds per person (mostly, however, in preserved forms like ketchup and sauces), for an increase of some 200 percent.

Actually, when it comes to nutritional value, tomatoes aren't the real power hitters that some other vegetables are. In fact, in a survey by M. Allen Stevens at the University of California, tomatoes were found to rank only 16th when the relative concentration of ten important vitamins and minerals were compared in all the common vegetables. Yet, tomatoes *do* contribute more good things to the average American's diet than any other vegetable simply because they outrank all the others in popularity.

In reality, the tomato and an armload of other popular "vegetables" aren't really vegetables at all. From a strictly botanical point of view, they're fruits—that is (to be scientifically exact), a matured seed vessel. It's a bit hard to think of pumpkins, eggplants and cucumbers as fruits, but that's what they are. In fact, this whole puzzling matter was once taken to the United States Supreme Court for clarification. Back in 1893 an importer of fresh produce protested the 10 percent duty charged on his West Indian tomatoes. The importer claimed they were fruit, which were duty free; the customs officials claimed they were vegetables, which weren't. "Botanically speaking, tomatoes are the fruit of a vine," the court concluded to set us all straight. "But in the common language of the people . . . [they're] vegetables." The importer didn't get his 10 percent back, but we got a double-barreled definition of tomatoes and their kin: They're fruit *and* they're vegetables.

Peppers. The glossy, deep green bell pepper of the backyard garden is especially valued for its vitamin C content; it contains more than twice as much as oranges do!

The many varieties of hot peppers — whose effect on the palate may range from a singe to a blister — are in the capsicum family and have been used for ages as medicine. Their specialness is attributed to capsaicin, the stuff that makes them hot. Scientists now believe that it may also work to inhibit blood clotting and thus protect against heart disease.

In one study, researchers in Bangkok, Thailand, took a look at the ability of capsaicin to affect fibrinolytic activity. Blood samples taken from 88 Thai subjects and 55 Americans showed that fibrinolytic activity was "significantly higher" among the Thais. Why? Because the Thais were accustomed to eating blazing hot food spiced with capsicum several times a day, the scientists guessed. They also noted that thromboembolism, or the potentially fatal blockage of a blood vessel by a clot transported from some other part of the body, is a relative rarity among Thais, while it's tragically common in the West.

Cucumbers. Cukes are fair sources of vitamin A and potassium — unless they're peeled; most of the A is in the skin.

Eggplants. Along with tomatoes, peppers and potatoes, the handsome, glossy eggplant is a member of the nightshade family. It's a fairly good source of potassium.

Sweet Corn. This vegetable offers moderate amounts of vitamin A, the B vitamins, some vegetable protein and certain trace minerals. Yellow corn, however, is far superior to white corn in vitamin A value. One ear of raw yellow corn contains about 910 I.U. of vitamin A, while the same amount of white corn contains only 21 I.U.

Squash. Most of the many varieties of squash are good sources of vitamin A, with Butternut and Hubbard squash leading the pack. Squash is also a good source of potassium. Butternut squash, for instance, has roughly twice as much as bananas, a traditional source of potassium.

Pumpkins. The jolly, orange, jack-o'-lantern is a good source of vitamin A, potassium and some trace minerals. The best nutritional bet in a pumpkin, though, comes in its seeds. They're fine sources of zinc, fiber and assorted minerals.

Mushrooms. Mushrooms are actually members of a group of organisms known as the filamentous fungi. Of the more than 2,000 fungi known to be edible, only about 25 species are widely consumed, and the little white button mushroom sold in supermarkets (the one called *Agaricus bisporus*) is the only one most of us know. Mushrooms are a surprisingly good protein source, and also contain fair amounts of iron, thiamine, riboflavin and niacin.

There's an old tradition in European folklore that mushrooms protect against cancer. And while "it's premature to go out and eat a lot of mushrooms because of their potentially antiviral or antitumor effect," says Kenneth Cochran, Ph.D., of the department of epidemiology and virus laboratory at the University of Michigan, he's convinced that this power is worth looking for. The button mushroom does seem to possess this property, Dr. Cochran points out, though it's too early to say exactly how or why it works.

Fruits

A true story. Almost.

The world's largest food manufacturer wanted to come out with a product that couldn't miss. Specialists of every kind were called in for their advice.

"First of all," advised one sales expert, "make it *sweet.* People love sweet things."

"Okay" agreed another marketing expert. "But make it *natural,* too. Natural is *in* today."

"Whatever you do," said the packaging consultant, "make it *colorful.* Use every bright color you can think of. Red, pink, purple, green . . .'

"Hold on a minute!" the medical expert complained. "People today are very conscious of health. This new product must be low in fat, low in salt . . ."

"And high in vitamins!" the nutritionist exclaimed. "I'd say we ought to concentrate on vitamins A and C. Good for the skin, disease resistance, you can see the results . . ."

"Forget all that nutrition stuff! Make it *crunchy!*" the snack-food expert called out.

"*Juicy!*"

"Put some fiber in it!"

"Watch the additives!"

"*Calories!* Whatever you do, keep down those calories!"

"Enough!" the client interrupted. "What do you think I am, a magician?"

"Well . . . aren't you?" the experts shot back.

" . . . Come to think of it, I am."

And so it came to pass that Mother Nature, Inc., came out with one of her biggest food triumphs ever: FRUIT.

Sweet, delicious, colorful? You bet. Fruit has all the sweetness of candy, without the bitter aftertaste of guilt.

Good for you? Mom was right, kids. Fruit doctors your insides like nobody's business. Gives you roughage to keep you regular. Delivers big shots of vitamins to build resistance, keep your skin smooth and help resist stress.

Calories? Well, let's look at it this way:

One piece of pound cake equals 142 calories.

Half a cantaloupe filled with strawberries and topped with yogurt equals 125 calories.

Compare fruit to something like a piece of chocolate cake at about 300 calories and you're talking about the kind of difference that can knock some real weight off your hips.

How about fat? To ingest the same amount of fat from say, cherries, that you would from just 1 ounce of potato chips, you'd have to cram down 565 of the sweet little beauties. Good luck. And don't forget a wheelbarrow for the cherry pits!

Concerned about salt? If high blood pressure runs in your family, you should be concerned. You should also know that fruit is one of your best dietary friends. For instance, milk isn't a high-salt food, but a cup still has 122 milligrams of sodium. By contrast, half a cantaloupe yields 33 milligrams and a large peach just 2 milligrams, while a whole pound of blueberries or watermelon contains only 5 milligrams.

Grapes

Fruit is also a wonderful source of potassium, a mineral especially important to people taking blood pressure medication.

Of course, these health-building treasures weren't handed out with exact equality.

In the food target at right, there's a fairly representative fruit basket laid out according to each fruit's ranking in total calories, fiber, iron, potassium and vitamins A and C. Like vegetables, however, *all* the rings are top quality. The target simply shows which fruits are the very best.

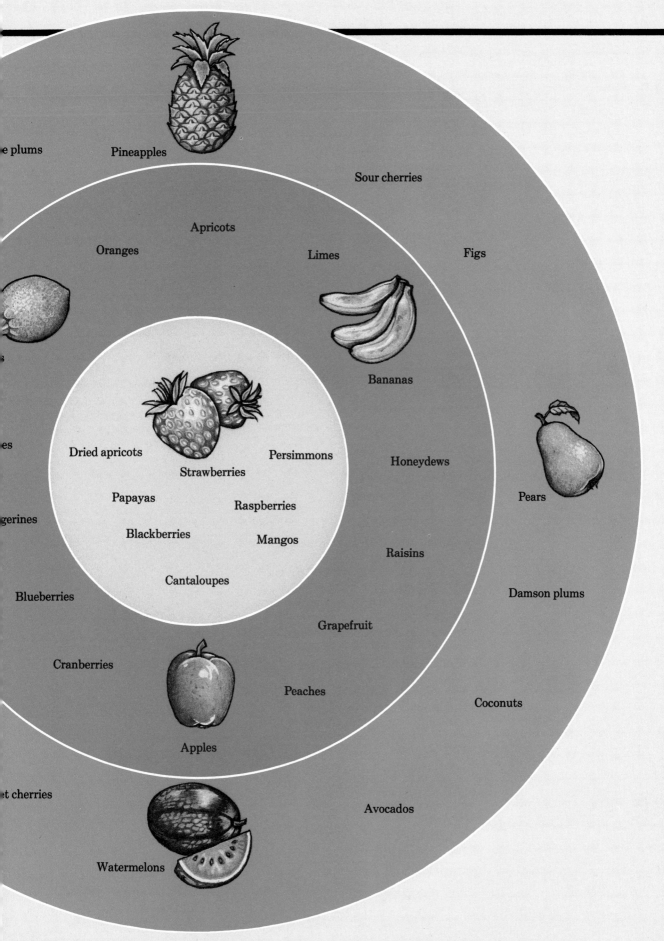

e plums

Pineapples

Sour cherries

Apricots

Oranges

Limes

Figs

Bananas

Dried apricots

Persimmons

Honeydews

Strawberries

Papayas

Raspberries

Pears

gerines

Blackberries

Mangos

Raisins

Cantaloupes

Blueberries

Damson plums

Grapefruit

Cranberries

Peaches

Coconuts

Apples

t cherries

Avocados

Watermelons

Seeds and Stones

Peaches

Native to China, the tender, fuzzy peach is now grown in temperate climates all over the world. Despite their sweetness, peaches are low in calories; a medium-size fruit has about 38. But they contain quite a bit of vitamin A.

Pears

Left to ripen slowly in a cool room, pears will become less grainy in texture. But if you can't wait to sink your teeth into one, place it in a paper bag. According to Gene Oberly, Ph.D., of Cornell University, the bag concentrates ethylene, a natural gas released by the pear that speeds ripening.

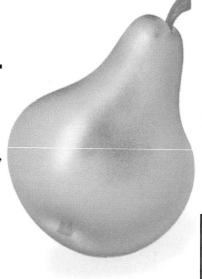

Grapes

Grape juice is a topical disinfectant, say scientists at the University of Wisconsin. If it's the *only* remedy handy, use it to bathe a wound.

Apples

They *do* keep the doctor away. A study at Michigan State University showed that the health of students who ate "an apple a day" for 3 years was "generally better than that of the student body as a whole." The most noted difference was fewer colds.

Is Your Smile Delicious?

Eating an apple reduces cavity-causing plaque on smooth surfaces of the teeth, but not between them. So it's better than nothing, but not as good as flossing and brushing. As a snack, however, it's sure to cause fewer cavities than sweets.

Apricots

The man in the moon likes apricots. They've been part of the menu on several NASA space flights (including the Apollo 15 trip to the moon) as puddings and in snack bars for a quick source of energy, vitamin A, vitamin C, iron and potassium. On earth, they're supposedly a favorite food of the Hunzas, a people of India famed for longevity.

Look beyond Laetrile for Answers

Laetrile is a distillation of apricot pits that a few doctors and cancer victims claim is a cure for the disease. It's popular enough to have been legalized in 27 states, and one scientific study says it has "completely eclipsed any other unorthodox therapy ever used for any disease in our time."

So much for the fanfare. Does it work? To find out, scientists from cancer centers all over the United States cooperated in a large study to test Laetrile. They gave the substance (along with the special diet and nutritional supplement program recommended by most of the doctors who believe in the drug) to 178 cancer patients. Only *1* of those patients had a regression of his tumor, which the doctors call "partial and transient." The rest continued to get worse.

As for the safety of Laetrile (apricot pits are loaded with cyanide), the doctors say that several of the patients had high levels of blood cyanide along with symptoms of poisoning.

So even though the apricot is a great food, as a cancer cure it's the pits.

Plums

It's no coincidence that something very desirable is called a "plum." This fruit gives you its great taste for only 32 calories, and throws in a bonus of vitamin A and potassium, too.

Cherries

Cherries—both sweet and sour—may cure gout. The first published account came from Ludwig W. Blau, Ph.D., who wrote that a bowl of cherries daily freed him from debilitating pain.

Nectarines

The nectarine is actually a kind of peach that has a smooth, waxy skin and extra-sweet flesh. There are 2 types: either clingstone, which means that the flesh must be cut away from the seed; or freestone, which means the stone pulls right out. Nectarines are a bit richer in vitamin A and potassium than peaches, but they're twice as high in calories.

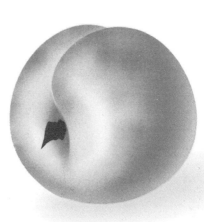

Citrus

Oranges

Orange juice gives you protection against colds and promotes healthy gums even more effectively than taking plain vitamin C, say researchers. OJ is great for people with high blood pressure; 1 glass delivers 496 milligrams of potassium.

Grapefruit

Biologists from Florida Atlantic University in Boca Raton have found that regular consumption of citrus fruits—including grapefruit—may reduce the risk of colon cancer. The scientists note that in Florida, southern California and Arizona the disease's rate is *half* the national average, and they believe that the easy availability of citrus fruits is the prime protecting factor.

Your OJ Could Be Cheating You of Vitamin C

Sure, fresh-squeezed orange juice is a great source of vitamin C. But what about juice made from frozen concentrate or the pasteurized juice that comes in a paperboard carton? To find out, New York researchers compared samples of all 3 kinds. The total vitamin C content didn't vary significantly among them, they found, but the vitamin's chemical form *did* vary. Pasteurized juice, these scientists found, has up to 30 percent of its vitamin C in a form that is biologically useless to humans and frozen juice has about 15 percent of its C in this unusable state. What's worse, mixing the frozen concentrate with water increased the amount of this useless form.

Tangerines

We call them tangerines because Tangiers was the port from which they were shipped to America in the early 19th century. And tangerine expert Ivan Steward, Ph.D., of the University of Florida Citrus Experiment Station, told us why he prefers the tangy fruits. "They taste good. They have lots of vitamin A [more than oranges], bioflavonoids, potassium and a host of healthful elements as yet undiscovered."

Limes

British sailors became known as "limeys" because limes were their shipboard safeguard against scurvy, the vitamin C deficiency disease that once ravaged whole navies.

Lemons

It's certainly *not* true—as the popular song claims—that "the fruit of the poor lemon is impossible to eat." The world production of lemons tops 1.6 million tons each year! Used to freshen everything from iced drinks to soap and perfume, the fruit is an excellent source of vitamin C.

Three Unusual Uses for a Lemon

1. Substitute lemon juice for vinegar in many recipes. The resulting taste will be fresher and brighter.
2. A squeeze or two of lemon juice will refresh the taste of canned, packaged or frozen vegetables.
3. Toss squeezed and grated lemons into the garbage disposal. They'll keep it clean and sweet smelling.

Berries

Blackberries

Blackberries are rich in minerals, vitamin C and the B vitamins. They're also quite high in fiber—it's roughly 4 percent of their total weight.

Loganberries

Loganberries are rich in vitamin C (1 cup contains about half the Recommended Dietary Allowance for an adult) as well as some B vitamins and calcium.

Blueberry Pickin' Time

Picking wild blueberries can be well worth the trouble. But remember: They may not be ripe just because they're blue (from green to red to blue is the spectrum of ripening). Ripe berries are sweet and ready to pull off at the slightest touch. The dark areas on the map above show where blueberries grow.

Mulberries

The white mulberry makes fairly poor eating, but red or American mulberries (which turn purplish-red when ripe) can be delicious. Mulberries contain small amounts of vitamin C and some potassium, iron and calcium.

Strawberries

"Doubtless God could have made a better berry," William Butler remarked after eating a strawberry for the first time, "but doubtless God never did." In addition to having a taste that inspires poets, strawberries are among the most nutritious of berries: ½ cup delivers about two-thirds of an adult's RDA for vitamin C.

Blueberries

Members of the heath family like cranberries, blueberries may grow on ground-hugging shrubs or high bushes. Blueberries are not quite as rich in vitamin C as raspberries or strawberries but, like all berries, they supply some B vitamins, minerals, a bit of fiber and very few calories.

Cranberries

The cranberry as a cure for urinary tract infections (UTI) has crossed over from a folk remedy to a medical fact (one report was published in the *Archives of Physician Medicine and Rehabilitation*). Drinking cranberry juice daily can clear up UTI because of the fruit's antibacterial properties and acidifying action on the urine.

Raspberries

There are nearly a thousand species of raspberries—many of which are wild—and their delicate fruits range in color from true red to black. Raspberries supply fair amounts of vitamin C and the B vitamins thiamine, riboflavin and niacin.

Melons

Watermelons

The juicy, pink-edged smile of a watermelon slice is one of summer's delights; its ample potassium actually makes it a good preventive for heat stroke. And the seeds are a folk remedy for high blood pressure, probably because they contain cucurbocitron, a substance that may help the problem.

Casabas

A globular fruit with pointed stem ends, a golden yellow skin and thick white flesh, the casaba melon is a late-ripening winter melon that is usually grown in California. Actually a muskmelon like the cantaloupe, it's a fair source of vitamin C and minerals. Casabas have the desirable ability to endure shipping and long-term storage without a loss of freshness or flavor.

Honeydews

The honeydew is a late-ripening winter melon that is unique in its ivory white or pale green skin and its sweet, firm, green flesh. It is a fair source of vitamin C (though not as good as cantaloupe) and minerals like potassium and calcium. Sweet as the flesh is, there are only 49 calories in 1 slice.

Cantaloupes

The succulent cantaloupe is extraordinarily rich in a form of carotene (the vitamin A precursor) that the body is able to use more completely than the carotene in various vegetables. That makes the melon a valuable fruit, since carotene is known to fight cancer, especially of the lungs.

Melon Ice Is Nice

This cool melon "cocktail" refreshes without the sweeteners and preservatives of soft drinks, and delivers plenty of vitamin C (a nutrient that helps you cope with boiling summer days).

The ingredients and tools are simple: a cantaloupe and a blender. Cut the melon into slices and then remove the skin. Now pare the slices into chunks and feed them one at a time into the blender. The result? Two cups of a refreshing, bright orange drink with a thick creamy head that's better still when chilled and served in frosted glasses.

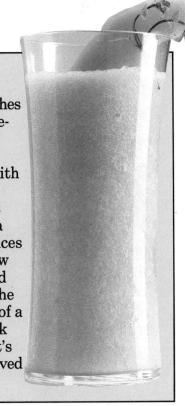

Tropical

Kiwi Fruit

The tart yet sweet kiwi is a rich source of vitamin C and contains proteolytic acid, which may help break up cholesterol and improve blood circulation.

Mangos

A medium-size mango supplies more than an adult's RDA for vitamin C and has only 76 calories.

Kumquats

Try this fruit raw—skin and all. But knead it a little to combine the sour pulp with the sweet rind.

Papayas

In a London hospital, strips of papaya successfully disinfected a wound after antibiotics had failed. The doctor who used the remedy took his cue from Africans who treat dirty ulcers with the fruit.

Persimmons

Japanese persimmons are particularly rich in vitamin A; a medium-size raw fruit supplies all of an adult's RDA.

Avocados

The buttery avocado has a nutty flavor. Except for olives and coconuts, no other fruit contains as much fat. Avocados also have vitamins A and C. Go easy on the guacamole if you're taking a drug called a monoamine oxidase inhibitor: Avocado can react with the drug and kick off hypertension.

Pineapples

Pineapple has a potent enzyme, bromelain. It's been used to aid digestion, reduce inflammation (perhaps working in much the same way as aspirin) and help clear up angina and heart disease by keeping blood platelets from clumping.

Three Steps to Paring Your Pineapple

1. On a cutting board, slice the pineapple into rings about ½ inch thick.
2. With a paring knife, peel the thorny skin off the edge of each ring, removing about ½ inch or less of skin and

flesh all the way around.
3. Slice each ring in half and then remove the hard, pithy core from each piece. A notch is usually the easiest cut to make here. Slice each half circle of fruit into serving pieces.

Pomegranates

Inside the leathery skin of each pomegranate lie thousands of tiny seeds, each wrapped in its own tart, crimson pulp. (To eat them, you have to pick them out one by one.) The pulp and seeds of an average-size pomegranate add up to 104 calories and are a good source of potassium.

Dried

Figs

In laboratory studies, a steamed distillate of figs has slowed the growth of tumors.

Dates

Actually a single-seeded berry, the date is such a rich and nourishing food that it's considered the "bread of life" by the desert people of Arabia. Dried dates are 64 percent sugar, so go easy on them: A quarter cup of pitted dates delivers a whopping 132 calories.

Bananas

From infancy on, bananas—dried or fresh—are an excellent food and healer. Since they're low in fat and sodium, people with heart or kidney disease should keep them on the menu.

Scouting Out Sulfur Facts

Dried fruits may be treated with sulfur dioxide to preserve their fresh color. But sulfuring dried fruits saves more than just appearance. It helps keep vitamin C from being baked out of the fruit along with the water. There's a drawback, however. Studies have shown that 1 in 20 asthmatics may be sensitive to the substance, so if you have the condition, avoid sulfured dried fruit.

Apples

Drying concentrates the pectin in apples, making them extra-good for your heart. A quarter cup checks in at about 58 calories, with plenty of iron and calcium.

Raisins

It takes 4½ pounds of grapes to make 1 pound of raisins, so this dried fruit packs a nutritional punch with lots of potassium, iron and B vitamins. They're also a good source of quick energy.

Prunes

The proverbial natural laxative, the prune is actually a dried red or purple plum ("prune," in fact, means "plum" in French). Prunes are fairly rich in fiber, which accounts for the laxative effect. They also have lots of iron, vitamin A and B vitamins. All that good nutrition comes wrapped in calories, though—a quarter cup contains 115.

Apricots

The finest-quality dried apricots—the most nutritious of dried fruits—come from California and Australia. Dried apricots are extraordinarily high in vitamin A: a quarter cup provides almost the entire RDA for an adult. They also pack 2½ grams of fiber—higher than a fiber-rich apple.

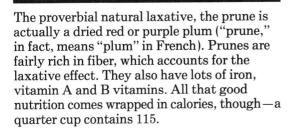

Grains

From the Mexican *tortilla* to the Indian *chapati*, the Chinese *pao ping* or the Arabic *balady*—bread is the "staff of life" in a thousand different languages. But the theme common to all those variations is grain: All bread, plain or fancy, white or brown, leavened or unleavened, is basically a paste made from grain that has been heated until it's firm.

But grains have a significance beyond bread. They are some of the most versatile foodstuffs on earth. In 1977, after a ten-year study of worldwide dietary patterns, the Agency for International Development observed that more than a third of the world's population obtain more than half of their daily calories from wheat alone!

Other grains, perhaps less well known to you, are equally important. On this food target you'll find some of these unfamiliar grains at the center of the bull's-eye. Along with bran and wheat germ, those extraordinarily healthful wheat components often removed during milling, you'll find amaranth, the "mystical grain" of the Aztecs just now making its American debut, and millet, a grain that has been more commonly fed to parakeets than to humans in the past. Yet the health-building power of these grains is too potent to be ignored.

But wheat is the king of them all—along with many of the B vitamins, especially thiamine and riboflavin, it contributes minerals like iron (for healthy red blood cells); potassium (for your heart muscle); magnesium (for nerves, muscles and kidneys); and zinc (a versatile mineral associated with enhanced sexual functioning, a clear complexion and rapid wound healing).

What's more, wheat bran is *the* best source of dietary fiber, a food element whose importance to health ranges from an ability to lower cholesterol and fight heart disease to the power to combat colon cancer, diverticular disease and other digestive disorders.

You'll find white flour and white bread in the outer ring of the food target because these foods are far more useful to grocery store owners than they are to the human metabolism. Stripped of the most healthful (and most perishable) parts of their grains, white flour doughs rise better than their whole grain counterparts, and their products stay fresh longer than whole grain baked goods. But when it comes to nutritional value, there's just no contest between white bread and the hardy, textured whole grain bread—often completely unleavened—that has been a staple food for millennia. The ancient antecedent of the spongy, air-filled white stuff we call bread today apparently got its start in Egypt, when it was discovered (probably by accident) that mixing soured dough with fresh produced a lighter, fluffier loaf. As a result, leavened bread became a sought-after status symbol: The hard, flat cakes of olden days were left for the peasants, but people who aspired to higher things sought out the latest leavened delight.

When mechanization hit the baking industry during the 19th century, leavened bread was taken a step further: By removing the germ or seed portion of the kernel in milling, bread that would stay fresher much longer was developed; and by removing the bran or heavy, fibrous covering of the kernel, doughs that rose better came into being. Thus white bread was born.

Unfortunately, we now know that the price we paid for this status and convenience was a heavy one: Wheat germ and bran are among *the* most healthful foods known to man.

144

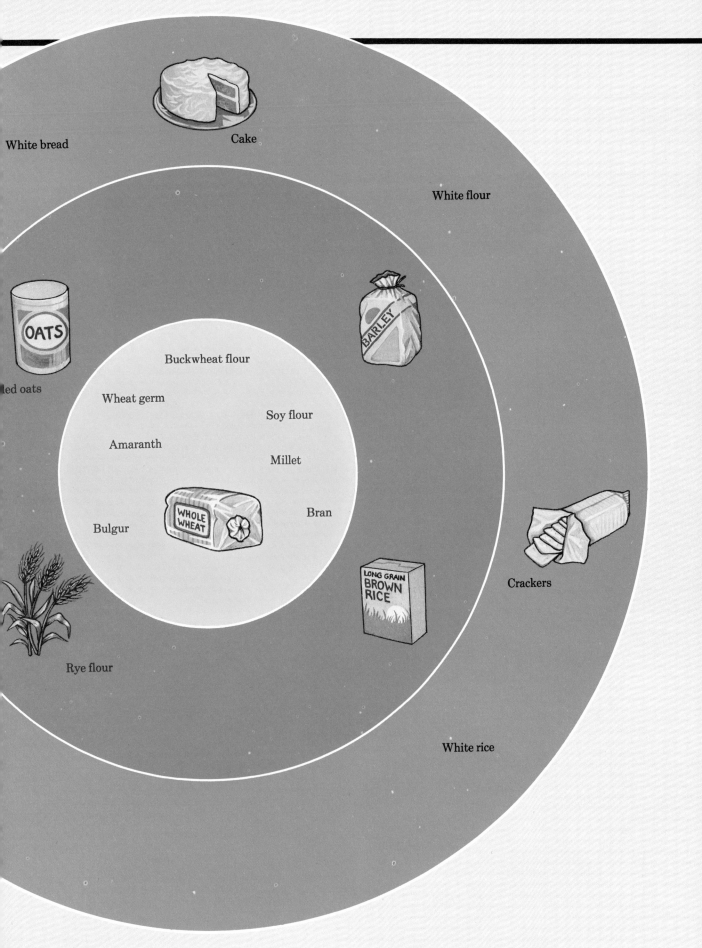

White bread

Cake

White flour

OATS

Rolled oats

Buckwheat flour

Wheat germ

Soy flour

Amaranth

Millet

WHOLE WHEAT

Bran

Bulgur

BARLEY

LONG GRAIN BROWN RICE

Crackers

Rye flour

White rice

The wheat germ is actually a tiny embryo nestled at the base of the wheat berry, and it's loaded with the nutrients needed to power the growth of the berry into a plant. That's why it's so rich in B vitamins—it naturally has five times more B_6 than "enriched" white bread, plus, for instance, iron, magnesium, potassium and protein (ounce for ounce, as much protein as T-bone steak!). It's also a good source of zinc, a mineral many older people don't get enough of, and an excellent source of vitamin E.

Wheat germ is a great food in its own right, either raw or toasted. You can also sprinkle it on cereals or casseroles—in fact, just about any dish is complemented by its nutty flavor. It is quite perishable, though, and should be refrigerated after the jar is opened.

Whole wheat flour, when used in breads, pastas, pies and other baked goods, can supply the second healthful component of wheat often removed by modern milling: bran. Bran is one of the great healthful foods because it is a terrific source of fiber. What's so great about fiber? Read on.

THE FIBER STORY

Researchers are now discovering that a "fiber deficiency" has been linked to a wide range of health problems, complaints that range from constipation to heart disease.

Denis Burkitt, M.D., a British surgeon who spent 20 years working in Africa, was among the first to recognize the importance of fiber for health. Intrigued by differences in dietary habits—and patterns of disease—between native Africans and people from industrialized Western countries, Dr. Burkitt began studying the geographical distribution of the chronic, noninfectious diseases that are rampant in civilized countries: bowel cancer, heart disease, constipation, gallstones, diabetes, hemorrhoids, hypertension, diverticular disease and varicose veins. Many of these conditions, he found, are virtually unknown in primitive societies. Heart disease, for example, kills about one man in four in Western countries. Yet, says Dr. Burkitt, "in African cities only occasional cases are found and these are always among the most Westernized part of the community." Similarly, cancer of the large bowel is the second most common cause of cancer

---

A Whole Wheat Bread That's Easy to Bake

Many home bakers complain that whole wheat bread is hard to make. But it doesn't have to be. Try this easy recipe and see if your whole wheat loaf doesn't come out a whole lot better.

Makes 4 loaves

  1 tablespoon honey
  ½ cup warm water
  2 tablespoons dry yeast
  12 to 13 cups whole wheat
      flour
  5 cups hot water
  ½ cup honey
  ⅔ cup oil

Dissolve the honey in warm water and sprinkle the yeast on top—but don't stir it. When the yeast mixture bubbles, combine it with half the flour, the hot water, honey and oil in a large mixing bowl. Blend with a mixer on low speed. Add the remaining flour slowly until the dough reaches the consistency of a cookie dough. Knead for 10 minutes on low speed with mixer. Oil hands and countertop and mold the dough into 4 loaves, then place them in 9 × 5 bread pans greased with oil and lecithin. Cover the pans, set them in a warm place, and allow the dough to rise.

Preheat the oven to 350°F. When the dough has increased in size by one-third, bake the loaves for 40 to 45 minutes. Then remove the loaves from the pans and tap them on the bottom; if they sound hollow, they're done. If they're not done, put them directly on the oven rack for a few more minutes.

Remove the loaves from the oven and cool them on wire racks.

death in North America, while in Third World countries, it's far less common. In case after case, the pattern holds.

What was making the difference? Certainly, Dr. Burkitt now admits there is no one reason. But he believes that dietary fiber is a major contributing factor. Perhaps *the* major factor. "The food component that changes most with adoption of Western dietary habits is the indigestible fiber," he writes. "Two and a half times more fiber . . . is consumed in Third World countries than in Western communities . . ."

A growing body of research has supported the pioneering work of Dr. Burkitt with clinical findings. In one Dutch study, for example, 871 middle-aged men were studied for ten years. Seventy-six percent of the deaths seen during the ten-year study period came from cancer or heart disease. However, the researchers noted, "men with a low intake of dietary fiber had a three times higher risk of death from all causes [of death] than men with a high intake . . ." Writing in the *Lancet*, the researchers concluded their report by suggesting that "a diet containing at least 37 grams of dietary fiber per day may be protective against chronic diseases in Western societies." (A cup of 100 percent bran cereal, one apple, one potato and ½ cup cooked spinach would supply about 37 grams.)

Another study examined the effect of high- and low-fiber diets on the recurrence of recently healed ulcers of the small intestine. Eighty percent of the patients on low-fiber diets had another bout with ulcers before the study's six months were up, but only 45 percent of those on a high-fiber diet experienced a recurrence. "A diet rich in fiber may, therefore, protect against duodenal [small intestine] ulceration," the scientists concluded.

How can you take advantage of these findings? "In the American diet, adding a good source of cereal fiber such as wheat bran would be the best approach," says Bandaru S. Reddy, Ph.D., of the American Health Foundation.

The very richest source of fiber is miller's bran—that is, the bran

that is removed during the milling process and is 44 percent fiber. Whole grain bread weighs in at between 8 and 11 percent fiber, and some fiber-rich cereals can go as high as 29 percent. Many health-conscious people have been putting this research to work by having high-fiber cereal at breakfast, switching from white to whole wheat bread, and adding heaping spoonfuls of bran to soups, fruits and salads.

As fiber has made the health headlines over the past few years, some authorities have claimed that a high-level intake can actually *hurt* you. How? By blocking the absorption of minerals: A substance in fiber called phytate can grab up minerals like zinc and calcium and haul them out of the body before the intestines know what hit them. Or so these experts say. If you hear this kind of info, ignore it—it's not a *practical* fact. No study has shown that a diet rich in fiber causes a long-term mineral problem. Only in certain Middle Eastern people whose diet is 80 percent unleavened bread is phytate a serious health problem.

"People have been eating whole grains and beans for hundreds of years. Obviously, these foods don't cause mineral deficiencies," says Pericles Markakis, Ph.D., a food scientist from Michigan State University who specializes in fiber and mineral metabolism.

GOING WITH THE GRAIN

So far we've been talking mainly about the virtues of wheat. But there are many other grains that are—or *should* be—important to human health. Some, like wheat, rye and oats, are certainly familiar to you. Others, like millet and buckwheat, have been used primarily as animal feed in the past, but recent research shows that they deserve a place in your diet because of some special nutritional characteristics.

Bulgur. For many centuries, residents of the Middle East and the Andes have prepared wheat in a way that so changes its character that many people regard it as a separate product. The Incas called it *Moté*,

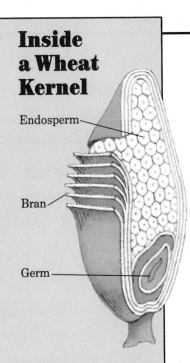

Inside a Wheat Kernel

Endosperm

Bran

Germ

Like all seeds, the wheat kernel or "berry" is actually an embryo with an attached life support system. The egg, or *germ*, is a tiny speck (representing only 3 percent of the whole kernel) that contains all the nutrients needed to spark its growth into a new plant. The starchy *endosperm* (about 83 percent of the kernel and its central body) is the source of white flour and most of the kernel's protein. The whole package is wrapped in a high-fiber hull, called the *bran* (about 14 percent of the kernel).

but you may know it as bulgur, a familiar accompaniment to many Middle Eastern dishes.

Since ancient times, bulgur has been prepared by first boiling or roasting the raw wheat grain and then spreading it out to dry in the sun. The hard, dry wheat berries are then rubbed by hand to remove some of the bran, sprinkled with water and then cracked in a mortar and pestle. Modern milling techniques have refined and streamlined these steps, but they remain basically the same.

The result is a hard, partially dehulled, cracked wheat that swells up during cooking to roughly double its size and is amazingly versatile. Bulgur can be eaten for breakfast as a cereal, used as an extender in meat, poultry or fish dishes, added to bread dough or pancake batter and added to soups as a rice or noodle substitute; it can even be eaten plain.

Astoundingly, many of the nutritional benefits of raw wheat are retained during the production of bulgur. The amounts of the B vitamins riboflavin and niacin are nearly equal in wheat and bulgur, as are iron and calcium. It also retains a full 75 percent of its fiber.

Millet. These tiny yellow kernels are probably more familiar to you as birdseed. But it's foolish to say that millet is simply "for the birds." As is true of all grains, millet is a good source of the B vitamin thiamine and of the minerals iron and magnesium. And you don't have to peck millet out of a tiny cup. It can be used as a rice substitute, as a hearty breakfast cereal, or as an addition to stews, soups, bread dough and other baked goods.

Rice. Most of the rice you'll find in supermarkets is white rice—something that is a mere ghost of its former self. Mother Nature made *all* rice brown, but man has decided that he needed a change of color, and so he scrubbed the nutrient-rich brown bran off the grains.

What difference did it make? Consider this: Ounce for ounce, brown rice has almost three times more fiber than unenriched white rice. Almost five times more thiamine. Three times more niacin. Twice as much pantothenate. Three times more B_6. Twice as much iron. Three times more magnesium. Fifty percent more zinc. Five times more vitamin E. In short, there's no comparison.

Maybe Mother Nature knew what she was doing.

Rye. Though rye may wind up in whiskey about as often as it does in bread these days, that's a state of affairs that should be changed. Rye is a nutritious cereal grain, and rolled into a flake it can be added easily to granola-type cereals. Coarsely ground

Toast is no match for wheat germ sprinkled over cereal in the battle for good morning nutrition. Even with nutritional fortification, white bread falls short in fiber (for good digestion), folate (a must for those on the Pill) and potassium (to help lower high blood pressure), while being over 500 times higher in sodium.

Wheat Germ Tops Toast in Breakfast Value

	Calories	Fiber (g.)	Thiamine (mg.)	Riboflavin (mg.)	Niacin (mg.)	Pantothenate (mg.)	Vitamin B_6 (mg.)	Folate (mg.)	Calcium (mg.)	Iron (mg.)	Sodium (mg.)	Potassium (mg.)
1 Tablespoon of Wheat Germ	22.5	1.5	0.1	—	0.3	0.1	0.1	20.3	4.5	0.6	0.2	51.3
1 Slice of White Bread	61.4	0.4	0.1	0.1	0.9	0.1	—	8.1	29.0	0.7	118.2	25.8

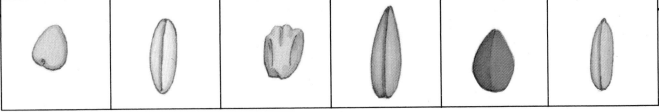

rye meal and finely ground rye flour can be blended with other kinds of flour to produce new tastes in bread and other baked goods.

Light rye is like white flour: It's chemically bleached, has next to no bran, and is a nutritional washout. Pass it by.

Buckwheat. It's grain*like,* but it's not a grain. Strictly speaking, it's a fruit, and that means that unlike wheat and rice, the buckwheat seed has no bran or germ; it's simply a kernel wrapped inside a shell. The kernel, called a groat, is the edible part. Buckwheat groats are usually served as a breakfast cereal, in puddings or as a stuffing for meat or poultry.

More popular, though, is kasha— *roasted* buckwheat groats. Kasha has a nutlike flavor and is a traditional Eastern European food.

Nutritionally speaking, buckwheat is superb. Its protein efficiency is better than any grain; buckwheat is especially well endowed with the amino acid lysine, a substance that most of the other grains lack. By combining buckwheat with oats, wheat or rice, you can create a very high-quality protein source. Buckwheat is also a fair source of the B vitamins, especially B_6, and iron.

Oats. The grain is unique because it emerges from the rigors of processing with most of its nutritional bounty intact. Rolled oats, the form sold for cooked oatmeal, is steamed and flattened by rollers before being packaged, and yet the result is still nutritious enough to be considered a whole grain product. The so-called quick cooking oats are precut, steamed and flattened even more; and instant rolled oats are quick oats with guar gum added, a substance that thickens them to oatmeal-type consistency in less than a minute. Although the more processed varieties don't lose many nutrients, they often gain sugar and artificial ingredients, so your best bet is still plain old rolled oats.

OATS LOWER CHOLESTEROL

You know, of course, that wheat bran speeds wastes through the intestine, but it does little to lower cholesterol levels in the blood—something that oat bran probably can do. In fact, scientific studies show that oat bran can lower low-density lipoprotein (LDL) cholesterol in the blood (the harmful stuff of which hardened arteries are made) while it raises (or leaves intact) the levels of high-density lipoprotein (HDL) cholesterol (the beneficial form of blood lipid).

One of the studies that looked at oats and cholesterol took place at the department of food science and nutrition at Queen Elizabeth College in London. Researchers there asked ten people to eat an oat-filled diet for three weeks, alternating it with four weeks of an oatless regime. The rolled oats were consumed as old-fashioned oatmeal at breakfast and in bread recipes created especially for the experiment. They ate enough of each to average about 4 ounces of pure rolled oats each day.

During the days of the study, the blood cholesterol levels of all the subjects were carefully monitored. When the results were totaled and averaged, it was found that the students' cholesterol levels had dropped an average of 8 percent.

In another study, American researchers tested the effect of oat bran in the diets of eight men whose cholesterol levels were relatively high and causing concern. These men ate strict oat and oatless diets in ten-day cycles so that during an oat-filled period they averaged about 3 ounces of bran a day; the bran was baked into muffins or blended into hot cereal.

At the end of the trial, the men had experienced an average drop of 13 percent in their cholesterol levels, a decrease that occurred largely because of a welcome 14 percent decline in LDL concentrations.

From left to right, the grains shown above are millet, oats, bulgur, rye, buckwheat and rice. The rice here is long grain, which is perfect for side dishes, salads and stews. Medium grain and short grain cooks up slightly sticky and moist and works best in puddings or as an extending and binding ingredient in meat loaves or croquettes.

The Morning Line on Sugar

Would you feed your kids a plate of cookies for breakfast? Maybe you should—it might be *more* nutritious than what they're eating now if they're sharing the breakfast table with Sugar Bear or Count Chocula. A sugar cookie, for instance, is 27 percent sugar; some sweet cereals are nearly *60 percent*. And that much sugar can sour health.

Breakfast is probably the most important meal of the day. For one thing, blood sugar levels need replenishing. And sugar isn't how to do it. That sweet dose romances your blood sugar way up—and then drops it, leaving you in a funk of fatigue. For another, the body should get at least one-third of its daily nutrients in the morning—sugar has next to no nutrients. Not a vitamin. Hardly a mineral. So which 10 cereals have the least sugar? And which 10 are the sugary worst? Here's the lineup.

LOWEST

Puffed Rice (any brand)

At 0.3 percent sugar, this cereal bears no resemblance to a cream puff.

Shredded Wheat (any brand)

At 0.5 percent sugar, it won't shred your kids' teeth.

Puffed Wheat (any brand)

It has 2.5 percent sugar. Not too bad.

Cheerios

A cheery meal to greet the day—only 3 percent sugar.

Kix

Your kids can get their breakfast kicks without getting their health kicked around. 4.3 percent sugar.

Corn Chex

You won't have to check your health at the kitchen door. Only 4.5 percent sugar.

Wheat Chex

A low-sugar cousin to the corn variety—also 4.5 percent.

Rice Chex

In this case, three's not a crowd. The most sugary of the Chex cereals at 5.1 percent.

Toasties

Pop them into your mouth without guilt. 5.4 percent sugar.

Grape-Nuts

You'd have to be nuts to eat a breakfast that's much more than 7 percent sugar—the amount in Grape-Nuts—but many other cereals are.

HIGHEST

Sugar Smacks

At 55.8 percent sugar, it smacks of candy.

Apple Jacks

These apples have been hijacked to sugar land. 52.4 percent.

Froot Loops

They can't spell "fruit." They can spell "sugar." 48.9 percent.

Sugar Corn Pops

A corn pop by any other name would taste less sweet. 46.5 percent sugar.

Super Sugar Crisp

It's a bird, it's a plane—no, it's a cereal with 45.2 percent sugar. That's no hero.

Cocoa Krispies

A chocolate bar in a bowl. 44.6 percent sugar.

Cap'n Crunch's Crunch Berries

He picked them off a sugar tree. 44.2 percent sugar.

Lucky Charms

Sweet, yes. Charming, no. 42.4 percent sugar.

Cookie Crisp

The name says it all. 42.3 percent sugar.

Cocoa Pebbles

These pebbles are really rock candy. 42.1 percent sugar.

Nuts and Seeds

In 1972, a Japanese archaeologist found milletlike seeds in an ancient tomb—seeds which had lain dormant in the dark for 4,000 years. He "excavated" them, put them in some water—and they sprouted!

That event was graphic proof that few foods are more highly concentrated bundles of life force than seeds and nuts. They *have* to be, since they must engineer and nourish one of nature's miracles: the unfolding of a living plant from a tiny kernel. Nuts and seeds, in short, are practically bursting with life—and all the nutrients that sustain life.

The more than 300 kinds of nuts that grow around the world vary nutritionally, of course, but most of them are good sources of the B vitamins thiamine and folate and the minerals iron, magnesium and zinc. Many nuts are also well supplied with vitamin E as well as protein and fiber. They're also loaded with calories, since the infant plant needs fats and starches to fuel its growth; raw peanuts are 48 percent fat, pecans an incredible 71 percent.

Still, nuts beat most other snack foods hands down. Compare 20 almonds to 20 potato chips, for instance. The chips deliver 228 calories, the nuts 120. The almonds also supply more protein, more calcium, more iron and more fiber—and almost no salt, compared to the whopping 400 milligrams in those potato chips.

This story would be a little different, though, if you were munching roasted, highly salted nuts out of a can. Up to 72 percent of thiamine may be lost in the roasting of peanuts, and a University of California study showed almonds lost about 25 percent of their vitamin B_6 content when roasted. Salted nuts—peanuts, in particular—may also contain up to 82 times more sodium than nuts in their natural state! As for fat, there's really no great difference between raw, dry-roasted and oil-roasted nuts. Raw nuts, however, have the lowest fat content, followed by dry-roasted and then oil-roasted nuts.

GOOD THINGS IN SMALL PACKAGES

Seeds like those of celery, coriander, cumin and mustard appear to have been among the first flavor-enhancing "spices" used by humankind; celery seed was mentioned by the Greek poet Homer as early as 800 B.C. But seeds enhance the spice of life in other ways, too, through their health-building supply of nutrients.

Like nuts, seeds are good sources of protein—pumpkin seeds, for example, are 29 percent protein, almost as much as porterhouse steak!

Cashews

Seeds are also well endowed with fiber (unhulled sesame seeds, with more than 6 percent fiber, are among the best), polyunsaturated fat, B vitamins, calcium, potassium, iron and zinc. Pumpkin seeds, in fact, have been used as a natural source of zinc in the treatment of swollen prostate glands, a common disorder among middle-aged men that can cause impotency and is known to be responsive to zinc.

Unfortunately, seeds are also heavyweights when it comes to calories. A quarter cup of sunflower, sesame or pumpkin seeds (that's roughly three handfuls) weighs in at about 200 calories. Practically speaking, though, it's a lot harder to "eat yourself sick" on pumpkin seeds than it is on cream-filled cupcakes or potato chips. In fact, says

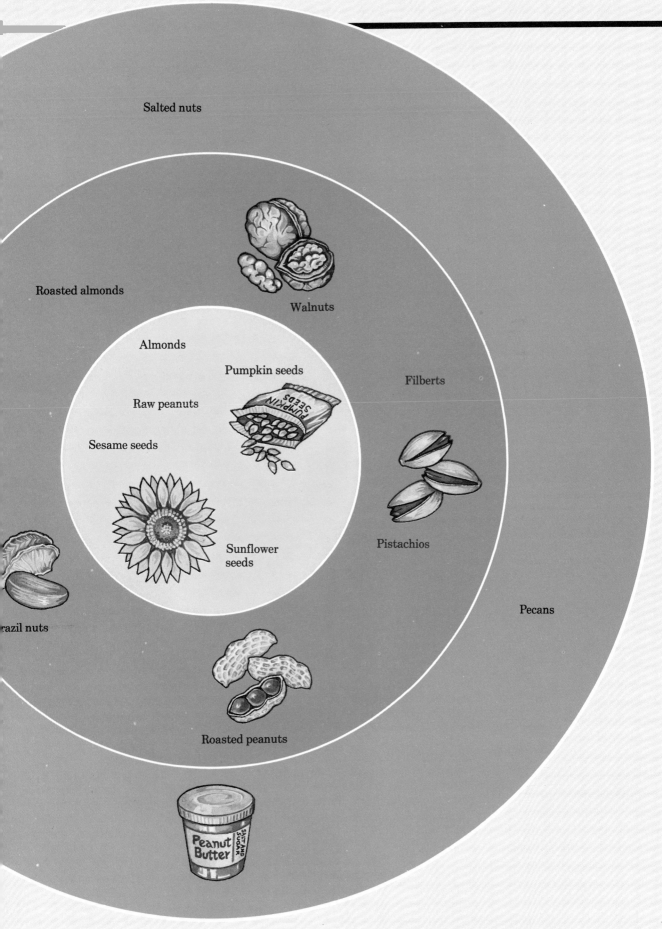

Salted nuts

Roasted almonds

Walnuts

Almonds

Pumpkin seeds

Filberts

Raw peanuts

Sesame seeds

Pistachios

Sunflower seeds

Pecans

Brazil nuts

Roasted peanuts

Peanut Butter SALT AND SUGAR

Clockwise from the lower left-hand corner, these nuts and seeds are Brazil nuts, pecans, peanuts, pistachios, filberts (hazelnuts), sesame seeds, pumpkin seeds, sunflower seeds, walnuts and cashews, with almonds in the middle. You'd be nutty not to include these in your diet—they're packed with protein, vitamins B and E and fiber.

John Douglass, M.D., a California internist who prescribes sunflower seeds for healing, "I've had a standing $5 bet going for anyone who could eat a pound of sunflower seeds in an hour. I haven't lost my $5 yet!" Still, moderation in all things is a virtue, even when it comes to seeds and nuts.

Calorie content, in the form of total fat content, was one of the things we measured when ranking the nuts and seeds for the food target shown on the preceding page. We also considered each one's protein content, its sodium, fiber, vitamin E, zinc, calcium and niacin content.

Though peanuts and almonds and sunflower, pumpkin and sesame seeds are all hefty sources of calories, they contain such extraordinary amounts of protein, fiber, polyunsaturated fats and practically the entire chart of vitamins and minerals that they can only be considered "bull's-eye" foods. Others, like filberts (hazelnuts) and pistachios, are good foods, but less nutrient dense. In the outer ring, you'll find nuts whose fat content outweighs their nutritional payload to the point where they're best eaten sparingly.

THE PROBLEM WITH PEANUT BUTTER

You'll find peanut butter—something four out of five American homes depend on as a basic food—in the outer ring. Though nourishing, most commercial peanut butters contain too much salt and sugar. And an interesting study reported in the *New England Journal of Medicine* has shown that the tremendous amount of fat in peanuts is even more completely absorbed by the body when the nuts are mechanically ground down to make peanut butter. And the *fats* in peanut oil (nuts ground down to liquid) are even better absorbed than the peanut butter itself! Another problem with peanut butter is that in order to prevent its oils from separating and rising to the top of the jar, many commercial manufacturers add hydrogenated vegetable oils, which are partially saturated—the type of fat that's been linked to heart disease. Fortunately, plain old peanut butter—topped with a layer of separated oil—seems to be making a comeback.

Almonds. Almonds are an important part of many vegetarian diets, because they contain 19 percent protein plus B vitamins, vitamin E, magnesium, iron and fiber. They're more than 50 percent fat, true, but these fats are mostly unsaturated and rich in linoleic acid, a component of fat associated with lowered blood pressure and good cardiovascular health.

Peanuts. They contain fully 26 percent protein, on a par with meat and cheese. Though lacking in vitamins A and C (like all nuts and seeds), peanuts are tremendously rich in B vitamins, especially niacin and thiamine, vitamin E, iron, magnesium, potassium and fiber.

Pumpkin Seeds. Don't scoop them out of your Halloween jack-o'-lantern and throw them away; they should be roasted and eaten. An amazing 29 percent protein, pumpkin seeds are good sources of iron, zinc and B vitamins.

Sesame Seeds. These small seeds are usually used as an ingredient, as a garnish, or ground into butter (tahini). But they're big on nutritional value, providing nearly 19 percent protein, plus unsaturated fats, vitamin E and the B vitamins. They're also providers of a substance called sesamol, an antioxidant some researchers believe can protect against cancer and help slow aging.

Filberts. Among nuts, the filbert (hazelnut) is second only to almonds in calcium content. Filberts are about 13 percent protein and nearly 70 percent fat; they provide good amounts of potassium, iron, B vitamins and vitamin E. To remove the skin from shelled filberts or almonds—a process called blanching—simply cover them with boiling water for a few minutes, drain the water, put the nuts in cold water and then rub off the skin with your fingers.

Brazil Nuts. These nuts are very high in two categories: thiamine and calories. At better than 65 percent fat, about ¼ cup of Brazil nuts (stripped of their tough, wrinkled hulls) weighs in at nearly 229 calories.

Pistachios. Especially rich in protein (about 20 percent, behind only peanuts and walnuts), pistachios also deliver plenty of iron, potassium and thiamine.

Walnuts. At a little better than 20 percent protein, black walnuts trail only peanuts. They're also particularly rich in iron, potassium and vitamin E. Unfortunately, they're nearly 60 percent fat.

Cashews. Though often thought of as a nut, the cashew is actually a fishhook-shaped seed that dangles from the tip of a strange fruit called a cashew apple. They're especially rich in magnesium.

Pecans. Pecans, scrumptious as they are, are fairly low in protein (a little better than 9 percent) and high in fat (about 72 percent). In fact, they're the fattiest nuts around: ¼ cup delivers almost 186 calories! So sugar isn't the only reason pecan pie tends to sink directly to your waistline.

Try a Different Nut Butter

Peanut butter, of course, is the king of nut butters. But there are others that shouldn't be ignored—like cashew, almond, pecan, walnut or filbert butter.

To make your own nut butter, grind 1½ cups of unsalted nuts in a food processor or electric blender, turning the machine off every 10 seconds. Continue grinding the nuts down until they're a thick, fudgelike paste. Then add light vegetable oil (start with 1 tablespoon and add more if necessary) and blend until smooth. Turn the machine off every 30 seconds during the final stage (for a total grinding time of about 3 minutes in a food processor, 5 in a blender). Then add 1½ tablespoons of oil and blend for another 30 seconds.

Sunflower Power

With their huge, amiable faces bobbing in the summer sky, sunflowers grace many a backyard garden. Their name, *Helianthus*, comes as much from their sunny corona of yellow petals as it does from their habit of facing the sun as it travels across the sky during the summer months.

But the sunflower is more than just a pretty face. Its visage is densely packed with seeds, whose familiar zebra-striped hulls hide one of nature's nutritional gold mines. They're so rich in vitamins, minerals, protein, polyunsaturated fat and fiber that the American Indians used them for centuries as a medicine to relieve chest pains, decrease water retention, prevent or expel worms, improve eyesight and provide energy. An Indian brave was said to have been able to travel farther on a pouch of sunflower meal than on any other food.

At least one modern-day doctor believes the Indians were onto something. John Douglass, M.D., is the country's unofficial "sunflower king": He's recommended sunflower seeds to over 5,000 patients over the past decade, to help lower blood pressure, improve cardiovascular health, suppress allergic reactions and even help them quit smoking without packing on the pounds.

"I've had patients come in with blood pressure so high it scared me," Dr. Douglass says. "Sometimes there would also be extreme edema [water retention]. Because sunflower seeds are naturally high in potassium and low in sodium, they act as a diuretic [an agent that drains excess water from tissues]. This in turn can help lower blood pressure, too. Within a couple of months their blood pressure improved dramatically and the edema was gone."

How do sunflower seeds pull off these healing performances? Probably through a combination of things, Dr. Douglass believes. They're excellent sources of B vitamins, for one thing, including hard-to-get B_6, plus niacin and pantothenate. They supply respectable amounts of vitamin E, crucial to circulatory health. They're loaded with minerals, too, like calcium, iron and potassium, as well as fiber, whose role in the prevention of a host of "civilized" disorders ranging from ulcers and heart trouble to constipation and high blood pressure is increasingly well documented. And fully 24 percent of the sunflower seed's tiny kernel is protein—a percentage comparable to beef. In fact, adding 15 percent sunflower meal boosts the protein content of whole wheat bread by over 50 percent.

Unfortunately, the sunflower seed is as concentrated a source of calories as it is of nutrients—it exceeds even chocolate fudge in that department! Yet that may be one part of its magic, since much of the unsaturated fat in sunflower seeds is of the class called

19 normal subjects, reducing the risk of excessive clotting— something that could be important to those prone to blood clots and other heart problems.

"I tell my patients to eat about 1 to 2 cups of sunflower seeds (shelled, raw and unsalted) per day," Dr. Douglass says. "I also stress the importance of daily exercise, and eating raw foods such as salads and fruits."

A SEEDY STOP-SMOKING PROGRAM

"I put so much pressure on my patients to give up smoking that I sometimes think they quit just to get me off their backs," Dr. Douglass laughs. But to make the quitting easier, he adds, he also recommends sunflower seeds. "They won't do the whole job, but I have found that sunflower seeds can be helpful for many people." Sunflower seeds, he explains, mimic the addictive and dangerous effects of tobacco on the body— without being addictive or dangerous. Tobacco, for example, temporarily decreases the smoker's allergic reactions; some smokers even develop respiratory problems after they quit, apparently because these allergic reactions have been kept in check by the antiallergic effect of tobacco. Sunflower seeds mimic this physiological action and make quitting easier, Dr. Douglass says. Tobacco also perks up the brain by releasing glycogen (a form of sugar) from the liver at the same time it acts as a sedative to calm you down. But then . . . so do sunflower seeds.

"Go to a store that sells raw, shelled sunflower seeds and buy 3 or 4 pounds," Dr. Douglass advises the aspiring nonsmoker. "Stash several ounces of the seeds in your purse or pocket and every time you get the urge to light up, reach for a handful of seeds instead. The sooner you start munching, the sooner you'll be an ex-smoker."

Raw sunflower seeds are better than roasted ones, he adds.

"Sunflower seeds are highly nutritious, beneficial to health in many specific ways, tasty and inexpensive."
—John Douglass, M.D., specialist in internal medicine and coordinator of health improvement services at Kaiser-Permanente Medical Center in Los Angeles.

linoleic acid, a substance associated with lowered blood pressure in study after study.

German researchers studied 650 healthy men, for example, and found the correlation between increased linoleic acid in their diet and a drop in blood pressure to be "strongly significant." In New Jersey, researchers found that a mere 1.2 percent increase in dietary linoleic acid for one month was all it took to lower the systolic blood pressure in 28 mildly hypertensive adults. And in another study, products made with pure sunflower seed oil were found to alter the blood chemistry of

Dairy

It's no wonder the family farm of yesterday almost always had a flock of chickens scouring the barnyard and a cow or two in the barn. Dairy products are among the most nourishing foods, and a fitting complement to almost any meal. Eggs provide the most nearly perfect proteins of any food, plus a feast of life-sustaining vitamins and minerals. We'll talk about both those foods in this section, but let's look at milk first.

Milk and the amazing array of products made from milk are fine sources of protein and calcium.

But dairy products also contain varying amounts of animal fat, ranging from the 80 percent in creamery butter to the less than 1 percent in some skim milk. (The minimum amount of fat in whole milk is regulated by law in each state, but it's generally between 3 and 3.5 percent.) Fat is one of the factors we've taken into account in evaluating each of the dairy products in the food target—too much of it is bad for you. We've also looked at protein (milk products should be a good source); calories (for those who watch their weight); riboflavin (a B vitamin important for healthy skin and blood); and calcium (a mineral necessary for strong bones, and one found mainly in dairy products).

Along with fat content, milk and milk products have another shortcoming as a food: Some people can't digest the milk sugar (lactose) in milk, and suffer abdominal pains, bloating and diarrhea when they drink it. Sometimes mistaken for an allergy, this lactose intolerance is actually caused by lack of an enzyme (lactase) that splits milk sugar. Without the enzyme, lactose is left intact in the digestive system, where it provides a home for the nasty intestinal bacteria that cause the uproar. Lactase is found in high levels in newborns, for the obvious reason that the baby's main source of nutrition is milk. During childhood, those enzymes mysteriously decline in most of the world's population, especially in people of Mediterranean, black and Asian ancestry. Still, one specialist says of the widespread disorder: "It's very underrecognized." So if you have chronic indigestion, look to milk products as a possible cause.

A more serious problem is the role fats from dairy products may play in the development of heart disease. High levels of cholesterol in the blood are a major risk factor for heart disease, and there's a strong link between high-fat diets and high cholesterol levels. Some studies, in fact, suggest a *direct* link between high consumption of dairy products and increased risk of heart disease.

But the story on dairy products and heart disease isn't quite that simple. It's been found, for example, that the Masai herdsmen of Africa—who live almost exclusively on milk—have very low cholesterol levels. Other studies with Americans have suggested that drinking milk may actually *lower* cholesterol counts. In fact, several different substances have been suggested as candidates for the mysterious cholesterol-lowering "milk factor."

Yet other studies have produced conflicting results. In one such study, reported in the *American Journal of Clinical Nutrition*, skim milk, yogurt and whole milk were tested on a group of schoolboys for three weeks. Yogurt and whole milk caused cholesterol levels to *rise;* skim milk produced a steady drop. Yet even skim milk isn't a surefire cholesterol antidote. A study reported in *Nutrition Research* found that drinking 2 quarts of skim milk every day for a month didn't

Sherbet

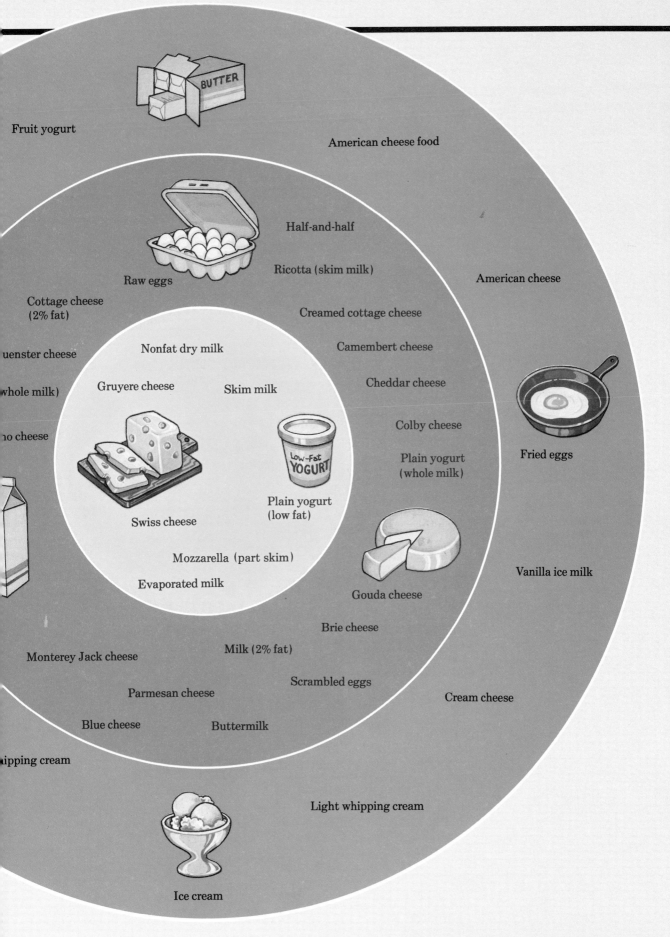

Fruit yogurt

American cheese food

Half-and-half

American cheese

Raw eggs

Ricotta (skim milk)

Cottage cheese
(2% fat)

Creamed cottage cheese

uenster cheese

Camembert cheese

Nonfat dry milk

whole milk)

Cheddar cheese

Gruyere cheese

Skim milk

o cheese

Colby cheese

Plain yogurt
(whole milk)

Fried eggs

Low-Fat
YOGURT

Plain yogurt
(low fat)

Swiss cheese

Vanilla ice milk

Mozzarella (part skim)

Evaporated milk

Gouda cheese

Brie cheese

Monterey Jack cheese

Milk (2% fat)

Scrambled eggs

Parmesan cheese

Cream cheese

Blue cheese

Buttermilk

ipping cream

Light whipping cream

Ice cream

159

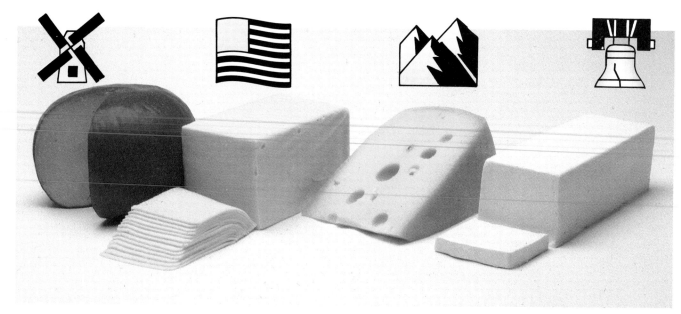

There's a world of difference in these 4 cheeses. An ounce of Swiss has 272 milligrams of calcium—over a third of an adult's RDA—while cream cheese has only 23 milligrams. But that same amount of cream cheese has more fat than any of the others. As for salt, the American cheese scores highest with over 330 milligrams of sodium per ounce, while Swiss is lowest with 74. For total calories, though, an ounce of Swiss has the most—107—with Edam right behind at 101.

lower cholesterol. (A surprising finding in the light of these statistics: Whole milk contains 13 times more saturated fat and 7 times more cholesterol than skim milk.)

In short, scientists have yet to figure out the heart disease/milk connection. But their studies do indicate this:

If you have heart disease, or there's a history of it in your family, stick with skim milk and other low-fat dairy products. If you don't have heart disease, and neither do many of your relatives, don't be afraid of whole milk—but don't drink a quart of it a day, either. The American habit of washing down every meal with a glass of moo juice is a bit extreme; it shouldn't be drunk—well, like water. But milk still can be a healthful *part* of your diet.

"Studies are now beginning to show that intake of calcium from dairy products can make a real difference in blood pressure levels," says David A. McCarron, M.D., associate professor of medicine and director of the hypertension clinic at Oregon Health Sciences University in Portland.

Dr. McCarron and two research associates compared calcium intake of 44 people with normal blood pressure to that of 46 people with high blood pressure. Those with normal blood pressure drank more milk—about three glasses a day—and ate more cheese and yogurt than

people with high blood pressure, so they consumed significantly more calcium.

"The easiest, most efficient way to get calcium is to drink milk and eat cheese and yogurt," says Dr. McCarron. "You'd have to eat an awful lot of greens, cereals, grains, beans and nuts to get even a small portion of the calcium that's concentrated in dairy products."

Until now, people with high blood pressure have been steered away from dairy products because they contain sodium and cholesterol. But Dr. McCarron feels that the protective effect of calcium overrides the harmful effect of sodium.

"By shunning dairy products, people have been inadvertently restricting their intake of what could be an important factor in control of high blood pressure," says Dr. McCarron.

MILK IN THE RAW

Most of the milk in the supermarket is pasteurized—heated to destroy any infection-minded bacteria that might be swimming around. But some milk is sold raw. The folks who like it say it's more natural and nutritious. And they're right about the nutrients: Pasteurizing knocks off bacteria *and* some vitamin C, thiamine, biotin and B$_{12}$. But is raw milk *safe*? After all, a little more vitamin C isn't worth a bout of food poisoning.

The answer is probably yes—if the milk comes from a dairy that's certified to produce it. That kind of dairy (and there are only a handful in the United States) has stricter regulations than those that sell the pasteurized variety. Certified raw milk must start with a lower bacteria count than milk intended for pasteurization. And it's tested every day for contamination, as compared to the once-a-month testing of pasteurized milk. So if you want to drink raw milk, just be sure it has the word "certified" somewhere on the container.

SHOULD YOU SAY "CHEESE"?

Anybody who's forgotten about that carton of milk in the back of the refrigerator knows that milk *changes*—in taste and texture. So it's not surprising that almost every culture in the world discovered cheesemaking and developed one or more varieties of this unique food, among them the mozzarella and ricotta of Italy, France's Brie, blue and Camembert, Belgium's odorous limburger and Holland's delicate Edam, England's Stilton, America's colby and of course, Switzerland's Swiss.

Like milk, cheese provides a lot of high-quality protein, calcium and other nutrients. But it has drawbacks—loads of fat, calories and salt. That's because cheese is a *concentrated* food: It takes about 5 quarts of milk to make 1 pound of cheese. Cheese contains, for example, roughly as much protein as meat—but far more fat.

How much fat you'll find in a given cheese depends on the kind of milk used to make it. The milk may have been extra-rich, whole, 2 percent, skim, or—fattiest of all—milk with added butterfat. But whether the cheese contains a lot of fat or a little, most of it is saturated; and too much of *that* in your diet has been strongly associated with increased risk of heart disease. So go easy. Especially on cream cheese, a product that's one-third fat. Many slicing cheeses like Muenster, Monterey Jack and Swiss are right behind, with between 20 and 30 percent fat.

Eggs Won't Scramble Your Health

Every member of 2 groups of people added an egg a day to his or her diet for 3 months. As you can see from the graph, the average cholesterol level of both groups hardly budged—more proof that eggs won't scramble your health.

Creamed cottage cheese, on the other hand, contains only about 4 percent milk fat, and some low-fat varieties can be as low as 0.5 percent.

Cheese also packs a hefty dose of sodium, averaging something like 200 milligrams to the ounce. Processed cheese spreads may be twice that high. Other cheeses overendowed with salt include Greek feta cheese, cheddar, Roquefort and blue cheese. If you're on a salt-restricted diet, you may want to avoid cheese entirely.

Looking at one kind of cheese—cheddar—sums up the health problems and pleasures of cheese. A 2-ounce serving contains about 352 milligrams of sodium. It also provides nearly 228 calories, almost twice as much as the same amount of choice porterhouse steak. On the plus side, it delivers 408 milligrams of calcium, or almost half the RDA for an adult man, and a very respectable 600 I.U. of vitamin A. Cheese, in short, is a powerful, nutritious food—but one you should eat in moderation.

You can "say cheese" more often by eating low-fat cheeses, which have become more available. You can now find cheeses that are low in fat, cholesterol, salt or a combination of all three. In many of these cheeses, the milk fat has been replaced by vegetable fat, which contains no cholesterol and is usually less saturated.

But no matter what kind of cheese you eat, it probably won't give

Margarine or Butter: The Better Choice

Which is better for your heart, butter or margarine?

Granted, butter is a natural product while margarine can be loaded with additives. But butter's *fat* is mostly saturated; margarine's is mostly polyunsaturated. That means margarine is the winner. Here's the proof.

A study published in the medical journal *Lancet* focused on residents of Belgium. In the north of the country, people had begun to substitute margarine for butter. In the south, butter consumption was 4 to 5 times higher. And so was the average level of cholesterol

in the blood *and* the risk of heart disease. In fact, life expectancy for men in southern Belgium—because of increased risk of heart disease—was more than 2 years less than that of men in the north.

So if you want to butter up your heart, use margarine.

you cavities. According to Charles Schachtele, Ph.D., a professor at the University of Minnesota, cheese prevents decay by blocking sugars and carbohydrates from forming an acid environment where cavity-causing bacteria would thrive.

When volunteers at the university munched on cheese and then swigged sugar water, the acid balance in their mouths returned to normal, non-cavity-promoting levels within a matter of minutes.

Aged cheddar, Monterey Jack and Swiss were the most protective cheeses tested.

THE POWER OF YOGURT

In Hindu mythology, the God of Medicine is pictured rising out of an ocean of milk. His first command was probably, "Let it be yogurt."

Luckily, health-minded mortals can create yogurt, too. By adding friendly bacteria known as yogurt cultures (there are three—*Lactobacillus*

bulgaricus, Streptococcus thermophilus and *Lactobacillus acidophilus* —and any one will do) to whole milk and letting the milk incubate for a few hours at low heat, you wind up with a completely new product loaded with health-giving properties. For instance, those friendly bacteria may help restore the bacterial flora in your digestive tract that help you digest food—flora that can be trampled by drugs, infections and other bodily insults. But yogurt has also been shown to help fight off infection, heal cold sores, lower cholesterol and even (in experimental conditions) inhibit the growth of cancerous tumors.

Yogurt is also a good source of B vitamins like folate, niacin, B_{12} and biotin. And it's low in calories (if you avoid the sweetened, fruit-filled kind): A cup of plain yogurt made from whole milk has 108 fewer calories than cottage cheese, a food usually considered a dieter's dream. Look for brands containing *live* bacteria cultures; some yogurts are heat treated or pasteurized, which destroys the bacteria. Freezing, however, doesn't do them much harm: A recent study of ten samples of frozen yogurt showed all ten had active cultures.

THE EGG CONTROVERSY

A chicken should be proud of her egg. It supplies a fair amount of vitamin A and a hearty sampling of *all* other nutrients (except vitamin C). It's also low in calories: A large egg contains about 80, of which 60 come from the yolk.

Eggs supply such a nearly perfect protein that they're used as a reference standard for evaluating the quality of protein in all other foods. In fact, virtually every bit of an egg's 12 percent protein is digested and put to use in your body.

But if eggs are such standouts, why do so many doctors take a stand against them? One word explains it: *cholesterol.* Egg yolk is one of the richest sources of cholesterol in the American diet, so it's a natural target for those concerned about the link between high levels of cholesterol and an increased risk of heart attack and stroke. The American Heart Association, in fact, has recommended that Americans try to limit their cholesterol intake to no more than 300 milligrams a day—or the amount in a single egg. But other researchers have questioned the wisdom of shunning the egg because of all the other nutrients it provides—and because of the fact that some studies have shown eggs *don't* raise blood cholesterol or triglycerides.

In one study, for instance, 116 male volunteers added two eggs a day to their normal diet for three months, then stopped eating eggs entirely for three months. Tests measuring their blood fat levels at the end of each experimental diet period showed that "no significant increase in mean [average] serum [blood] cholesterol was found nor was there a significant association of dietary cholesterol intake with serum cholesterol." In other words, more eggs didn't mean more cholesterol.

In another study, cholesterol levels were measured in a group of volunteers five hours after eating two eggs. Result? "In the majority of patients," say the researchers, "the serum cholesterol level did not change significantly."

But other researchers have found eggs *do* increase cholesterol. Scien-

tists at Texas A&M University tested the effect of four different diets on the cholesterol levels of 29 middle-aged men. The men ate various combinations of red meat, fish, poultry and eggs—and 15 of them showed no big change in cholesterol levels on any of the diets. But the 14 others registered "significantly higher" cholesterol concentrations when eggs were added to either a red meat or a fish and poultry diet.

The bottom line here is the same as it was for milk: People with heart disease or a family history of it should avoid eggs; they're not worth the risk. Everybody else can eat them—but not every day. Try to vary your breakfasts so that when you eat eggs—maybe once or twice a week—they'll be a treat instead of a routine.

By the way, if you are on a cholesterol-restricted diet you can't get away with eating eggs by preparing them a special way. Says Dean Fletcher, Ph.D., chairman of the department of human nutrition at Washington State University, "The yolk of the egg is the source of cholesterol, and whether it is boiled, scrambled, fried or poached seems to make no difference."

Picture-Perfect Yogurt

To make your own yogurt, start by heating fresh milk to just below boiling. A quart of milk will make a quart of yogurt; you can use whole milk, skim milk or even half-and-half. Each will produce a yogurt with its own distinctive taste and texture.

Next, allow the milk to cool until tepid. The ideal temperature for yogurt bacilli is 112° F, but anywhere from 90° to 120° F will do. If you don't have a thermometer, test the milk on your wrist (it should feel lukewarm, not hot). Then stir in 2 to 3 heaping tablespoons of plain, prepared yogurt with live cultures and beat until it's blended with the milk.

Finally, pour the milk into the containers of your yogurt maker (if you have one) and let it incubate 4 to 6 hours, or until firm. You can also incubate yogurt in a wide-mouthed Thermos, or in a covered glass or earthenware bowl set in a warm place (like an oven preheated to 120°F, then turned off). The important thing is to maintain an even temperature and not to disturb the culture while it's forming.

Source Notes

Chapter 1
Page 6

"The Fattening of America; Consumption of Calories, Protein, Fat and Carbohydrate in the United States" adapted from *The Changing American Diet*, by Letitia Brewster and Michael F. Jacobson (Washington, D.C.: Center for Science in the Public Interest, 1978).

Page 7

"Too Much Salt? Consumption of Sodium in the United States" adapted from "Perspective of Food and Drug Administration on Dietary Sodium," by Fred R. Shank et al., *Journal of the American Dietetic Association*, January 1982.

Page 7

"Too Much Sugar? Consumption of Caloric Sweeteners in the United States" adapted from *Sugar and Sweetener Outlook and Situation*, by Economic Research Service (Washington, D.C.: U.S. Department of Agriculture, 1982).

Page 10

"Med School Fare: Undernourished; Medical School Curriculum" adapted from *1981-82 AAMC Curriculum Directory*, Lynn Farley, ed. (Washington, D.C.: Association of American Medical Colleges, 1981).

Page 11

"Factory Foods Gaining Favor" adapted from "Review of Trends in Food Use in the United States, 1909 to 1980," by Susan O. Welsh and Ruth M. Marston, *Journal of the American Dietetic Association*, August 1982.

Chapter 2
Page 17

"Charting Your Kids on a Healthy Course" adapted from "Physical Growth: National Center for Health Statistics Percentiles," by P. V. V. Hamill et al., *American Journal of Clinical Nutrition*, March 1979.

Chapter 5
Pages 56-60

Vegetable and fruit information substantially compiled from *The Greengrocer*, by Joe Carcione and Bob Lucas (New York: Pyramid Books, 1974).

Chapter 7
Page 78

"Vitamin C Content (mg.) of Raw, Steamed and Boiled Vegetables" adapted from *Nutritional Evaluation of Food Processing*, by Robert S. Harris and Endel Karmas (Westport, Conn.: Avi Publishing Co., 1975) and *Nutritive Value of American Foods in Common Units*, Agriculture Handbook No. 456, by Catherine F. Adams (Washington, D.C.: Agricultural Research Service, U.S. Department of Agriculture, 1975).

Chapter 8
Page 84

"Nutritional Potencies in a Healing Garden" adapted from *Nutritive Value of American Foods in Common Units*, Agriculture Handbook No. 456, by Catherine F. Adams (Washington D.C.: Agricultural Research Service, U.S. Department of Agriculture, 1975) and *McCance and Widdowson's The Composition of Foods*, by A. A. Paul and D. A. T. Southgate (New York: Elsevier/ North Holland Biomedical Press, 1978).

Chapter 9
Page 97

"Nutrition in the Fast Lane is Slippery Going; Percentage of Recommended Dietary Allowances in Fast Food Meals" compiled from information supplied by companies whose products are described.

Page 98

"Salt in Snack Foods: A Better Shake" adapted from *Nutritive Value of American Foods in Common Units*, Agriculture Handbook No. 456, by Catherine F. Adams (Washington, D.C.: Agricultural Research Service, U.S. Department of Agriculture, 1975) and *The Sodium Content of Your Food*, Home and Garden Bulletin No. 233 (Washington, D.C.: Science and Education Administration, U.S. Department of Agriculture, 1980).

Page 99

"Potassium Scores" adapted from *Nutritive Value of American Foods in Common Units*, Agriculture Handbook No. 456, by Catherine F. Adams (Washington, D.C.: Agricultural Research Service, U.S. Department of Agriculture, 1975) and *Provisional Table on the Nutrient Content of Beverages*, by Rena Cutrufelli and Ruth H. Matthews (Washington, D.C.: Human Nutrition Information Service, U.S. Department of Agriculture, 1981).

Chapter 10
Page 106

"America's Beefing Up; Consumption of Beef in the United States" adapted from "Review of Trends in Food Use in the United States, 1909 to 1980," by Susan O. Welsh and Ruth M. Marston, *Journal of the American Dietetic Association*, August 1982.

Page 107

"Meat Puts on the Pressure" adapted from "Effects of Ingestion of Meat on Plasma Cholesterol of Vegetarians" by Frank M. Sacks et al., *Journal of the American Medical Association*, vol. 246, no. 6, August 7, 1981, p. 640. Copyright 1981, American Medical Association.

Page 110

"Fat in Beef Cuts" adapted from *Composition of Foods*, Agriculture Handbook No. 8, by Bernice K. Watt and Annabel L. Merrill (Washington, D.C.: Agricultural Research Service, U.S. Department of Agriculture, 1975) and *Nutritive Value of American Foods in Common Units*, Agriculture Handbook No. 456, by Catherine F. Adams (Washington, D.C.: Agricultural Research Service, U.S. Department of Agriculture, 1975).

Page 113

Cave painting photograph from a reconstruction by Anne Louise Stockdale. Reprinted courtesy of American Heritage Publishing Co. and James Mellart.

Page 140

"Blueberry Pickin' Time" map compiled from information from the U.S. Department of Agriculture and adapted from *Modern Fruit Science*, by Norman F. Childers (New Brunswick, N.J.: Horticultural Publications, Rutgers University, 1973).

Page 148

"Wheat Germ Tops Toast in Breakfast Value" adapted from *Provisional Table on the Nutrient Content of Bakery Foods and Related Items*, by Catherine McQuilken and Ruth H. Matthews (Washington, D.C.: Science and Education Administration, U.S. Department of Agriculture, 1981) and *Composition of Foods*, Agriculture Handbook No. 8, by Bernice K. Watt and Annabel L. Merrill (Washington, D.C.: Agricultural Research Service, U.S. Department of Agriculture, 1975) and *Nutritive Value of American Foods in Common Units*, Agriculture Handbook No. 456, by Catherine F. Adams (Washington, D.C.: Agricultural Research Service, U.S. Department of Agriculture, 1975).

Page 161

"Eggs Won't Scramble Your Health" adapted from "Effect of Dietary Egg on Serum Cholesterol and Triglyceride of Human Males," by Martha W. Porter et al., *American Journal of Clinical Nutrition*, April 1977.

Index

Photography Credits

Cover: Carl Doney. Christopher Barone: pp. 52, upper right and upper left; 53, upper left and lower right. Carl Doney: 28; 33; 38; 52, lower left; 53, upper right; 73; 116. T. L. Gettings: 31; 34, upper left, lower left and lower right; 35; 53, lower left. Mitchell T. Mandel: 36; 40; 49; 58; 72; 78; 102; 140; 142; 146; 150; 161; 163. Margaret Smyser Skrovanek: 8; 19; 24; 29; 34, center left; 34-35; 45; 48; 54; 57; 64; 74; 82; 92, upper left and center left; 93, upper right, center, lower right and lower left; 94; 109; 111; 124, top row, photos 3 and 4 and bottom row, photos 1, 2 and 4; 138; 154. Christie C. Tito: 92, lower left; 93, upper left; 124, top row, photo 1; 131; 136; 160. Sally Shenk Ullman: 1; 14; 26; 92, center right; 121; 123; 124, top row, photo 2 and bottom row, photo 3; 126; 128; 130; 132.

Illustration Credits

Susan Blubaugh: pp. 5; 16; 17; 20; 30; 32; 35; 38; 44; 61; 63; 67; 70; 79; 80-81; 85; 86; 87; 88; 96; 97; 98; 99; 106-107; 108; 121; 125; 127; 147; 148; 149; 155; 161; 162. Joe Lertola: 2; 8; 10; 12-13; 18; 37; 43; 46-47; 60; 66; 68; 69; 71; 76; 77; 100; 110; 117; 131; 136-137; 138-139; 140; 141; 142; 143; 160.

The food target illustrations on pp. 104-105; 114-115; 118-119; 122-123; 134-135; 144-145; 152-153 were done by Joe Lertola; the illustrations on the targets were done by Kathi Ember.

Rodale Press, Inc., publishes PREVENTION®, the better health magazine.
For information on how to order your subscription,
write to PREVENTION®, Emmaus, PA 18049.